Every

Pilgr
to Ce
and Ireland

Every Pilgrim's Guide to Celtic Britain and Ireland

ANDREW JONES

Liguori

LIGUORI, MISSOURI

Imprimi Potest:
Richard Thibodeau, C.Ss.R.
Provincial, Denver Province
The Redemptorists

Published by Liguori Publications
Liguori, Missouri
www.liguori.org
www.catholicbooksonline.com

ISBN 0-7648-0846-X
Library of Congress Catalog Card Number: 2001098357

Originally published in 2002 by The Canterbury Press Norwich,
St Mary's Works, St Mary's Plain, Norwich, Norfolk, NR3 3BH.

Printed in Denmark
06 05 04 03 02   5 4 3 2 1
First U.S. edition

Contents

Contents

IRELAND

SCOTLAND

THE ISLE OF MAN

Dedication

TO THE ONE WHO SHOWED ME
HOW TO CONNECT TRUTHFULLY
THAT INNER JOURNEY OF THE HEART
WITH THE OUTER PILGRIMAGE OF LIFE

I FOUND THE LINK TO BE LOVE AND
FRIENDSHIP

THANK YOU

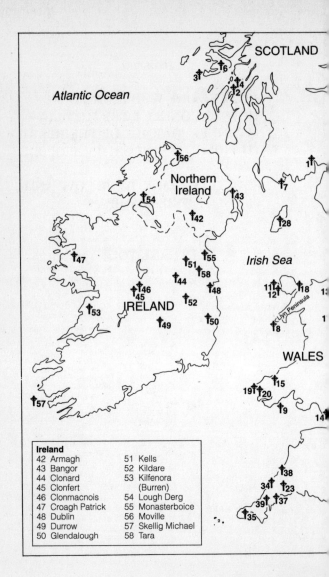

SCOTLAND

Atlantic Ocean

3 ✝ ✝6
✝4
2

✝56

Northern
Ireland

✝1
✝7
✝54 ✝43

✝42

✝28

Irish Sea

✝47 ✝55
✝51
✝44 ✝58 11 ✝ ✝18
✝46 ✝48 12
45 ✝ ✝ Llyn Peninsula
53 ✝ IRELAND ✝52
✝49 ✝50 ✝8

WALES

✝15
19 ✝ ✝20
57 ✝ ✝9

14

✝38
34 ✝ ✝23
39 ✝ ✝37
35 ✝

Ireland

42 Armagh	51 Kells
43 Bangor	52 Kildare
44 Clonard	53 Kilfenora
45 Clonfert	(Burren)
46 Clonmacnois	54 Lough Derg
47 Croagh Patrick	55 Monasterboice
48 Dublin	56 Moville
49 Durrow	57 Skellig Michael
50 Glendalough	58 Tara

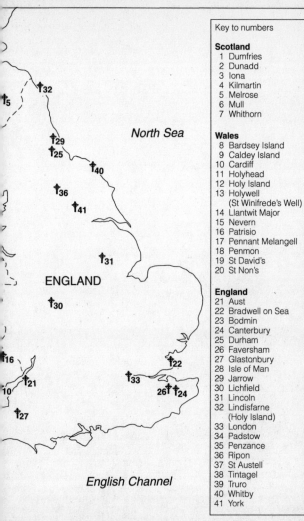

North Sea

ENGLAND

English Channel

Key to numbers

Scotland
1 Dumfries
2 Dunadd
3 Iona
4 Kilmartin
5 Melrose
6 Mull
7 Whithorn

Wales
8 Bardsey Island
9 Caldey Island
10 Cardiff
11 Holyhead
12 Holy Island
13 Holywell
   (St Winifrede's Well)
14 Llantwit Major
15 Nevern
16 Patrisio
17 Pennant Melangell
18 Penmon
19 St David's
20 St Non's

England
21 Aust
22 Bradwell on Sea
23 Bodmin
24 Canterbury
25 Durham
26 Faversham
27 Glastonbury
28 Isle of Man
29 Jarrow
30 Lichfield
31 Lincoln
32 Lindisfarne
   (Holy Island)
33 London
34 Padstow
35 Penzance
36 Ripon
37 St Austell
38 Tintagel
39 Truro
40 Whitby
41 York

Preface

by the Rt Revd F. J. Saunders Davies

This is an invaluable addition to the series of Every Pilgrim's Guides. When early Christians could not afford the money or the time to go on pilgrimage to Rome or to the Holy Land, they found impressive centres of pilgrimage in Britain. In this diocese of Bangor, Bardsey became such a centre and we still know the routes they took from north and south.

Andrew Jones was born on one of these routes on the Llŷn Peninsula. He probably took it all for granted in his youth, but on returning to his native area he has been struck by the power of this ancient tradition. Like so many of our contemporaries he has sensed the link between the inner pilgrimage of the heart and the outer journey of life. He opens up a path between foot and heart.

Although he wears his scholarship lightly, there is a lot of information in this Guide. He has researched the lives of the saints and the churches where they are commemorated. All this is designed to help us to enter into the world of Celtic Britain, to get to know the saints and to walk where they walked. In that process we find that we share their journey. It is the journey of God's people throughout the ages, a journey along the way of the cross, the journey of exodus, leading from captivity to freedom, for individuals and for groups. To assist us on this journey Andrew Jones provides a biblical reading and some devotional material related to each centre visited.

This is also a practical guide, giving clear directions to ensure that we reach our destination, and pointing out the details we should note. Our efforts to discover the narrow path or cross the busy highway will be well rewarded with this Guide at hand.

The Reverend Andrew Jones deserves a warm tribute for preparing this Guide to so many key centres in Britain and Ireland in the midst of all his other duties as parish priest and rural dean. This is clear evidence of the energy that can be engendered when life is experienced as a pilgrimage.

Saunders Davies, Bishop of Bangor

Author's Preface

Under each heading there will be a brief historical outline of the church and of the saint(s) associated with it, references to some of that church's artefacts and links with the Celtic tradition, a selected piece of devotion or meditation and some practical notes on location and directions.

All biblical references come from the New Revised Standard Version (NRSV) (Oxford University Press, 1995).

The sections are arranged in a geographical sequence, but a comprehensive index at the end enables immediate reference to each individual place and site.

The general information supplied – in particular contact names and addresses, opening and closing arrangements – has been carefully checked at the time of writing, but inevitably some details may vary from time to time.

Acknowledgements

Several people have enabled this work to continue. I am indebted to my parishioners in Llanbedrog, Llannor, Llangian and Llanengan who have been very patient as I have both tried to be a priest to them and searched for spare time to continue this work. I am grateful for the support of the Right Revd Saunders Davies, my Bishop, and to Canon Donald Allchin, Dr Jonathan Wooding, Sr Verena CHN, Sr Cintra CSH, and Sr Iwona MSCK (from Poland, who accompanied me on some of these journeys). I am also grateful to my father, Tomos Jones, and Monica Madour for the line drawings and to Sr Verena CHN, the Revd Evelyn Davies, Faith Taylor and Edward Jones for the photographs, some drawings, for additional material and support.

Introduction

There have been two major influences behind the writing of this book. The first is the geographical area in which I am currently privileged to serve as parish priest: the Llŷn Peninsula in north-west Wales. The privilege is accentuated by the fact that it is also the area where I was born and in which I grew up; my very being is saturated in the ethos of this holy Celtic space. This is not only an area of outstanding physical beauty but also one where the spiritual beauty of the Christian tradition has been vibrant for 1,500 years and where the increasing pilgrimage traffic in our own day witnesses the urge in modern-day Christians to rediscover the historical importance and significance of pilgrimage, both as a popular pastime and as a different way of being church in the twenty-first century. The opportunity of sharing in other people's pilgrimages, of participating in many different kinds of pilgrimages and of actually leading pilgrimages with various groups and individuals convinces me of its vitality and that here lies a major 'life-line' for the contemporary church.

The second influence is my own, on-going and more specific research project. For some time I have pursued the quest to identify the shape, character and some important features of the early church in Celtic Britain, and particularly in Wales. I see myself as having two main tasks in this project:

- to identify a coherent and distinctive process of theological reflection which operated in Britain during the early part of the first millennium AD;
- to show that the authors and practitioners of that distinctive early British theology almost certainly regarded themselves and their emerging tradition as part of the mainline orthodox Christian theology which was operating in Europe at the same time. One only needs to read the ninth-century *Juvencus* manuscript of the Gospels which contains a number of glosses and notes in the margins in Latin, Welsh and Irish. One of the Welsh poems contained in the glosses praises God as Trinity, as Creator, Redeemer and Sanctifier. It is also probably the oldest text of a theological poem existing in Welsh. To tell one of my forefathers here in north-west Wales during the sixth century that he was practising a different kind of religion to what was happening in Rome at the same time would have horrified him. However, in many ways it was different, though not intentionally so. It's to do with the space, the land, the ethos, and the air of places; that's what gave the Christian in Celtic Britain and Ireland a distinctiveness.

To visit the various British and Irish sites associated directly or indirectly with the early church in the Celtic period has therefore been of crucial importance to my overall work. Hopefully the general investigation will eventually bring me round in a future project to ask questions about what kind of Christians worshipped in the churches at that time – what were their concerns, their worries, their priorities and so on.

Basil Hume, in his book *Footprints of the Northern Saints* (Darton, Longman and Todd, 1996), asked:

> What is life all about?
> What are we here for?
> Where is it all leading to?
> What happens after death?

These are questions which haunt people in our day. The early northern saints brought answers to these questions and those answers are as relevant today as they were in their time.

The very act of pilgrimage today echoes questions that come to each of us from that deeper journey of the heart: what is the reason for my being? It is not a coincidence that many who go on pilgrimage are people who are themselves at critical stages of life.

This book therefore is the fruit of two major influences: of confronting issues surrounding the increasing number of people wishing to become pilgrims as well as my own pilgrimage of life and my own wish to know more about the early church in Britain. To do justice to both of these things meant my comparing, for example, what was happening in north-west Wales with the east coast of Ireland; what was happening on an off-shore island in the west of Scotland with what was happening on an another island off the Northumbrian coast in the east of England; and all of this at about the same time: the period between about 300 and 1100, a time when there were significant events happening throughout western and eastern Christendom. A time also in which lines of communication between the East and the West were stronger than most modern people care to think.

The intention of this book is simply to provide a basic introduction to some of the main places and people associated with the development of the early church in Britain and Ireland during the Celtic period in the hope that the modern pilgrim will be better able to make the connections between then and now, them and us, and maybe to feel that the link is vital. For in many ways it is precisely in the rediscovery of the Church's past, particularly at those times when the life of the Church was vibrant and challenging, that Christians find new ways of discovering a vision for the contemporary Church and for the future. Although R. S. Thomas was referring to a different period, for me his words, 'This

is the springtime of the imagination; it offers hope', could well
apply to this particular period.

PILGRIMAGE IN A THEOLOGICAL CONTEXT

Christians can justifiably regard themselves as a *pilgrim people of
God*. Indeed, in the Bible this idea of the spiritual life as a journey
is expressed often. Through the centuries, pilgrims have come to
sacred places to seek healing, inspiration and redirection. Often it
has been a quest by simple, practical and concrete-minded people
to find 'stepping-stones' between themselves and the geographically
distant and spiritually abstract concepts of the Christian religion. In
that sense 'pilgrimage' as a way of becoming church in a different
way is not a new phenomenon. It is actually as old as the Church
itself, and as a Christian practice it has probably always challenged
the Church. This challenge has often focused on that ambivalent
relationship between one's inner spiritual journey of faith and the
outward, more physical journey of life.

It is so often true that an outward pilgrimage is a sign of an
inner journey, of repentance, resurrection and rebirth – the journey
of the heart which is held in the Creator's hands. It is rooted in
the conviction that life itself is a process of continual change and
movement. Christians are never static; they carry within themselves
a sense of expectancy, of looking forward in hope.

The writer to the Hebrews framed that reality in memorable
words:

> Therefore, since we are surrounded by so great a cloud of
> witnesses, let us also lay aside every weight and sin that clings
> so closely, and let us run with perseverance the race that is set
> before us, looking to Jesus the pioneer and perfecter of our faith
> . . . (Hebrews 12.1–2)

Here is expressed that marvellous journey of the Christian soul on
a continuing pilgrimage into the heart of God – a pilgrimage which
will never be completed here on earth, but continues in God's
eternal Kingdom.

Places such as Bardsey, Iona, Lindisfarne and Glendalough, in
particular ways, are associated with pilgrimage, but in reality the
pilgrim path is located everywhere and never just in sacred places.
The question that faces every pilgrim is: are participants open to
being truly *pilgrims*? Are they prepared to live with some of the risks
and uncertainties and loose ends which pilgrimage always entails?
The pilgrim can never have everything neatly 'sewn up' – there is
always the exploration, the search, the movement, the questions and
the challenge; after all, that's life!

PILGRIMAGE IN THE CELTIC TRADITION

The problem of defining what is meant by the term 'Celtic' centres mainly on the relationship between aspects of life such as culture, ethnicity and language. The evidence to show that a Celtic people did exist is largely three-fold:

- archaeology;
- documentary sources;
- linguistic material.

These three categories of evidence combine to present us with a Celtic world which, by the last few centuries BC, appears to have stretched from Ireland to eastern Europe and beyond, to Galatia.

Early linguistic evidence for the Celts is extremely sparse before the Roman period because northern Europe was virtually non-literate during most of the first millennium BC. When writing was adopted in the Celtic world in the late first millennium, it appeared almost entirely in Latin. Early Celtic linguistic evidence, such as it is, consists of inscriptions, coins and the names of places and people contained within classical documents. These early sources suggest that by the time of the Roman occupation, at the end of the first millennium BC, Celtic languages were spoken in Britain, Gaul, north Italy, Spain and central and eastern Europe.

There are major problems in actually defining 'Celtic', primarily because it is a term that means different things to different people. The archaeological approach to the Celtic question is different from that of the linguists and that of the anthropologists. So the varied types of evidence at our disposal – archaeological, linguistic and literary – themselves cause problems of determination. However, on the whole, the ancient sources present the modern seeker with a picture of a Celtic world which, in its heyday (the later first millennium BC to the second/third centuries AD), stretched from Ireland and Spain in the west and Scotland in the north to the Czech Republic and Slovakia in the east and northern Italy in the south – and even beyond Europe to Asia Minor. The study of the nature of that Celtic culture and how it expanded from its original central European heartland is a vast area and significant contributions are currently being made.

What eventually became of the Celts?

During the fifth century AD the Roman Empire in the west disintegrated and with that collapse of centralized power the Celts also apparently disappeared from all but a few peripheral regions in the extreme west. The areas of Europe previously under Roman influence, and in which Celtic and Roman culture had merged, were overrun by a new Germanic culture which seems largely to have obliterated Celtic tradition in central Europe, Gaul and much of Britain. After the collapse of Roman power, the western areas that had been on the fringe of Celtic tradition became its focus and remained its focus: Wales, Ireland, Scotland and Brittany. Only there (together with Cornwall and the Isle of Man) did distinctive Celtic langues survive, and it is these areas which, during the later first and earlier second millennia AD, produced a vernacular Celtic mythic tradition on the one hand, and literary and archaeological evidence for early western Christianity on the other. In both the mythic and early Christian traditions the link between sacredness and place proved to be vital.

This book is chiefly concerned with some of the practical aspects of this early Christian tradition in the western areas between about 400 and 1066. There is no doubt that the Christian tradition here was both different and unique. It's not that the Celtic tradition set out to be different but rather, that the geographical conditions, the social circumstances, the political developments, the common linguistic background, and the distinctive history, language, and culture greatly influenced the development of a Celtic religious conscience.

Consequently, there does seem to be a special vision within the Celtic tradition that characterizes the actual spirituality of the Celtic peoples. In an interesting anthology of prayers and blessings from the Celtic tradition, *Threshold of Light* (Darton, Longman and Todd, 1986), A. M. Allchin and Esther De Waal identify three of those special characteristics:

- an astonishing confidence that this world is God's world, that nature and grace belong together;
- an awareness of the reality of evil and the need for a radical repentance – this is where the cross comes in and especially the high Celtic Crosses of triumph;
- a powerful sense of the closeness of eternity to the things of everyday.

So much in the Celtic tradition points to the idea that the God of the Celts was primarily an immanent God; a God who was very close and present all around them. It appears that this was as true for people as it was for places and spaces. Cintra Pemberton in her book *Soulfaring: Celtic Pilgrimage Then and Now* (SPCK, 1999), says:

> The numinous qualities perceived in certain places in the natural world were revered and respected. When Christianity arrived, the physical place where one would die and see God face to face tied in with earlier Celtic beliefs and was thus extremely important.

That connection, therefore, between sacred place and the concept of pilgrimage, is crucially important; but not only in the Celtic tradition. All over the world and in all kinds of traditions pilgrims have been drawn to particular sites and spaces and it is this that, in turn, creates a 'pilgrim route'.

Clearly, this is not an exclusively Christian idea. In fact there are sites in Britain that show that pilgrimage was at the heart of pre-Christian ritual and worship; it is of course as old as humanity itself. Similarly, the Jewish tradition is saturated with the practice of pilgrimage. The Old Testament is steeped in references to sacred places to which Jews travelled on a regular basis to sing, to pray and to venerate. The ministry of Jesus also takes the idea of pilgrimage seriously and his visits to the Temple in Jerusalem were part of an ancient tradition belonging to his people. This was soon adopted into Christian practice and by the fourth century AD it was big business and extremely popular, not least in the emerging Celtic Christian way of worship.

Again, in her *Soulfaring*, Cintra Pemberton states that there were four major aspects of Celtic pilgrimage:

- missionary outreach
- an apparently aimless wandering for God
- the search for one's place of resurrection
- the imitation of Jesus through a fierce asceticism

In Britain the shift of attention from pre-Christian pagan and Celtic sites to Christian happened reasonably quickly. Some sites were even shared for a while and this seems to have been especially true of many Welsh and Cornish places. On the whole, local saints attracted local pilgrims and the idea of pilgrimage in Britain 'took off' initially as a local interest. But soon many of these places achieved a much wider importance and popularity. The selection of sites in this book attempts to explore just some examples of places which drew international pilgrims. Similarly, British pilgrims travelled to sacred sites in Europe such as Rome, Jerusalem and Syria.

PILGRIMAGE TODAY

Pilgrimage for many people is not just about religion. Throughout history it has been regarded as a kind of 'escape from reality'; a means of avoiding constraints and tensions. Things haven't changed! Modern groups of pilgrims will have a variety of participants with all sorts of strange and wonderful reasons for being there. Many people who begin their pilgrimages for non-religious reasons speak retrospectively about being 'surprised by joy'; such journeys touch places of personal interior pain, uncertainty and vulnerability.

Cintra Pemberton in her *Soulfaring* makes an interesting point about the link between being 'pilgrims' and 'tourists'. She says that 'the line between tourist and pilgrim can sometimes be very fluid'.

Occasionally someone says 'I started out as a tourist, but after a few days I realized I had become a pilgrim'. When this happens, it usually is a result of a shift in the person's inner focus; what may have begun as curiosity or an intent for increased education or some other goal has become unmistakably an experience of the Holy. This can happen on a conventional tour or in any other kind of travel, and the person is deeply enriched by the shift.

In their book *Sacred Britain* (ICOREC Piatkus Press, 1997), Nigel and Martin Palmer explore the changes in the way modern pilgrims travel the pilgrimage routes. They note that today most people never complete the whole 'traditional' routes, although remembering of course that even the course of these routes over the years has changed. The Reformation destroyed many of the pilgrimage routes as well as the actual idea of pilgrimage. Some of the paths today lie under motorways and housing estates. But this does not necessarily make a great deal of difference. The modern interpretation of the route is still as valid. Nor do modern pilgrims use the same mode of travel – it's much easier today. But what is crucial is that this does not change the fundamental idea and blessing of pilgrimage today. The process may have been speeded up and made much easier but the basic ingredients are the same. Pilgrims with sorrows and joys, pains and delights, certainties and doubt still travel together along the ancient routes and to the sacred spaces and continue to share and grow. The crucial issue is still how open people are to what they might find both externally and within themselves.

PRACTICAL INFORMATION

At the end of each chapter there is a section devoted to practical aspects of the particular site or church. Telephone numbers and e-mail addresses are given so that each group co-ordinator or leader can make the necessary contacts well in advance.

PREPARATION

Most pilgrimages happen in groups; groups vary in size and intention. Initially some time needs to be devoted to the process of getting to know each other. This can happen in all kinds of different ways: social activities, worship, time apart, study, outings. In this time of preparation, the sharing of past stories, present situations and future hopes will prove to be fundamental to the consolidation of the group and plenty of time and effort will need to be given to this. This kind of initial sharing will make the various unexpected experiences 'along the way' meaningful and manageable.

Once the initial 'gelling' takes place, the second preparatory stage will entail some learning. This will mean that so much 'on the way' will make more sense and even time will be saved. This may involve learning sessions as part of social occasions or even specially prepared lectures, visits or slide and video presentations. Part of this will also be given over to consultation: consulting the group about visits to various places, especially if there are choices; discussion about participants' previous experiences – this too will make a difference as to whether all the proposed visits are relevant or whether particular places should be left out.

The planning of worship will also need to be taken seriously and dealt with well in advance. It might be useful to appoint someone to take responsibility for the various acts of worship. However, it is at the early planning stage that these arrangements should be made. A programme of worship – participants, contents, nature of the act of worship and so forth, resources available, space for self and group expression – needs to be finalized before departure. It might be the group's wish to produce a booklet which will contain the hymns, prayers, themes and places of worship and which each pilgrim can comfortably carry during the pilgrimage. There are some suggestions for meditation at the end of each chapter in this book which can be used alongside further material planned by groups or individuals. This will ensure a smooth running of the worship at the various sites.

There is also the administrative side to pilgrimages. It is hoped that the closing sections of each chapter in this book will help in the process of smooth planning: pre-booking entry tickets and checking on times, costs and seasonal variations as well as the different facilities available is crucial. An important aspect to remember is that some participants will appreciate the chance to help in much of the planning and share in the smooth running of the pilgrimage, once the actual travelling begins.

A pilgrimage never finishes. The return home is often the new beginning of lasting relationships and the process of relating and story telling. Each group should bear this in mind when planning debriefing sessions: to make sense retrospectively of some aspects of the pilgrimage; to share the story again; to relate the experience to others; to share photographs; to have regular reunion parties. The return is often as much fun as the preparing and as the travelling: a pilgrimage is all about the preparing, the travelling and the returning.

WORSHIP

There are a number of books available to help pilgrims to plan their worship in the Celtic tradition. I have found the following to be useful:

David Adam, *Borderlands*, SPCK, 1999
Jim Cotter, *Prayer At Day's Dawning*, Cairns Publications, 1998

Jim Cotter, *Prayer At Night's Approaching*, Cairns Publications, 1998

Esther de Waal, *The Celtic Way of Prayer*, Hodder and Stoughton, 1996

Brendan O'Malley, *God at Every Gate*, Canterbury Press Norwich, 1997

Brendan O'Malley, *A Welsh Pilgrim's Manual*, Gomer Press, 1989

Brendan O'Malley, *A Celtic Eucharist*, Canterbury Press Norwich, 2001

Margaret Pawley, *Prayers For Pilgrims*, Triangle, 1991

Martin Robinson, *Sacred Places, Pilgrim Paths*, Harper Collins, 1997

Mick Sharp, *Holy Places of Celtic Britain*, Blandford, 1997

Ray Simpson, *Celtic Worship Through the Year*, Hodder and Stoughton, 1997

Shirley Toulson, *Celtic Journeys*, Fount, 1995

Shirley Toulson, *The Celtic Year*, Element, 1996

Martin Wallace, *The Celtic Resource Book*, National Society/ Church House Publishing, 1998

Wild Goose Worship Group, *A Wee Worship Book*, Wild Goose Publications, 1999

Wild Goose Worship Group, *The Pattern of Our Days*, Wild Goose Publications, 1999

Wild Goose Worship Group, *The Iona Abbey Worship Book*, Wild Goose Publications, 2001

Useful music resources (tapes and CDs):

Duck Baker and friends, *The Music of O'Carolan*, Shanachie Records

Patrick Ball, *Celtic Harp*, Vols 1–3, Fortuna Records

Derek Bell, *Carolan's Favourites*, Claddagh Records

Alec Finn, *Blue Shamrock*, CBM Ltd, Atlanta Records

Sammy Horner, *Celtic Praise*, Vols 1–3, Kingsway

Ann Heyman and A. Kinnaird, *Irish and Scottish Harp Music*, Temple Records

Llio Rhydderch, *Melangell*, Flach Studio

Sileas, *Harpbreakers*, Lapwing Records

Various Artists, *Celtic Legacy, Celtic Odyssey*, Narada Productions

Celtic Expressions of Worship, Vols 1–2, Kingsway

Worship at holy sites varies widely, ranging from a liturgical renewal of baptism vows and Eucharist to free-form healing services, candlelit hymn singing, prayer vigils, liturgical dance, intercessions of all kinds, and many other creative expressions of prayer. Worship during a pilgrimage is both natural and essential. The actual pilgrimage is a sacrament: the outward, visible journey is a sign of the inward, spiritual path that helps to reach out toward God and it in turn deepens one's relationship with God.

Each pilgrimage will vary in number, duration and needs. The devotional aspect will thus also vary; from simply an opening and closing prayer, to acts of spiritual devotion and the use of silence 'along the way'. So much is available for the modern-day pilgrim; prayer books, anthologies of prayer and devotional writings, translations of classical, ancient and medieval writers, poetry, experimental liturgies and litanies, all kinds of song books and choruses, collections of meditations of varying length and topics, sets of personal and communal acts of penance, thanksgiving and intercession . . . The list is unending and the resources are readily available and plentiful. The key is: that the group prepares carefully and together.

PATRONAL FEASTS

The following is a list of the patronal feasts of saints included in this book:

January

1 Gwynhoedl
6 Hywyn
7 Cedd
15 Paul of Thebes
17 Antony of Egypt
31 Melangell (some
   celebrate 28 May)

February

1 Brigid
1 Seiriol
9 Engan

March

1 David
2 Chad
3 Non
5 Perran
17 Patrick

April

7 Brynach
21 Beuno

May

16 Brendan
19 Dunstan
27 Augustine of Canterbury

June

3 Kevin
4 Pedrog
9 Columba
20 Julius and Aaron

July

28 Samson

August

26 Ninian
31 Aidan

September

4 Cuthbert
9 Ciaran

October

10 Paulinus of York
12 Wilfrid
24 Cadfarch

November		December	
1	Cadfan	5	Cawrdaf
2	Aelhaearn	11	Cian
3	Winifrede	12	Finian
6	Illtud	28	Maughold
8	Cybi		
14	Dyfrig		
17	Hilda		
21	Paulinus of Wales		

DATES AND HISTORICAL SURVEY

Paleolithic (Old Stone Age): earliest human existence to
  c. 10,000 BC
Mesolithic (Middle Stone Age): *c.* 10,000 BC – *c.* 4500 BC
Neolithic (New Stone Age): *c.* 4500 BC – *c.* 2300 BC
Bronze Age: *c.* 2300 BC – 800 BC
Iron Age: *c.* 800 BC – Roman Period
Roman Period: AD 43 – AD 410
Early Medieval Period: AD 410 – AD 1066
Medieval Period: AD 1066 – *c.* AD 1485

SOME IMPORTANT DATES

AD 43	The Romans occupy Britain
45	St Paul preaches to the Celts of Galatia
70	Fall of Jerusalem
103	Justin Martyr writes that 'there are Christians in every part of the Roman Empire'
178	King Lucius, a Christian convert, builds a church on what is now the site of St Peter's, Cornhill, in London
190	Tertullian writes that 'Christianity in Britain has penetrated even those parts the Roman army cannot conquer'
210	Origen writes that 'the power of God our Saviour is even with them in Britain'
250	Martyrdoms of St Alban, Julius and Aaron
313	Edict of Milan Christianity tolerated throughout the Roman Empire
314	At the Council of Arles three Celtic Bishops attend from York, London and Colchester
325	Council of Nicaea
350	Athanasius writes about the purity of faith of the British bishops
375	Anglo–Saxon settlements begin in Britain
400	John Chrysostom writes that 'there are many churches and altars in Britain'
410	Romans leave Britain for the last time

Wales

Introduction to Wales

The martyrdoms of Aaron, Julius (probably in Caerleon, south-east Wales), and Alban can be dated to about the middle of the third century, and along with the record of British bishops (London, York and Colchester or Lincoln) present at the Council of Arles in 314 this information helps to show that Christianity was an early phenomenon in Britain.

Christianity took root in Britain in several ways:

- Roman soldiers
- commercial relations, especially with Gaul
- various wars and settlements
- the veneration of European saints such as Martin of Tours
- the influence of monasticism
- relationship with heresy such as Arianism and Pelagianism
- the immigration and the emigration movements

The arrival of Christianity in Wales is directly related to all of these seven influential factors.

The actual shape, character and quality of the life of the early church in Celtic Britain remains to be defined, but the evidence available points to the existence of a strongly Romanized church, most prevalent among the Romano-British elite, the people most directly in contact with these seven factors of influence. It was a church whose language was probably overwhelmingly Latin and whose structure, based on local centres of population, generally reflected the Roman pattern of civil organization, at least initially.

Whatever the shape of this early church, it was sufficiently developed to generate a sophisticated, vibrant and influential religious life. Seven crucial sources of information tell us this:

- the slightly later literature of the period (much of it written retrospectively)
- church dedications
- the string of holy wells
- cross-inscribed stones and standing crosses
- grave markers
- shrines
- place names including the names of fields

This church survived until the first half of the fifth century when, after the official withdrawal of the Roman forces in 410, the Celtic areas of Britain came under increasing pressure from vigorous assaults of the Irish from the west, the Picts from the north, and, most importantly, the Germanic or early English peoples who were seizing land from the east. Over a period of time the territory of this early Celtic church sharply contracted in the face of increasing pagan advances. The kingdom to the west and the north of the country (then known as Brythonic), which offered the invaders most resistance, got smaller because of the generally remote and inaccessible character of its terrain. The early church in Celtic Britain, therefore, began to be cut off from the rest of the world and took on the aspect of an insular foundation.

From the fifth century onwards, Christianity was probably restricted to Strathclyde and Cumbria in the north, through Wales, to Devon and Cornwall in the south.

It appears that the Welsh part of this early church was keen to maintain, as far as possible, the historical link with the old Roman civilization and with the religion that Rome had introduced, and it is worth noting that the very term *Welsh* is an early English word that means 'Romanized Celt'. One of the most influential spiritual impetus for the early church in Celtic Wales was the example of the monks of the Middle East, which came *via* southern Gaul. The *Lives* of the early Welsh saints contain many references to the monasticism of the desert and it clearly provided a powerful role model in Wales, as it did in other parts of Celtic Britain. It is likely that during

the fifth and sixth centuries individuals inspired by these ideals sought solitude and a life of work and prayer, attracting to themselves like-minded followers who established communities about them, as had been the pattern in fourth-century Egypt. In course of time, some such communities developed into small towns. There is some evidence to suggest that the communities of the far west (for example, Bardsey, Caldy, and St David's), which were closer to Ireland, maintained a more ascetic life-style as opposed to becoming townships.

As was the case in Ireland, the 'Celtic' period in Wales ended principally with the arrival of the Normans, who brought with them many of the traditions of European Christianity. For the first time the major religious orders of the Catholic Church, especially the Cistercians and the Augustinian Canons, took root in Wales. The new integration into European ways brought change, but it also greatly encouraged a Welsh national consciousness and represented an expansion of Welsh cultural horizons.

Introducing Llŷn

and the Pilgrim Paths to Bardsey, St Beuno and St Cadfan

THE LLŶN PENINSULA

This area of north-west Wales has attracted generations of visitors but much of its history and culture remains hidden and undiscovered. It's not an area scattered with grand churches, but for centuries its people have built, maintained and prayed in buildings which reflect a wide variety of architectural styles and cultural influences. Throughout the Llŷn Peninsula there are ancient expressions of a distinctive Celtic tradition and devotion offering crucial links back to the Celtic Church which survived in this area until the thirteenth century.

As in all other parts of Britain where there are early Christian sites all these churches have suffered the ravages of time. Of course not all the churches are ancient but most of them on the Llŷn Peninsula preserve clues as to the spirit of an earlier church which may formerly have occupied that or a nearby site.

The Peninsula also has a wide repertoire of Welsh saint dedications, but on the whole little is known of most of them. Many may have been early missionaries bringing the faith to the people of ancient Britain, whilst others may have been

hermits living simple lives of devotion in this area. Still others may have been donors of land upon which the first churches were built. The ancient Welsh word *llan*, for instance, means a consecrated enclosure within which worship and burial took place. It came to mean the church of the founding saint and villages that have grown up around these churches often share the name of their original church.

By following the ancient Pilgrimage Trail towards Bardsey, for devotional reasons or just out of interest in architecture, history or culture, today's pilgrim is assured of a rich and rewarding experience.

As well as its religious and spiritual attractions, Llŷn's coastline is rich in natural beauty, wildlife and maritime heritage, and its self-contained position, at arm's length from the outside world and shielded by the mountains of Snowdonia, makes it a stronghold of Welsh tradition and language.

Neolithic (New Stone Age), Bronze Age and Iron Age settlers left evidence in the form of *cromlech* (burial chambers), round huts and stone forts, which scatter the length of the Llŷn Peninsula. In common

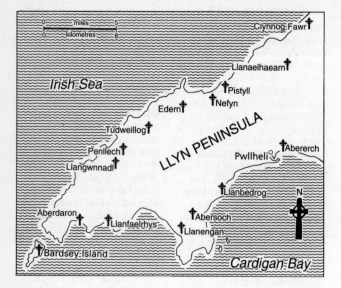

with other Celtic outposts in Ireland, Scotland and Brittany, there's an inexplicable yet irresistible impulse that draws people westwards to Llŷn.

THE TWO ANCIENT PILGRIM PATHS OF LLŶN

On the western tip of the Peninsula lies Bardsey, the Island of 20,000 Saints. In its Christian religious context the island is almost certainly an early Celtic foundation; it was one of the best known of the pilgrimage sites in Britain during the Middle Ages. Traditionally there were two pilgrim routes leading to Bardsey and today there is a great resurgence of interest in walking (and driving) these routes towards Bardsey across the Llŷn Peninsula.

During the twelfth century a number of important references confirm the significance of both the island and the pilgrimage routes:

- Pope Callixtus II (1119–24) declared generous indulgences for those undertaking these routes; he proclaimed that three pilgrimages to Bardsey were equal to one pilgrimage to Jerusalem.
- Giraldus Cambrensis (Gerald of Wales) accompanied Archbishop Baldwin during his tour of Wales to preach the Third Crusade in 1188. Gerald remarks on the prolific number of pilgrims travelling towards Bardsey.
- A poetic expression of the spirit of Welsh re-awakening accompanied the rise of the Princes of Gwynedd during the twelfth century. Meilyr Brydydd, the court poet of Gruffudd ap Cynan, King of Gwynedd (1055–1137), for example, in his deathbed lament expresses a wish to be buried on Bardsey and links the island's spiritual importance to the resurrection and the saints.

Although both routes have places of 'pilgrim-gathering' further away such as those at Bangor Cathedral to the north (Deiniol *c.* 525, its patron saint, is believed to have been buried on Bardsey) and Tywyn to the south (Cadfan *c.* 570, its patron, was the first Abbot of Bardsey), this section will focus primarily on the pilgrimage churches on the Llŷn Peninsula.

The Northern Pilgrimage Route

ST BEUNO, CLYNNOG FAWR

As a missionary, St Beuno is probably the most significant saint of North Wales and his contribution to the growth of the early church in this area is of paramount importance. It was he and his disciples who evangelized most of the northern part of Wales and it is probably due largely to them that the pilgrim routes on Llyn are so firmly established.

Beuno was born into a princely family in mid-Wales during the second half of the sixth century. His *Life* was written quite late: it survives in a fourteenth-century Welsh version. In it Beuno is introduced as a model powerful Christian. The *Life* also gives information on how Beuno was prepared for a life of mission in the church in the south. His chapel at Llanfeuno under Clodock in the Black Mountains is evidence for his early ministry in that area. When his father died Beuno received land from a local prince on which he built his first monastery, probably near Berriew in mid-Wales. After a long period in the area of Powys, the Severn Valley, the Dee Valley, the Flint coast and Holywell, Beuno eventually turned his missionary interest to Llŷn in the north-west.

On arrival in the north-west Beuno asked King Cadwallon of Caernarfon for land on which to build a church, but Cadwallon cheated him and Beuno cursed the king. The king's cousin, Gwyddaint, offered him his own township of Clynnog. Beuno probably built his first church beside the stream there in 616. Soon that small chapel was to develop into the most important and thriving monastic settlement of North Wales; it was this that became the heart of Beuno's cult. When Beuno died in about 642 he was buried beneath the adjacent Clynnog chapel. His grave immediately became a shrine, and those who were sick bathed in the waters of his nearby holy well and were laid on his tomb for the night. Both the well and the chapel are easily accessible today.

The Celtic monastery founded by Beuno continued in existence as a *clas*, or collegiate church (monastery and college: an institution peculiar to the Celtic Church) until the Norman period (post 1100). At that time it became a 'portionary' church, which meant that it was served by a number of different clergy. The status of being a cross between a parish church and a college, rather than a monastery, enabled Clynnog Fawr to escape dissolution during the reign of Henry VIII. It became the largest, wealthiest, and most important church in this part of Britain.

The present building dates from the late fifteenth century and was probably built to offer shelter and service to the increasingly vast crowds of pilgrims.

A few references to some of the features in this church will be useful:

- There is a fifteenth-century rood screen in the chancel with carved misericords.
- It boasts an especially fine wood ceiling above the nave.
- The chancel and transepts were built in c. 1480, the nave and porch in c. 1500, the vestry and Beuno's Chapel in the mid 1500s, the cloister between the main church and the chapel in c. 1610 and the lychgate in c. 1750.
- The medieval Beuno's Chest stands in a glass case in the nave. This was hollowed out from a single ash tree trunk for people to place offerings to atone for crimes; the carved inscription reads: *Here I offer to God four pence for my private sins on which account the Almighty is now punishing me.* People also offered money from the sale of animals considered to belong to Beuno. At birth some Welsh calves and lambs have a slit in their ears known as 'Beuno's mark'

(*Nod Beuno*). Until the late eighteenth century, farmers brought these animals to the church wardens on the Sunday after Whitsun; they were sold, and the money was placed in the chest.

- On the south-west side of the church stands Beuno's Chapel. This forms an almost separate building and is connected to the main church by a narrow cloister. Some time in the eighteenth century this cloister was used as a kind of parish prison. It has an unusual vaulted roof, which probably recalls early Celtic work. The chapel, originally much smaller, was the site of Beuno's tomb until 1796 and between 1827 and 1849 was used as a school by Eban Fardd, a well-known Welsh poet who is buried on the north side of the churchyard. Leaning against the wall in the chapel is Beuno's Stone (*Maen Beuno*), a flat, roughly-shaped boulder incised with a Latin Cross, dated to the fifth century. Traditionally, pilgrims kneel before the

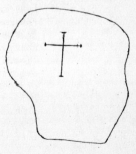

stone, trace the outline of the cross with their fingers, and then make the sign of the cross on themselves.

Outside the church there are two important features:

- On the west side stands a flat pillar approximately six feet high and on its face (not its head!) lies a unique kind of sundial. In its top is a round hole (for the use of a moveable marker) and below it a semicircle divided into four equal parts; these symbolize four times for worship: the beginning of the day, mid-morning, mid-afternoon and the day's end. This type of dial is known in Ireland but this is the only example in Wales. It dates from the tenth or eleventh centuries.

- About a hundred yards from the church on the left side of the A499 leading to Pwllheli is St Beuno's Well. Its square pool of clear water is surrounded by an open-roofed stone well-house. Take great care as you walk along this busy road and as you step out of the well area.

The church is open daily from March to November with a good exhibition on pilgrimage and on the history of this church.

Contact number: 01286 660547

Suggested Devotion

Luke 24.13–31: The Emmaus Road

The Call to Worship, from *The Iona Community, Liturgy for Holy Communion A*, in Wild Goose Worship Group, *A Wee Worship Book*, (The Iona Community, 1999), pp. 80-1:

> *GATHER US IN,*
> *From corner or limelight,*
> *From mansion or campsite,*
> *From fears and obsession,*
> *From tears and depression,*
> *From untold excesses,*
> *From treasured successes,*
> *To meet, to eat,*
> *Be given a seat,*
> *Be joined to the vine,*
> *Be offered new wine,*
> *Become like the least,*
> *Be found at the feast.*
> *GATHER US IN!*

ST AELHAEARN, LLANAELHAEARN

The church in Llanaelhaearn is named after its seventh-century founder, St Aelhaearn (the saint of the 'iron eyebrow'), and is situated in the centre of the village about five miles from Clynnog along the northern pilgrim route. Aelhaearn and his two brothers, Llwchhaearn and Cynhaearn, were the sons of Hygarfael, a leader in Powys. All three sons refused a military career and chose to follow Beuno. Clearly this was the next stop for the pilgrims *en route* to Bardsey.

The present church, built on earlier foundations, is in the form of a cross and was greatly restored in 1892. Its most important features are its early Christian inscribed stones both inside and outside. On the south of the church gate can be found a roughly hewn pillar stone inscribed vertically in Roman capitals. There is also a memorial stone for Aliortus, a Christian from Elfed (a distant Celtic kingdom around the West Riding), dating back to about 500, on the interior north wall of the church, and a memorial stone for Melitus, about 500, in the churchyard on the right side of the path. Also in the churchyard wall there is a stone with an incised cross dating back to the seventh or eighth century.

On the left of the B4417 to Llithfaen is the well of St Aelhaearn in a stone housing. Most medieval pilgrims would have stopped here before facing the strenuous climb over part of the Eifl mountain. Once that difficult part was behind them, pilgrims would find a welcome break at the monastery and hospice at Pistyll, dedicated once again to Beuno.

Suggested Devotion

Psalm 121: I will lift my eyes to the hills

From 'The Road Ahead' by Thomas Merton, in Margaret Pawley, *Prayers For Pilgrims* (Triangle, 1991), p. 30:

> *My Lord God,*
> *I have no idea where I am going.*
> *I do not see the road ahead of me.*
> *I cannot know for certain where it will end.*
> *Nor do I really know myself . . .*
> *. . . Therefore will I trust you always*
> *Though I may seem lost in the shadow of death.*
> *I will not fear, for you are ever with me,*
> *And you will never leave me*
> *To face my perils alone.*

A little further up the hill on the right of the B4417 stand the three peaks of the Eifl hills (in English these are referred to as 'the Rivals'). The most easterly is Tre'r Ceiri (the Town of the Giants), an exceptionally well-preserved fortress rising to 1,591 feet. Excavations have shown that the site was occupied during the latter part of the Roman period, and perhaps earlier. It also has a Bronze Age cairn (a heap of stones representing a monument or landmark). It is possible to climb to the top of Tre'r Ceiri fairly easily. About 400 yards up this steep road on the right side of the B4417 is a lay-by for parking. Simply walk a further 50 yards or so after parking alongside the right hand side of the road and a public footpath leads gently upwards.

Details for access to the church are on the notice-board.

Contact number: 01286 660547

ST BEUNO, PISTYLL

Medieval pilgrims would probably have turned towards the coast by taking what is today the right turning on the crossroads in Llithfaen, through Nant Gwytheyrn (the valley of Vortigen, currently the Welsh National Language Centre and well worth a visit), following the coastal path towards the church in Pistyll. Modern pilgrims would do well to stick to the B4417 through the village of Llithfaen for

three miles until they come to a spacious lay-by on the left; across the road a narrow lane on the right leads to the church and the sea. The farm at Pistyll was excused from paying tithes because it offered hospitality to pilgrims.

This is another church founded by Beuno in the sixth century. It is possible that he

established this place originally as a sanctuary of peace or retreat for himself in the same way as St Kevin did at Glendalough in Ireland and St Antony in the Egyptian desert. The present church was probably built in the twelfth century and lies significantly in a grassy hollow beside a stream, typical of many Welsh coastal chapels that relied on the sea for travel and water for both healing and nourishment. The church, whose very simplicity is part of a characteristically Celtic charm, has some interesting medieval artefacts:

- On the north wall of the chancel are the remains of

a medieval wall painting, possibly of St Christopher, the patron of travellers.

- The font has interesting features: the overlapping circles carved in relief around the basin, the scalloped rim, and the double row of beading suggest strong Celtic influences; it is probably twelfth-century.

- The west side of the church is almost certainly twelfth-century and the east fifteenth-century. For protection from sea winds, there are no windows on the north side, apart from a later small window near the altar, sometimes referred to as a leper's window.

Two very interesting traditions associated with Pistyll are Lammas and healing.

The season of Lammas begins on 1 August, the time of the Druidic festival of Lughnasadh, held in honour of the great god Lug, who is commemorated in the Roman name for Carlisle, Luguvalium – the fortress of Lug. In the late twelfth century Giraldus Cambrensis, then Archdeacon of Brecon, described a strangely mutated Christian version of this festival, which took the form of a frenzied circle dance round the churchyard on the feast of the local saint, Almedha, which fell on 1 August. The purpose of the ceremony was prayer to ensure that the corn should be safely gathered in. 'Lammas' is derived from the Anglo-Saxon *hlaef-mas*, the Mass Loaf. It was the custom for this to be made from the first flour ground after the harvest. It was a time of great feasting and celebration, praying for and anticipating a successful harvest.

At some stage the church at Pistyll resumed the practice of celebrating Lammas. It is still celebrated today. On the Sunday closest to 1 August the church is decorated with all kinds of symbolic breads and the floor is strewn with rushes cut from the surrounding hillsides.

Suggested Devotion

Deuteronomy 16.1-4: Coming into God's Land

Matthew 13.1-23: Parable of the Sower

From 'Bread of Tomorrow', by Janet Morley, in *Praying with the World's Poor* (SPCK, 1992), p. 93:

> *Come to this table*
> *To meet the Living God . . .*
> *. . . Come to find, to meet, to hold*
> *The living, loving God*
> *Made new for us in bread and wine.*

This church has also been associated very much with the ministry of healing. Pilgrims used to rest at the adjacent monastery, at the inn, or at the hospice on nearby Cefnedd Hill. The twenty-acre field called Eisteddfa (place of rest) next to the larger Cae Hospice field would have held a larger number of accommodation huts for those who needed to rest after receiving medicinal aid. Lepers were probably confined in a smaller building on Cae Hospice Pennla. Growing on the hillsides in the surrounding valley are the offspring of the same herbs and medicinal plants that grew there during the Middle Ages. Some are common plants used as familiar remedies, but many are rare or endangered species of considerable historic significance. Before approaching the church one notices the remains of a mill pond, believed to have once been a dammed pond providing fish for the hospice and monastic community. Slightly upstream from the fishpond is the fresh spring that is Pistyll's holy well.

Pistyll Church is usually open all year.

Contact number: 01758 720494

ST GWYNHOEDL, LLANGWNNADL

From Pistyll pilgrims travel along the B4417 through Nefyn, Edern and Tudweiliog (all of which have interesting ancient churches) and into Llangwnnadl, turning right before the narrow bridge, at a postbox on the right and signpost to Porth Colmon. The founder, St Gwynhoedl, was a sixth-century missionary, whose probable burial place in the north-east of the church is marked by a stone carved in late medieval Latin. A commemorative stone dating back to the seventh century and probably used to mark his burial place stands today in Plas Glyn-y-Weddw Art Gallery at Llanbedrog. The stone bears the name *Vendesteli*, the contemporary Celtic form of the later Welsh Gwynhoedl.

Gwynhoedl is reputed to be one of the sons of the Welsh chieftain Seithenyn. Like his brothers, Gwynhoedl was a member of the *clas* of Dunawd in Bangor on Dee. Again this church is strategically located near the sea – the main means of travel at that time – as well as being close to a river that provided water for living and for baptism.

During restoration work on the church in 1940, a large stone with a Celtic Cross was found when plaster was removed from the interior of the south wall. Traces of red colouring not only tell us that the cross was originally painted, but enable a fairly accurate dating to about 600. Also dating from the same time is a bronze handbell, one of

the very few surviving in Wales. The original is in the National Museum of Wales in Cardiff, but a replica is in the present church and can be rung.

The original building was made of wattle, mud and timber, and remained until Norman times when a stone building was erected. The first edifice was a simple rectangle with a small window above the altar and a door in the west wall. During the Middle Ages the shrine of Gwynhoedl became very popular for pilgrims heading for Bardsey. The field adjacent to the church is called Cae Eisteddfa: a place of rest or a place to sit. Popularity made it necessary to enlarge the church.

The church is open daily.

Contact number: 01758 730450

ST HYWYN, ABERDARON

Although the medieval pilgrim would have kept close to the coastline heading for Anelog and Uwchmynydd, the B4417 is an easier route to Aberdaron.

Aberdaron was and still is for many the end of the journey for those heading to Bardsey. Because of the tides and currents, crossing to the island is not a straightforward

---

Suggested Devotion

Matthew 11.25-30: Come to Me

'Roads' by Ruth Bidgood, in *Selected Poems* (Seren, 1992):

> *No need to wonder what heron-haunted lake*
> *lay in the other valley,*
> *or regret the songs in the forest*
> *I chose not to traverse.*
> *No need to ask where other roads might have led,*
> *since they led elsewhere;*
> *for nowhere but this here and now*
> *is my true destination.*
> *The river is gentle in the soft evening,*
> *and all the steps of my life have brought me home.*

experience. During the Middle Ages, pilgrims often had to wait a long time. Aberdaron was thus heavily populated with a monastery, several chapels, inns, local dwellings and the church.

Hywyn is believed to have accompanied Cadfan, one of the princes of Armorice in Brittany, who was, with Einion, prince of Llŷn, one of the founders of the religious community on Bardsey during the sixth century. Cadfan was the first Abbot of Bardsey. Hywyn was the son of Gwyndaf Hen and his wife Gwenonwy of Brittany, cousin to Cadfan and probably the confessor to the religious community on Bardsey.

Shortly after its foundation, the community at Aberdaron developed into a distinctive Celtic *clas*. It became an important one, the abbot being lord of a considerable area and holding extensive properties in Llŷn. Although the policy of the Normans was to break up this *clas* organization and reduce them to ordinary parish churches, the *clas* at Aberdaron survived and, like Clynnog, continued as a portionary church.

There has always been a close relationship between Aberdaron church and Bardsey and it is probably the canons of St Mary's Abbey on Bardsey

that conferred the status of portionary church on St Hywyn's, or at least approved it in order that the portioners, or secular priests, of Aberdaron, who later became canons of the collegiate church, could take spiritual charge of the tenants of the abbey properties on the mainland; but at what date is unknown. The first certain information as to the existence of a portionary church at Aberdaron occurs in a document dated 12 July 1252, purporting to be an agreement between the abbot and canons of Bardsey and tenants of the abbot on the mainland.

In the church there are two very important stone monuments to Christian priests and monks dating from *c.* 500. The first reads: *Veracius Priest lies here*; and the second: *Senacus Priest lies here with many brethren*. Both were found in the shallow valley of the headwaters of the river Saint, near the farm now called Gors under Mynydd Anelog (Anelog Mountain). The reference to *many brethren* suggests that the stones came from the cemetery of an early religious community in this area.

The church is usually open during the day.

Contact number: 01758 760229

Suggested Devotion

Psalm 23: The Lord's my shepherd

Mark 1.14–20: Jesus Calls Four Fishermen

The Southern Pilgrimage Route

The tracing of the southern route is more complex. The coastline of Meirionydd, Ardudwy, Eifionydd and the south side of Llŷn is very different to that of the north with wider river estuaries. Even today one has to travel quite some distance inland to cross the Dysynni, Mawddach and Dwyryd rivers and much land has been reclaimed along the whole of the coast of Cardigan Bay.

By the sixth century Cadfan had established a *clas* at Tywyn between the river Dyfi and the Dysynni estuary. From his religious community priests and missionaries founded churches along the whole of the coastline north and south, as well as inland. Along with other saints, Cadfan established a monastery on Bardsey and from that time onwards the southern route from Tywyn to Bardsey became as important as the one from Clynnog Fawr on the northern coast of Llŷn.

ST CYBI'S WELL, LLANGYBI

The church of St Cybi in Llangybi became an obvious place of gathering and resting.

The well near the church was an important centre for healing. It is the most elaborate of its kind in Wales. The two well chambers are of ancient date and may have originally served as baptismal centres. A stone standing against the lychgate leading to the church and engraved with a primitive cross (possibly seventh- or eighth-century) suggests a religious foundation with strong Celtic links.

St Cybi was a sixth-century Cornish missionary whose life is written in two Latin manuscripts. Cybi's chief foundation was Caer Gybi (Holyhead), where he established himself within the walls of a dismantled Roman fort. The *clas* which he founded there had a long history; it continued as a collegiate church throughout the Middle Ages.

Access to the well is easy and Llangybi can be found by leaving the A497 from Cricieth on to the B4354 through Chwilog and then right to the village of Llanarmon, and then to Llangybi. The well is well signposted.

Contact number: 01766 523222

Suggested Devotion

Mark 1.1–13: John the Baptist and the Baptism and Temptation of Jesus

From 'Pilgrim, fainting in the tempest', translated by Alan Gaunt from Ann Griffiths' 'Bererin Llesg gan rym y stormydd', in *Always From Joy* (Stainer and Bell, 1997):

> *. . . In your feeble state remember:*
> *ankle deep, the stream will rise*
> *like a great unfathomed river,*
> *measured for you in the skies;*
> *only resurrection's children*
> *swim in floods so deep and wide;*
> *fathomless and shoreless waters,*
> *from Bethesda's mighty tide . . .*

ST CAWRDAF, ABERERCH

Abererch was popularly supposed to be the resting place of those who did not make it to Aberdaron, but whose health suffered during the journey or who even died *en route*. This was also the traditional resting place for those carrying others who wanted to be buried on Bardsey; special prayers would be said here for a safe crossing. The church, dedicated to Cawrdaf and to Cadfarch, is first mentioned about 1250–75 when it belonged to the Beddgelert Priory.

Because of its influence on the general development of the early church in this area during the Celtic period as well as its significant later wealth and land ownership, it is worth mentioning the Beddgelert Priory. Abererch Church is the westernmost church for which the Priory had responsibility. The Priory was regarded in medieval times as almost the oldest monastery in Wales, and must have begun as a Celtic community in the sixth century. When Giraldus Cambrensis described it towards 1200 it was still unconnected with any regular order. Characterizing it as the kind of religious community which existed before the Benedictine or other rule, Giraldus alludes to it as an example of Cistercian pressure, its independent existence threatened by the new abbey of Aberconwy. It adopted the rule of the Augustinian Canons probably soon afterwards. Its prior and convent are mentioned from the mid-thirteenth century onwards. But the change probably took place early in the first half of the century to judge from the style of the earliest features of the church, the erection of

31

which may well have followed the new association with a widespread order. The monastery was accidentally burnt down during Edward I's war of conquest (1282). The king's commissioners paid compensation in 1284, and in 1286 Anian, Bishop of Bangor, authorized an appeal for rebuilding the house, as the oldest monastery in all Wales next to Bardsey, and one much used by pilgrims and travellers from west to north Wales and from Ireland to England.

According to tradition Cawrdaf was a prince, the son of Caradog Freichfras, prince of Brecon in the sixth century, and was trained for the priesthood by St Illtud at his large monastery in Llantwit Major. It is also suggested that Cadfan was a disciple of St Seiriol. The present building was built in the fourteenth and fifteenth centuries on the foundations of a much older building. Abererch is named in the 'Stanzas of the Graves' which refers to the graves of the 'warriors of Britain' and may have been composed in the ninth century. A mid-thirteenth-century copy survives and notes that Rhydderch Hael (The Generous), a hero of north Britain, was buried there. The church is listed in the Norwich Taxatio (1254) as 'Abher of the deanery of Lleyn'.

Contact number: 01758 612305

Suggested Devotion

Wisdom 3.1–9: The Souls of the Faithful are in the Hands of God

John 11.21–27: I am the Resurrection and the Life

From 'Cofio' ('Remembering') by Waldo Williams, translated by Tony Conran, in *The Peacemakers: Waldo Williams* (Gomer Press, 1997):

> *Before the sun has left the sky, one minute,*
> *One dear minute, before the journeying night,*
> *To call to mind the things that are forgotten*
> *Now in the dust of ages lost from sight . . .*
>
> *. . . Often when I'm alone and it's near nightfall,*
> *I yearn to acknowledge you and know each one.*
> *Is there no way fond memory can keep you,*
> *Forgotten ancient things of the family of man?*

ST PEDROG, LLANBEDROG

From Abererch travel through Pwllheli on the A497 and the A499 towards Abersoch, and you will come to the village of Llanbedrog. The church is located on the road leading to the beach.

Pedrog was a sixth-century Welsh saint and a missionary in Wales, Ireland, Cornwall and Brittany. The church's proximity to the sea and its nestling situation suggest strongly that this was an obvious resting point on the southern route and it is a good example of coastal chapels typical along the Welsh coast. The present church is a very simple structure; its nave and foundations are thirteenth-century; the chancel, font, west window and screen are fifteenth-century.

Pedrog (also referred to as Petroc, Petrox and Perreux) was born during the last part of the fifth century and ministered as an important missionary during the first half of the sixth century. He probably received his early education in Ireland where he studied secular literature and theology for 20 years (possibly with St Kevin at Glendalough). He returned to Wales in about 518 and then made his way to Cornwall, probably followed by a group of Irish Christians. His first achievement was to establish a small house of prayer called Petrocstow (Padstow) in Cornwall and he spent about 30 years exercising a preaching, praying and teaching ministry there. In 540, after a seven-year missionary journey and pilgrimage, he moved 'up river' to Bodmin. Some sources claim that during the seven-year period he travelled to Rome, Jerusalem and India, but he almost certainly also returned to Wales to establish churches at this time. In Wales there are three churches which bear his name: Llanbedrog on the Llŷn Peninsula, Ferwig in Cardiganshire, and St Petrox in Pembrokeshire. There are a further 17 dedications in Devon, 6 in Cornwall and 8 in Brittany.

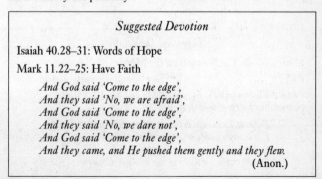

Suggested Devotion

Isaiah 40.28–31: Words of Hope

Mark 11.22–25: Have Faith

> *And God said 'Come to the edge',*
> *And they said 'No, we are afraid',*
> *And God said 'Come to the edge',*
> *And they said 'No, we dare not',*
> *And God said 'Come to the edge',*
> *And they came, and He pushed them gently and they flew.*
> (Anon.)

After his 'missionary journey' Pedrog returned to Cornwall and established a large religious monastic community in Bodmin. It is said that this monastery was active for 1,000 years after his death. Pedrog spent the rest of his life as the abbot of this community but also probably visited his other 'communities' such as the one in Llanbedrog on the Llŷn Peninsula. Tradition has it that he died on 4 June 564 and was buried at Bodmin.

The church is usually open.

Contact number: 01758 740919

ST ENGAN, LLANENGAN

Further along the A499, through Abersoch, is the small village of Llanengan. Here is undoubtedly one of the most important churches on the southern route and a popular resting place for pilgrims to Bardsey. Apart from Llanfaelrys, the small coastal church near Aberdaron, this is the only church from which pilgrims could and still can see Bardsey.

The present church is mainly fifteenth-century and the tower was built in 1534. It has had important links with the abbey church on Bardsey. The religious community on Bardsey was destroyed in 1537 and there may well be some significance concerning the closeness of the dates of the Bardsey abbey destruction and the Llanengan rebuilding and restoration. It is possible that the bells which hang here came from Bardsey as did the choir stalls behind the medieval screen and the money chest near the door.

There are two holy wells at the far end of the churchyard beyond the west boundary wall. Healing was to be received by bathing in one and drinking from the other.

From Llanengan the route continues to Aberdaron either by returning to the B4413 or via the narrower coast road through the village of Rhiw.

Contact number: 01758 740919

Suggested Devotion

Matthew 5–7: The Sermon on the Mount

From 'Dewi Sant' ('St David') by Gwenallt, translated by Patrick Thomas, in A. M. Allchin et al., *Sensuous Glory* (Canterbury Press, 2000), p. 100:

> *There is no border between two worlds in the Church;*
> *The church militant on earth is the same*
> *As the victorious Church in Heaven.*
> *And the saints will be in the two-one Church . . .*

UWCHMYNYDD AND ST MARY'S WELL

By continuing through the village of Aberdaron to the very tip of the Peninsula the Island of 20,000 Saints, Bardsey, can be seen.

The weather was as unpredictable in the medieval period as it is today. In the event that medieval pilgrims were delayed for a long time many of them possibly walked from Aberdaron to Uwchmynydd and to a small coastal chapel dedicated to St Mary (now totally ruined) where they could spend part of their waiting time and see Bardsey albeit from a distance.

The coastal path from Aberdaron to Uwchmynydd can still be walked today. Simply park in the village of Aberdaron and walk on to the beach, turn right towards the coastline and walk to the corner. The outline of the path can be seen clearly from a distance and the local authorities have recently made the pathway safe for walkers. As well as leading you to the tip of the Peninsula the path also leads to the picturesque cove called Porth Meudwy (The Hermit's Port). This is clearly an ancient place from which many pilgrims sailed to Bardsey and is the popular departing place for Bardsey today.

There is nothing left to see of St Mary's Chapel today but from above, from the top of Uwchmynydd, the outline of the chapel with possibly the location of its apse, its surrounding buildings and its boundary wall can be picked out. In the cliffs below St Mary's Chapel, and at the point where the island is closest to the mainland, is St Mary's Well. The walk down to the well is dangerous. Follow the valley down towards the sea, but before arriving at the water's edge take the clearly defined upward footway (not an official-looking path) on the right, keeping right on the treacherous cliff edge until the well can be seen. Medieval steps hewn in the rocks will take you to the water's edge. The well is carefully tucked into the rocks on your right-hand side.

Suggested Devotion

John 21: The Resurrection

From 'Ffynnon Fair' ('St Mary's Well') by R. S. Thomas, in *Laboratories of the Spirit* (Macmillan, 1975), p. 45:

> *They did not divine it, but*
> *they bequeathed it to us:*
> *clear water, brackish at times,*
> *complicated by the white frosts*
> *of the sea, but thawing quickly . . .*

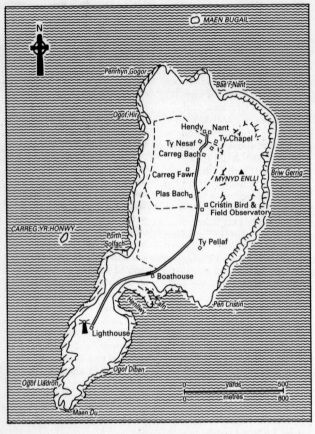

Bardsey

Bardsey Island/Ynys Enlli

Bardsey (*Ynys Enlli* in Welsh, 'the Island of the Tides') is a place of pilgrimage that has been of great importance throughout Welsh religious history. It is one of the largest islands off the coast of Wales and with its mountain (167m; 548ft), sea cliffs, beaches and lowland area, provides a wide variety of habitats for wildlife. Lying 3km from the tip of Llŷn, Bardsey is 1km across at its widest point and 2.5km long.

Tradition speaks of Cadfan as the founder of the earliest Celtic monastic settlement on Bardsey. But many rightly claim that it was almost certainly a place of spiritual significance in pre-Christian times. Cadfan also founded the church at Tywyn (across the water to the south-east). Both sites claim to be his burial place. In the church at Tywyn a stone bears the inscription in Welsh: *Beneath a similar mound lies Cadfan, sad that it should enclose the praise of the earth. May he rest without blemish.* This stone claims to be the oldest recorded example of written Welsh.

The earliest record of a monastic presence on the island is an inscription found at the foot of Anelog Hill which records the burial of '*Senacus the Priest together with many brethren*' and dates from the late fifth or early sixth century. Early Welsh monasticism, like

that of Ireland, was strongly influenced by fourth-century Egyptian models which stressed the hermit life as well as that of the community as an ideal form of radical Christian commitment. It is likely that Bardsey itself became the focus for these experiments, possibly attracting those who wished to retire into a more rigorous and solitary form of monastic life as a retreat or, as in the case of Dyfrig (or Dubricius, a sixth-century Welsh saint with jurisdiction over Caldey Island off the Pembrokeshire coast), as a preparation for death.

Such monastic settlements on the island must have suffered severely during the ninth and tenth centuries from Viking invasions; the name *Bardsey* is of Norse origin, meaning 'Bardr's Island'. The outlines of the Celtic foundations of small round huts on the mountain can be seen in the winter or early spring before the bracken grows. They are situated in a reasonably sheltered position on a level plateau with strategic views of the sea in three directions.

By the twelfth century Bardsey was already long established as a place of special significance in Welsh religious life. Giraldus Cambrensis speaks of it in this sense, revealing also that it was the home of *Culdee* groups (part of the ninth-century Irish monastic reform movement). On the basis of its reputation, Bardsey became a major centre of pilgrimage in Wales. This spirit of devotion is summed up by the twelfth-century Welsh Court poet Meilyr Brydydd, who celebrates the 'fair parish of Enlli's faithful' and speaks of it as a place of resurrection. Meilyr expresses his own fervent hope that his body will rest among the many saints who have died on the island and that he will on the last day rise with them to meet his Creator. The hermitic tradition of Bardsey is still maintained today: there are still solitary nuns on Llŷn and at special times on Bardsey.

Modern-day pilgrims can see the fragmentary remains of the thirteenth-century abbey of the Augustinian Canons who took over the ancient Celtic foundation. The roofless tower has recently been adapted for eucharistic celebration and several interesting carved stones of the early period are preserved there. Edward I visited the island with his court in 1284 but the monastery was suppressed at the Reformation in 1537. However, Christian faith and worship continued through the centuries and especially in the nineteenth century when the inhabitants were affected by the evangelical revivalist movements which swept through Wales.

Bardsey was bought by the Bardsey Island Trust in 1979 and today it can be seen as a working island with a small year-round population. Its 180 hectares are farmed in a way that balances sensitive ecological and environmental goals with modern farming techniques and most of the houses are let to summer visitors. The Trust now has responsibility for the island and maintains it as a place for religious and spiritual renewal and a centre for ornithology, marine biology, and other natural sciences.

Contact numbers:

Bardsey Island Trust office
01758 730740

Booking office 01758 760667

Suggested Devotion

Psalm 122: Now our feet are standing within your gates

Matthew 28: The Resurrection

From 'Marwysgafn', (the deathbed poem of Meilyr Brydydd, 1137, translated by Tony Conran, in *Poetry Wales* (Poetry Wales Press, 1986), pp. 139–40:

> . . . *The Creator who made me, he'll receive me*
> *Among true folk of the parish of Enlli* . . .

Dilyn Dewi:

Pilgrimages in the Welsh Celtic Tradition

Dilyn Dewi (Following David) is an organization in North Wales offering pilgrimages in the Welsh Celtic tradition. As well as group pilgrimages along ancient and medieval pilgrim routes, it also specializes in the development of study programmes, field trips and research opportunities for groups and individuals in the Welsh Celtic tradition.

The programmes provide:

- a study of the Celtic tradition in the physical and human setting of the land;
- opportunities to share with people from different areas, countries, traditions and cultures;
- exposure to the history and practice of the Celtic traditions;
- times of prayer, reflection and worship as a pilgrim in Wales;
- contact with 'living stones' of the local faith communities;
- an opportunity to explore the Welsh spiritual tradition in a living ecumenical and bilingual context;
- the retracing of ancient footsteps along the two medieval pilgrim routes to Bardsey, along with the chance to visit the island.

Dilyn Dewi offers a range of resources for individuals, religious groups and pilgrims, students and academics, and the programmes can be designed to suit particular requirements. Shorter one-, three- or seven-day programmes can be arranged for individuals and groups. Programmes can also be arranged for individuals and small groups who wish to explore the Celtic tradition in Wales through a time of sabbatical or personal reflection and study.

Today, the 'living stones' of Llŷn offer a warm ministry of welcome to all who wish to pilgrim through a cherished land. *Dilyn Dewi* makes full use of a web of ancient churches, 'modern' chapels, medieval footpaths, and groups of ecumenical and bilingual people to provide exciting and stimulating resources to explore the Celtic traditions.

In the light of this important historical background, *Dilyn Dewi* has three main aims:

- to meet an increasing demand in 'pilgrimage traffic'. More and more people are discovering ancient pilgrim paths all over the world. Many of these have become major tourist centres but also successfully manage to maintain a 'spiritual heart'. Here on the Llŷn Peninsula, Christians have travelled between the many early sites since the sixth century, reaching an important climax in the early Middle Ages. Some twelfth-century texts describe pilgrims arriving in vast numbers in order to see and to visit Bardsey;

- to provide a living focus for those who are searching for a connection between the physical and geographical pilgrimage and the inner and spiritual journey of life – this is true for both Christians and non-Christians. It is striking just how many people are finding it important to make this connection, and once the connection has been made so much in life either takes on a new meaning or simply begins to make some sense;

- to root the growing interest in Celtic history firmly within a vibrant Welsh context. Throughout the world people are retracing their roots back to one of the many Celtic traditions. The Irish and Scottish traditions have been well explored in recent years. Today the uniquely Welsh Celtic is 'fully awake' thanks to many of the contributors to the *Dilyn Dewi* programme, all of whom are experts in aspects of the Welsh Celtic tradition. *Dilyn Dewi* therefore invites pilgrims to participate in this unique tradition through the medium of pilgrimage. One important way for the Christian tradition to speak confidently and faithfully to the present is by recovering the Church's past; *Dilyn Dewi* believes that the renewed exploration of the intensity of the Christian Celtic period is a vital contribution to this end.

Contact numbers: 01758 740919 or andrewjon@supanet.com

e-mail: dilyndewi@supanet.com and the website at www.dilyndewi.co.uk

PRACTICAL INFORMATION

The above pilgrim routes can be done all at once or divided as appropriate. Because the routes involve a web of churches and wells as well as travel, the following practical tips and contacts are essential:

- Below each pilgrimage stop above you will find a useful contact number.
- Unless you're part of an organized pilgrimage or a participant in the *Dilyn Dewi* programme (which will 'tailor-make' pilgrimages as requested), you will find plenty of eating places, hotels and B&Bs near to all the pilgrim stops.
- There are many public toilets *en route*.
- The main places for shopping and activities in the area are Pwllheli, Porthmadog and Caernarfon.
- If you prefer to make accommodation (etc.) plans beforehand the following Tourist Information Offices may be useful:
  Pwllheli: 01758 613000
  Porthmadog: 01766 512981
  Caernarfon: 01286 672232.
- Be well prepared for wet weather.

- It is essential to have the Ordnance Survey Map for Llŷn Peninsula, No. 123, or the Explorer Series Map no. 12 and 13 as well as *Llŷn: Pilgrim's Trail* leaflet available from the Tourist Information Offices.
- There is a British Rail station at Pwllheli.
- Taxi numbers: 01758 740999, 740666 or 01758 713338.
- Local hospital: Bryn Beryl, Pwllheli (minor injuries) 01758 701122.
- Most of the churches on the pilgrim routes have information sheets and/or exhibitions; the one at Clynnog Fawr is particularly good as you start.
- For the suggested devotions it would be helpful to have a Bible at hand.
- Preparatory reading:
  Patrick Thomas, *Candle in the Darkness* (Gomer Press, 1997)
  Brendan O'Malley, *A Welsh Pilgrim's Manual* (Gomer Press, 1989)
  Mary Chitty, *The Monks of Ynys Enlli*, parts 1 and 2 (Aberdaron, 2000)
  Elisabeth Rees, *Celtic Saints* (Thames and Hudson, 2000)
  Cintra Pemberton, *Soulfaring: Celtic Pilgrimage Then and Now* (SPCK, 1999)

St Winifrede's Well

The life of medieval Welsh people was intimately concerned with water and connected with wells and well-chapels. Pilgrimages to these were made at all times of the year, but especially during the patronal festival.

Holywell is a town on the North Wales A55 coast road. It was here that St Beuno probably built his cell, on the site of the present parish church. Across the road, on top of Castle Hill, Beuno's well is almost inaccessible beneath undergrowth. Beside the parish church is the magnificent St Winifrede's Well (*Gwenfrewi* in Welsh). It is one of the most powerful of all British holy wells dedicated to a Celtic saint as well as claiming an unbroken line of pilgrimage activity since the seventh century. The twelfth-century *Life of Winifrede* describes her as Beuno's niece and says that she was born in the early seventh century of noble parents, from whom Beuno obtained land on which to build a church.

Winifrede's life story relates how, after being killed, she was miraculously restored to life. This event took place one midsummer's day: left alone in her parents' house, she was visited by a young man, Caradog. While out hunting, he had felt thirsty and stopped at the house to ask for water.

But when he saw the beautiful young woman, his interest turned from drink to sexual matters. Winifrede did not want his attentions and fled to a chapel nearby, where St Beuno was praying. Enraged, Caradog pursued her to the chapel door, where he cut off her head with his sword. Where the head fell, the rock opened and a spring rose up. St Beuno, hearing the conflict, ran to her aid and, seeing the severed head, set it again on the body of Winifrede. St Beuno then cursed Caradog and turned him into a pool of water, which sank into the earth. After her miraculous resurrection, Winifrede travelled from one holy place to another and finally returned to Holywell, where she set up a convent of nuns.

Winifrede's well has been a place of pilgrimage since medieval times. The well and chapel of Holywell had been granted in 1093 by the Countess of Chester to the monastery of St Werbugh (a seventh-century saint and founder of the shrine at Chester), and in 1115 her son, Earl Richard, made a pilgrimage to the well. In 1138 Winifrede's relics were moved from Gwytherin (the convent in which she died) to the Abbey of the Black Monks at Shrewsbury. There her relics were venerated by pilgrims until the dissolution of the

monasteries by Henry VIII and Thomas Cromwell in the sixteenth century. At that time Winifrede's shrine and its relics were destroyed by the orders of the government, all but one finger-bone which was saved, half being today preserved at Holywell, while the other half is in the possession of the Catholic church at Shrewsbury. The government, however, was powerless to put an effective stop to the pilgrimage to this well.

During the Middle Ages, not far from the sea on the flatlands at the bottom of the valley, stood the Cistercian abbey of Basingwerk. The abbey was founded in 1131 by monks from Savigny in France, but it became Cistercian fifteen years later. In its day it was large and wealthy, for it was founded primarily to protect the hundreds of pilgrims

visiting the well, and the alms of those grateful pilgrims swelled its coffers enormously. Archaeologists have found very early Saxon building remains at Basingwerk, so it is likely to have been a settled community even earlier, possibly as far back as the Celtic or even pre-Celtic period. The Roman road between Chester and Segontium (on the outskirts of present-day Caernarfon) passes nearby, and there is every reason to believe that the Romans, too, venerated the well as a sacred place, first as pagans and later as Christians, who no doubt used the waters for baptism. Today Basingwerk is only a ruin of red sandstone.

This place was a Catholic stronghold when Roman Catholics were persecuted during the eighteenth century. The well became a centre of resistance to Protestantism and

Daniel Defoe wrote that priests were very numerous here, but had to appear in disguise. At that time pilgrims from Lancashire visiting Holywell crossed the Mersey by boat, walked across the Wirral and the often treacherous sands of the Dee estuary at low tide, and climbed the narrow valley to the well. But by the late nineteenth century opposition had disappeared. In 1896 the chairman of the town council recorded publicly that in that year 1,710 sick and pitiful pilgrims had visited the well and had stayed at the welcome hospice which had been built in 1870. He also said that over 500 of those pilgrims had been medically tested and he was assured that a great many of them had received remarkable cures.

The well continues to be an important place of pilgrimage. It is, in reality, far more than a well, being a holy water shrine, contained within a two-storey late Gothic building built in *c.* 1500 by Lady Margaret Beaufort, mother of Henry VII. A small chapel extends from the hillside, while below it is a polygonal well chamber from which the holy waters flow. In the base of the well chamber are some curious stones that bear red marks symbolizing the blood of Winifrede. Tall pillars depicting scenes from Winifrede's life support the upper storey. The inner pool is star-shaped, with five recesses in honour of the well at Bethesda, where Jesus healed the sick. Pilgrims would usually pass through the waters three times, in memory of the ancient Celtic baptism rite of triple immersion, and in the belief that Winifrede would answer their prayers by the third time.

THE MAEN ACHWYNFAN CROSS

Just north of Whitford (A55 and A5151), near Holywell, is the great Maen Achwynfan Cross of the tenth century, one of the tallest in Wales. Its simple boldness, intricate knot patterns, slightly wobbly top cross and enigmatic figure on the lower panel make this one of the most intriguing of Welsh Celtic Crosses. It is unclear why it is raised here; perhaps it marked the site of some monastic cell out on the windswept flats.

PRACTICAL INFORMATION

Opening Times

- The well is open daily: summer 9am – 5pm (Sat 4.30pm), Winter 10am – 4pm.
- There is a small charge.

Services

- each weekday, Pentecost to late September 11.30am
- each Sunday, Pentecost to late September 2.30pm

Bathing in the Well

- Arrangements can be made with the custodian by telephone: 01352 713054.
- No bathing is permitted on Sundays and Bank Holidays.

Veneration of the Relic

- Arrangements should be made via parish priest: 01352 713181 (or the Presbytery).
- There is also a repository containing a wide range of religious books and goods.

St Winifred's Pilgrims' Hospice

- accommodation for approximately 30 pilgrims for short stays (full board)
- dining facilities for larger groups and/or individuals
- St Winifred's Hospice, New Road, Holywell, Flintshire (01352 710763)

Map

Ordnance Survey: Landranger Series no. 116

Suggested Devotion

John 5.1–9: The Healing at the Pool of Bethesda

Station or special prayers to be said at the well:

- Make the sign of the cross at the entrance.
- Proceed to the front of the well and make your intentions.
- Recite the Apostles' Creed.
- Recite one decade of the rosary while walking around the well or the pool.

Novena prayers to St Winifrede:

- Almighty and everlasting God, who didst enrich St Winifrede with the gift of virginity, grant us we beseech Thee by her intercession to set aside the delights of the world, and to obtain with her the throne of everlasting glory, through Christ our Lord. Amen.
- Almighty and everlasting God, grant we humbly beseech Thee, that St Winifred may obtain for us such spiritual and temporal benefits as are expedient to Thy holy service and our eternal salvation, through Christ our Lord. Amen.

Several medieval poets wrote poems about the well and St Winifrede (Iolo Goch, 1326–1402; Ieuan Brydydd Hir, 1440–70; Tudur Aled, 1480–1500). The following extract is from the work of Tudur Aled. It praises Winifrede, draws on the imagery of the waters of life and weaves a typically Celtic integrated religious teaching that links the physical world with the symbolic and the holy.

Translated by T. M. Charles-Edwards in his *Two Medieval Welsh Poems* (Gomer Press, 1971):

> *. . . The waters of baptism are*
> *the life support of the world,*
> *It is the fountain of the oil of faith.*

Penmon and Holy Island
St Seiriol and St Cybi

PENMON

From Beaumaris on Anglesey, take B5109 north for about 1 mile and turn right at the crossroads; continue for another mile, turn right at the T-junction and continue into the priory car park (follow signs for Penmon Point). The church is open all day throughout the year. This group of monuments on the site – sculpted Celtic Crosses, the twelfth-century church, the thirteenth-century priory and the holy well – encapsulates the development of Christian history on Anglesey.

The original monastery is reputed to have been founded by St Seiriol, one of the sixth-century missionaries, and a friend of St Cybi, who founded the monastery at the other end of Anglesey in Caer Gybi (Holyhead). There is an interesting story about these two saints, which is depicted on an icon in the Russian Orthodox church in Blaenau Ffestiniog. According to legend, these two men were in the habit of setting out in the morning to meet each other near Llanerchymedd, half-way between Penmon and Holyhead, returning home in the evening. Seiriol, going westwards in the morning and returning eastwards in the evening, always had the sun at his back; Cybi, on the other hand, always had the sun on his face; with the result that Cybi grew tanned while Seiriol remained fair; they became known as *Cybi Felyn* (Cybi the

tanned) and *Siriol Wyn* (Seiriol the fair).

The monastery prospered, and in the tenth century fine crosses were set up at its gates, but the Viking raids have destroyed all other evidence of this date. During the twelfth-century revival under Gruffudd ap Cynan (1055–1137) and Owain Gwynedd (1137–70), both princes of Gwynedd, the abbey church was rebuilt, and it remains the finest and most complete example of a church of this period in Gwynedd. In the thirteenth century the Celtic monasteries were persuaded by Llywelyn ap Iorwerth (1137–1240), another prince of Gwynedd, to adopt a more regular religious rule, and Penmon, like many others in Gwynedd, became an Augustinian priory. The priory survived the Edwardian conquest and expanded slightly, but was dissolved in 1538. The buildings passed into the hands of the Bulkeleys of Beaumaris, who enclosed much of the land as a deer park and built a fine dovecote (still standing). They also converted the prior's lodging into a house. Throughout this time the priory church remained in use, as it does today.

The two High Crosses are the only tangible evidence for the early medieval monastery. Both are now inside the church. One had been used as a window lintel in the later refectory; the other stood in the deer park but was moved to the church to prevent further weathering.

Both would probably have stood close to the gates into the monastic enclosure. The smaller cross is in the south transept; the one from the deer park is in the nave. Light switches to illuminate them and the nave are located in the north transept.

The small cross is carved from a single piece of stone: the head is a cross within a cross, a plain wheel-cross carved on a disc with very short projecting arms (one was probably cut off when it was used as a lintel). Apart from the cross and the two animal heads within the fret pattern on the sides, the decoration is entirely non-figural. The patterns vary, but the scheme is the same on both sides. The 'deer park cross' is larger and retains its original base, but the head is a separate piece. The decorative scheme is more complex and includes one figural panel in the manner of the Irish pictorial crosses which fulfilled a teaching role. Unfortunately weathering makes this very difficult to see, but earlier photographs show a figure between two standing beasts, who whisper into the ears of the figure. This is probably the temptation of St Antony in the desert, a favourite theme in these monasteries where Antony, the desert hermit (251–356), was so much admired. There are other figures, perhaps a hunting scene, on the bottom on the left-hand side. The very striking ring-chain motif on the back of the shaft was a particularly

47

popular pattern in the Isle of Man during the tenth century.

Both the crosses and the font (possibly originally the base of another cross) belong to a school of sculpture which absorbed stylistic traits from northern English, Viking and Irish art. They date from the late tenth or early eleventh centuries, perhaps from the relatively peaceful reign of Gruffudd ap Llywelyn (1234–44).

The cruciform church is the most complete twelfth-century church structure on Anglesey, built during the reign of Owain Gwynedd (1137–70), the golden age of Welsh independence. The nave is believed to be a little older than the tower (1140) and the transepts (1160–70). The large chancel was added by Llywelyn ap Iorwerth in 1220–40, perhaps because the newly reorganized Augustinian Canons needed this space, since the rest of the church remained in parish use. It was entirely rebuilt on the old foundations in 1855.

The surrounding buildings, probably conventual, date from the thirteenth century, when the positions of Penmon and its sister foundation on Holy Island (Ynys Seiriol in Welsh and sometimes called Puffin Island) were regularized. The cloister, now a garden, stood on the south side of the chancel – an unusual, easterly position which reinforces the idea that the nave was a public church. The eastern range of buildings

has gone, but the southern one, containing the refectory with dormitory above, still stands. Enter by a door in the south side which gives access to a cellar. A twelfth-century gravestone which had been used as a lintel to this door stands nearby. The beam-holes for the refectory floor and the large windows which lit this dining room can be seen above. Meals were accompanied by spiritual readings, and the reader's seat can be seen beside the window in the south-east corner. In the sixteenth century a califactory or warm common room was built against the end of the refectory (notice the straight joint and ground-floor fireplace). The western range was occupied by the prior's lodging, modified as a private house in the eighteenth century.

The holy well is a spring emerging from a cliff behind the church. It is reached by a path on the left, just beyond the car park, which skirts the monastic fishpond. Although it is the source of water for the monastery, the structures here are all relatively modern. The roofed inner chamber around the pool is of brick and dates from 1710. The lower courses and the open antechamber with seats to either side may be somewhat earlier, but no medieval finds were made during recent excavations. The so-called 'cell', beneath the cliff on the left, is of uncertain date and purpose.

THE ISLAND

Continue along the road past the dovecote and towards the sea and you reach the coast, off which is Holy Island. It has many names: Puffin Island; Priestholm in Norse, because of its monks and hermits; in Welsh Ynys Seiriol, after the sixth-century saint who established a monastery there. The remains of a church with a twelfth-century stone tower stand within Seiriol's monastic enclosure on the island. The tower had been built against a small memorial chapel over the burial of a muscular man of the late Middle Ages. A cloister can also be identified, constructed alongside the eastern part of a pre-existing church, most of the land surrounding the western part of the church being already occupied by the graveyard.

In 1237 Llywelyn Fawr, the prince of Gwynedd, gave the church at Penmon to the monastic community on the island, and in 1316 a canon of Bardsey became prior of the island community. This makes it clear that by that date the island was already a community of Augustinian Canons, as the appointment would not have been made had not the two houses been of the same order.

In 1188 Giraldus Cambrensis visited Anglesey on his tour of Wales and described in his *Itinerary* the monastic settlement on this island. He says,

> . . . there is a small island almost adjoining Anglesey which is inhabited by hermits, living by manual labour and serving God. This island is called in Welsh Ynys Lenach, or Priests' Island, because many bodies of saints are deposited there, and no woman is suffered to enter it.

There is no access to the island.

Contact number: 01248 811402

Suggested Devotion

Isaiah 49.1–6: The Second Song of the Servant

From 'Sea' by Brendan O'Malley, in *God at Every Gate*, (Canterbury Press Norwich, 1997), p. 58:

> *Let us adore the Lord, maker of wondrous works,*
> *great bright heaven with its angels,*
> *the white-waved sea on the earth.*

Pennant Melangell

St Melangell

St Melangell's Church is to be found in the hills at the head of the Tanat Valley not far from the village of Llangynog on the main Oswestry to Bala road, B4580 and B4391.

There has been a Christian church on this site for over 1,200 years and parts of the present building go back to about 800. By 1150 Pennant Melangell was already famous as a place of ancient pilgrimage and sanctuary. The present churchyard lies on a Bronze Age site where there are ancient yew trees probably dating back as long as 2,000 years. As a place of sanctuary, Pennant Melangell (the head of Melangell's valley) goes back to the seventh century and in recent years it has once again flourished as a centre of Celtic Christianity, offering healing, counselling and prayer.

The story of this remarkable place is rooted in the story of an equally remarkable young girl from the seventh century. In about the year 600 Melangell, the daughter of an Irish king, fled from a planned marriage which she didn't want, and lived alone for fifteen years in this remote valley devoting her time to prayer. She was not alone in this; many people in those early years left their homes and families in

obedience to the call of God and sought the place where God willed them to stay. A young man by the name of Brochwel, who was a prince of the area known as Powys, was out hunting when his dogs chased a hare into brambles. (Pre-Norman Wales was divided into three major kingdoms: Gwynedd in the north; Deheubarth in the south; Powys in the centre.) He found the hare sheltered and protected by a beautiful young woman deep in prayer. The dogs refused to attack and Brochwel, deeply impressed by Melangell's piety, granted her the valley as a refuge for ever. Melangell stayed for the rest of her life and eventually attracted a community of holy women about her. The legend of St Melangell derives from two seventeenth-century transcripts of a lost 'Life of the Saints'.

A number of interesting features emerge from this legend:

- The story of Melangell and the hare speaks about the clash between a violent and aggressive world and a way of life which puts its trust in God. It is a way of life that is prayerful and quiet, full of compassion and care for all living things. It makes vivid something of early Celtic

Christianity which stresses the sense that God is present and at work in all things and that he can be praised and glorified in and through the whole of creation.

- Such incidents are to be found in the lives of other women saints. It is evident that a woman living either alone or with only a few companions of her own sex in a primitive and in many ways brutal society would have been extremely vulnerable. The lives of St Dwynwen (seventh century) of Anglesey and St Winifrede (seventh century) of Holywell both turn on incidents where the local prince comes to carry them off by force. In all three we encounter male aggression on the one side, men and horses and dogs and weapons, and on the other side the vulnerability and weakness of the unprotected woman. Only the strength of prayer and faith stands between them and violent death.

- The special relationship established between the man or woman of prayer and the animal world is a common theme not only in the lives of the Celtic saints but in the lives of the saints right across the Christian world.

One of the publicity leaflets written by Evelyn Davies, the former Warden of the Shrine, crystallizes what the place is all about today:

And so once again Pennant Melangell has become a place of pilgrimage and prayer. There is something about the place, its peace, its feeling of presence, above all its magnificent scenery, which draws people of many faiths and of none. It is a valley of welcome and acceptance that asks no questions. Clearly its story speaks in a particular way to people concerned with animal welfare and with the care and conservation of the environment. It has a special resonance for those committed to the cause of ecology. The story speaks strongly also to those who are sensitive to the power and significance of prayer. The whole valley is so full of prayer; the prayers of Melangell; the prayers of the countless men and women who in many generations have come in quest of God. Here is a place of reconciliation of differences and of earth and heaven, God and humankind, the separated parts of the broken body of Christ.

A stone church was built around 1160, with an eastern apse over Melangell's grave, and her relics were placed in a Romanesque shrine which is the earliest surviving Romanesque shrine in Northern Europe. The place was a sanctuary protected by law; those seeking healing, refuge and forgiveness made generous donations at the shrine until it was broken up in the sixteenth century. From then on the Norman church underwent many changes. The apse was replaced by a square structure and pieces of the shrine were built into the walls of the church and lychgate.

In extensive renovations between 1988 and 1992 the reassembled shrine was put back in the chancel. The square-ended building was taken down, a new apse being built on the twelfth-century foundations of Cell-y-Bedd (the Cell of the Grave). The slab believed to have marked Melangell's original grave is set in the apse floor.

There are a number of notable things to see in the church:

- *Cell-y-Bedd* (the Cell of the Grave)
  Rebuilt in 1990 on twelfth-century foundations. Post holes of an earlier building are underneath the cobbled floor.
- *St Melangell's Grave*
  St Melangell was buried here in the eighth century. The grave slab has been painted white at some time.
- *St Melangell's Door*
  Built up in the sisteenth century to cover twelfth-century material and rediscovered in 1989.
- *St Melangell's Shrine*
  The oldest known Romanesque shrine in Northern Europe. Built in the twelfth century and reconstructed in 1991. It now contains the relics of Melangell.

Services:

Sundays (May–Oct): 3pm

Mon–Sat (all year): 9am morning prayers and intercessions for the sick; 6pm Compline

THE MELANGELL CENTRE

In the grounds of the church there is a centre which offers individual support and counselling for those who have cancer or other chronic illnesses, and who are being cared for in a hospital, hospice or at home. It also offers support for those who care for very sick people in the community. The centre is aware of the special needs of those who are too ill to come to the centre for counselling. Help is also offered to families and close friends following a death.

The aims of the centre are five-fold:

- to offer help to all people in need;
- to enhance the quality of life of the very ill and to treat the whole person;
- to encourage patients to take an active part in their own healing;
- to work with those who are very sick or dying and who need the extra support;
- to develop a ministry of support and care for all people.

In addition to this, since 1998, when the centre was opened, it offers **MORE**:

1. St Beuno, Clynnog Fawr (see pp. 20–1)

2. St Beuno's Church, Pistyll, decorated for the feast of Lammas (see pp. 24–5)

3. St Pedrog's Church, Llanbedrog (see pp. 33–5)

4. Bardsey from the Llŷn Peninsula (see pp. 37–8)

5. The Celtic Cross, Bardsey, commemorating the 20,000 saints buried on the island

6. Icon of St Cybi and St Seiriol, Blaenau Ffestiniog Russian
Orthodox Church (see pp. 46–7)

7. St Melangell's Church, Pennant Melangell (see pp. 50–4)

8. St David's Cathedral (see pp. 56–8)

9. Canterbury Cathedral, Kent (see pp. 85–90)

10. Holy Island, Northumbria (see pp. 96–9)

11. Durham Cathedral (see pp. 112–4)

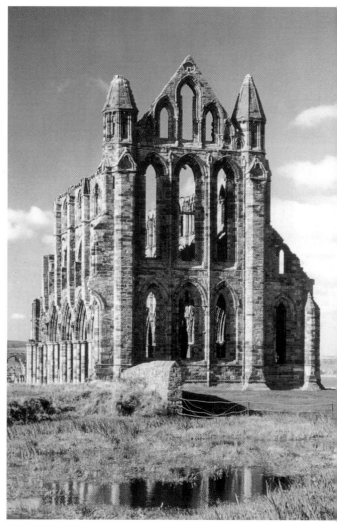

12. Whitby Abbey, Yorkshire (see pp. 101–3)

- **M**ission to all Christians
- **O**utreach to those of all creeds or none
- **R**econciliation and healing for those who are sick, sad, lost or lonely
- **E**ducation and creativity for those who wish to develop a better quality of life

The centre offers:

- a phone link: 01691 860455 (8pm – 10pm Mon, Tues, Thurs and Fri)
- individual and family counselling by appointment: 01691 860408
- a 'drop in' centre
- a quiet garden
- a ministry of healing

The centre is purpose built for disabled persons and wheelchair and day bed access is excellent. All help, counselling and care is free of charge.

THE MELANGELL WALK

Starting point: the Forest Enterprise car park at the bridge in Pont Llogel, on the B4395 (off the B4393) about 8 miles south-west of Llanfyllin.

In the valley and vicinity of the church there is a challenging 15-mile walk which traces a route between the Vyrnwy and Tanat valleys, trodden in centuries past by pilgrims, quarrymen and drovers. It's an undulating route, with gentle valley floor and moorland top sections linked by long climbs into and out of the area's valleys.

Suggested Devotion

Mark 7.24–37: The Healing of the Syrophoenician Woman and the Deaf Man

A Pilgrim's Prayer

We thank you Lord God
for the life and prayer
of your servant Melangell.
May her care and compassion
for all your creatures
inspire us in our day
with the same concern
for all that you have made.
May we with her learn
to find your glory
in the world around us
and in all that
you give us to do.
We ask this through
Jesus Christ Our Lord.
Amen.

Experienced walkers should find no difficulty in completing the walk in one day. Recreational walkers may find it best to split it in two, breaking the route at Llanwddyn, with its wealth of activities and facilities based around Lake Vyrnwy.

The walk starts at Pont Llogel, already on both the Glyndwr's Walk and the popular Ann Griffiths Walk, named after the renowned hymn-writer who lived locally. It climbs into Dyfnant Forest, cresting a ridge-top viewpoint before undulating through forest and along lanes to Lake Vyrnwy. Rising past Bronze Age remains, the route gains Hirnant Forest, unveiling views to the rugged Aran Mountains, the highest in Britain south of Snowdon itself. Beyond the forest, rough sheep pastures are crossed to reach the highest point on the route, 1,627 feet. Woodlands threaded with streams and waterfalls accompany the walk to its target, remote St Melangell's Church, hidden in the Tanat Valley. Quiet paths and lanes lead to Llangynog, from where a circular day walk allows exploration of the high ridges and secluded valleys of high Tanat. A booklet containing full details of the route with general information is available: *Pererindod Melangell: Kites, Cairns and Churches; a walk to a saint's retreat below the Berwyn Mountains,* published by Powys County Council (Llandrindod), 1999.

PRACTICAL INFORMATION

- The church is open daily: until 6pm (Easter–Oct); 4pm (Nov–April).
- On Sundays at 3pm there is a special pilgrimage service followed by tea.
- As there are many retreat days, quiet days and day courses it is advisable to book.
- There are no public toilets in the valley at present. Toilets in Llangynog village.
- Buses are unable to travel along the lane from the village of Llangynog. If you are travelling in a group, leave your coach in the village and either walk the two miles to Pennant Melangell, or contact Tanat Coaches at Llangedwyn on 01691 780212 or 780241 who can supply minibuses at very reasonable prices per person.
- There are many footpaths in the valley for walkers.
- All groups are welcomed and visits begin with an act of worship.
- The church shop sells cards, books and artefacts.

St David's
St David and St Non

THE SAINT

Since at least the tenth century (and probably earlier) the position of St David's Cathedral has been associated with the patron saint of Wales. Tradition has it that David founded a monastery here during the sixth century, hence the present Welsh name *Tyddewi* (David's House). It is believed that David was born here, and that Non, his mother, gave birth to him near the cliffs to the south of the cathedral now marked by the ruins of St Non's Chapel. It was said that his baptism took place at Porth Clais, where the river Alun enters the sea, and that a holy well sprang from the ground on the occasion, whose waters healed the blindness of the Irish bishop who baptized him.

After being educated by St Paulinus, he came back to Vetus Rubus where his uncle had a monastery, before founding his own at a place called Vallis Rosina. It was here that David died on 1 March about 589.

Vallis Rosina (*Glyn Rhosyn* in Welsh, 'the valley of the little marsh'), is an appropriate name for the wet valley bottom through which the river Alun flows to the sea. It was on a comparatively dry platform on the bend of the river that

the Celtic monastic community associated with David placed its church. The usual medieval name for St David's was Menevia (*Mynyw* in Welsh), derived from the Irish *muine*, 'a bush'. It vividly suggests the original state of the valley, dense with bushes and trees, before it became a settlement by a monastic community. It also reminds people of the deserted and waste places in which David and his contemporaries sought the solitude in which to pursue lives devoted to God.

David stood out among the monastic founders of the Celtic west. He expected his monks to spend their time not only in prayer and study but also in hard manual labour. As the eleventh–century *Life of David* has it, 'they place the yoke on their own shoulders' (rather than using oxen to plough the fields); 'they dig into the ground with mattocks and spades, they provide with their own labour all the necessities of the community'. They wore animal skins, had no possessions of their own, and lived on a diet of 'bread and herbs seasoned with salt'. Rhigyfarch, the son of Bishop Sulien, wrote the Latin *Life of David* about 1090. In it he emphasized the sanctity and orthodoxy of David.

David himself was even more ascetic than his monks, standing for long periods in cold water to subdue the flesh. It may have been this practice which led to his being known as 'David the Waterman' (in Welsh *Dewi Ddyfrwr*), as much as his habit of drinking only water.

The peninsula upon which St David's stands is significant as far as the development of the early church in Celtic Wales is concerned; it is situated at the junction of ancient sea and land routes linking Britain to Ireland and the Continent. This proximity to the western seaways brought pilgrims in large numbers to this spot, attracted by the asceticism, learning and devotion which characterized David and his community, and which was the foundation of his reputation for sanctity.

THE CATHEDRAL

The first church was burnt down in 645. Between then and 1097 the monastery was attacked, burnt or destroyed many times by the Vikings who used the western seaways. Two such raids led to the deaths of Bishop Morgenau in 999 and Bishop Abraham in 1080. Around 1090 the site was described as abandoned, the shrine stripped of valuables and masked by undergrowth. All that remains of the pre-Norman church are a few inscribed stones such as the Abraham Stone now built into the south transept wall.

The first Norman bishop,

Bernard, was appointed by Henry I and enthroned in 1115, when, in a political move to weaken Welsh autonomy, the Celtic monastic organization of the cathedral was changed to the ordinary diocesan type. David has been regarded as the patron saint of Wales since 1123, when Pope Callixtus II officially approved his cult and conceded, because of the dangers of the journey to Rome, that two pilgrimages 'to seek David' should be equivalent to one 'to seek the Apostles'. Bishop Bernard dedicated a new cathedral in 1131 and it was his church that Henry II visited in 1171 and 1172.

The present building, standing on the site of the sixth-century monastery, was begun in the 1180s and heavily restored in the late medieval and Victorian periods. The *St David's Chronicle* states that in 1182 Peter de Leia (bishop, 1176–98) began to rebuild the cathedral with the assistance of Giraldus Cambrensis who was canon of the cathedral and Archdeacon of Brecon. In 1188, he went around Wales with Baldwin, Archbishop of Canterbury to gather recruits for the Third Crusade.

At the Reformation, St David's thirteenth-century shrine, the stone base of which survives between the choir and the presbytery, was stripped of its jewels, ornamental wooden canopy and murals. The relics, which had stood on the shrine in a portable casket, were taken away. During the restorations of

1862–77, a walled-up recess was found in Holy Trinity Chapel, at the back of the high altar. It contained the mixed bones of a very tall man and a short one. The remains, now in a modern casket, are believed to be those of St David and his confessor, St Justinian.

St David's Cathedral Library is also a place of some significance. The pre-Norman church must have had an active scriptorium. It once possessed richly illuminated copies of the gospels, psalters, missals, service books, penitentiaries and copies of the writings of the Early Fathers. Part of this medieval library was later attached to St Mary's College. It formed part of the west cloister and was destroyed by fire. The book collection was kept in the Chancellor's house, now the Canonry, before being moved to the fourteenth-century Chapter House shortly after 1795. The room was

also used as the Cathedral Grammar School during this period. The Chapter House, above St Thomas's Chapel in the north transept, dates from Bishop Gower's time, around 1340, and is reached by a staircase of the same period. Today there are over 7,000 volumes in the library.

Other places of interest besides the cathedral in the St David's area include a fine fourteenth-century preaching cross in the centre of the city and several of the buildings, which date from the Middle Ages. Porth y Twr, the bell-tower, still guards the entrance to the cathedral precincts, and the original medieval city walls can be seen today. Next to the cathedral are the ruins of the fourteenth-century Bishop's Palace.

One author describes the palace as having been 'a medieval bed and breakfast', where the bishop could entertain the thousands of pilgrims who came to the shrine of St David. In exchange for their accommodation and the hospitality, pilgrims were expected to leave donations. The bishop's hospitality to his wealthy pilgrims must have been lavish. Impressive indeed are the remains of the kitchens and the great hall. The lodging spaces in the west range of the complex provided for the dozens of retainers brought by important visitors. The bishop had his own private chapel with carved heads at each of the corbels supporting the roof. The entire roof line of the palace projects a series of wonderfully varied carvings of heads, human and beast, and the surrounding parapet is unique in its use of coloured stone in a purple and white checkerboard pattern.

ST NON

St Non's lies about a mile south of St David's, overlooking St Non's Bay, one of the numerous bays forming the ten-mile stretch of St Bride's Bay, on the west coast of Pembrokeshire. From that early period pilgrimages were not only made to St David's itself, but also to chapels and other holy places in the area including St Non's.

St Non, Nun or Nonnita was the mother of St David and traditionally his father was Sant, a chieftain in Ceredigion who was grandson of Cunedda, a founder of the royal line of Gwynedd. St Non's father was Gynyr Gaer Gawch, Prince Pebidiog, said to be a 'regulus' of the district later called Dewisland. Gynyr was also father of St Gwen and St Guistliamus, Bishop of Old Menevia.

St Non was educated at Y Ty Gwyn (The White House) by Maucan, who may have received his training from St Patrick on his departure for Ireland. She is said to have moved later to a cottage on the site of St Non's Chapel where David was born in about 500. Shortly after the birth of David, St Non went to Brittany. Dirinon, of which she is patron saint, has a chapel and a well dedicated to St Non. The chapel contains her tomb, and it is one of the historic

OGHAM is a non-alphabetical form of stroke writing and is probably based on long and short dashes from or across a base line in groups of one to five. It does not contain organic letters – that is, ABC etc. It probably appeared during the Roman period and those who invented it were certainly familiar with the way some Roman grammarians classified letters. Ogham words were written on a drawn baseline, which provided a backbone, and most of it is set vertically. It is associated in the main with Ireland.

monuments of Brittany.

There are three interesting parts to the St Non site:

- St Non's Chapel
- The Holy Well of St Non
- The Chapel of Our Lady and St Non

Tradition has it that St David was born on this site during a great storm, but that the place of his birth shone with a bright light. A further tradition is that to relieve the agony of her labour pains Non supported herself on a stone that lay near her and that it retained the prints of her fingers. It is said that when the chapel was later built on that spot the stone was introduced as an altar.

The date of the foundation of the chapel is unknown, but is prior to 1335. Of the chapels subordinate to the cathedral, St Non's was the principal. It is likely that the chapel was abandoned before 1557, possibly converted to a dwelling house, and later the ground around it was used as a garden for leeks.

The chapel, which follows a north–south orientation, is marked by four ruined walls of different periods, certainly medieval if not earlier. In the south-west corner can be seen a stone with an incised linear Latin Celtic Cross. It dates from the seventh–ninth centuries and at one time was built into the east wall of the church.

A brass discovered in the chapel showed a chantry priest with his hands in the attitude of prayer. It is said to date to about 1370 and is one of the oldest in Wales. In the field around the chapel are five erect stones that are possibly part of a Bronze Age stone circle. Excavations have also uncovered some stone-lined coffins that may be early Christian graves.

THE HOLY WELL OF ST NON

Near the chapel is the Holy Well of St Non which tradition says sprang up at the birth of St David. It was regarded as one of the most sacred and famous wells in Wales and visited by many of the pilgrims to St David's. The water was considered to have healing and miraculous powers and was famous for its healing properties in connection with eye afflictions.

CHAPEL OF OUR LADY AND ST NON

Although it was only built in 1934, the architect intended the chapel to be a reflection of the old coastal chapels of Pembrokeshire as far back as the sixth century. The fabric of the chapel also contains many associations with much earlier religious buildings. The stones used were gathered from ruined cottages originally built from the ruins of the priory and the chapel of Whitwell, which stood south of the cathedral. Many of the carved and incised stones were let into the altar of St Non's, which also contains a white heart-shaped stone from the altar of St Patrick's Chapel.

PRACTICAL INFORMATION

Services in the Cathedral

Sundays: 8am / 9.30am (in Welsh) / 11.15am / 6pm

Weekdays: 7.30am Matins / 8am Holy Eucharist / 6pm Evening Prayer

Other Details

- The cathedral shop is open from 10am Mon–Sat (spring and summer).
- St Thomas's Chapel is reserved for prayer and quiet.
- Toilets are over the river, next to the Old Bishop's Palace.
- Detailed guides are available, including an excellent children's guide.
- The Cathedral Library is open throughout the year on Mondays, 2–4pm.
- St David's Cathedral Festival: May/June, contact 01437 720271.
- Organ recitals: 8.15pm Tuesdays July–Sept.
- Drama Festival: first half of August, contact 01437 720517.
- Doctor: 01437 720303 Hospital: 01437 764545 Police: 01437 720223.
- Tourist Information Centre: 01437 720392.
- Ordnance Survey Map: Landranger Series no. 157.

Contact Numbers and Details

Cathedral: 01437 720202

Cathedral Shop: 01437 720507

Cathedral Music: 01437 720128

Cathedral Library: 01437 720822

TWO HERITAGE PILGRIMAGES

There are very interesting Heritage Pilgrimages in the vicinity:

- The Bishop's Road
- Saints and Stones

Detailed maps of both trails are available from the Tourist Information Centre in St David's (01437 720392) and accompany OS 1:50,000 maps nos. 157 and 158, or OS 1:25,000 Outdoor Leisure nos. 35 and 36.

THE BISHOP'S ROAD

In the Middle Ages the diocese of St David's was the largest and richest in Wales. Its bishops were not only prominent in the church but also powerful in the affairs of state. To reflect their status they built on a grand scale and this pilgrimage journey takes you from their castle at Llawhaden to their palace at St David's.

The churches on the way vary in style, size, origin and location. Some display the characteristics common to the churches of north Pembrokeshire: a simple nave, chancel and bellcote, often with the addition of a nineteenth-century porch and vestry. Others show greater elaboration: towers, transepts, chapels, vaulting and arcaded aisles.

Whilst all the sites are old, the hand of time has been kinder to some churches than to others, so that for the least fortunate much of what is visible today belongs to nineteenth-century restorations. However, the indications of their true antiquity remain in the dedications to early saints, holy wells, inscribed stones and ancient fonts. Nonetheless each one has a story to tell and points us back to the Celtic age of faith.

There is evidence that the route from Llawhaden to St David's is older than the castle, which was first erected during the twelfth century to protect the episcopal estates which lay about it. Traces of a Roman road extend westwards from Carmarthen and during the Middle Ages pilgrims would have followed these tracks on their way to the shrine, guided by the ancient waymarkers and resting at hospices, indicated by place names at the present day. Having crossed the Taf river at Llandeilo Abercowin, the pilgrim might rest at Tavernspite or Whitland Abbey, Llawhaden, Wiston, Spittal and at Middle Mill, between Llandeloy and Whitchurch, to arrive, relatively refreshed, at the cathedral and the palace built by Bishop Henry Gower (1328–47).

SAINTS AND STONES

The saints and stones of the churches along this pilgrimage have their origins in the early Christian traditions of North Pembrokeshire, when, from the fifth century onwards, missionary saints and holy men began to establish communities. Traces of these may still be seen in the circular enclosures, or *llanau*, constructed of massive boulders, which later became the churchyards. The tradition of marking burials with inscribed stones was handed down from the Bronze Age and continued at this time in commemoration of local Christians. Originally many were carved with simple square or ring crosses or carried an inscription, which gave their name and sometimes status and antecedents in Ogham or Latin letters. Later, elaborate ornaments of knot and scroll work enhanced these impressive memorials.

The early churches were probably built of wood and turf: small cells from which the founder saint or his followers could carry out their ministry. As they became established, stone structures replaced them. These too were often rebuilt as the Normans tried to absorb or extinguish the old traditions, even replacing some of the dedications to native saints.

This pilgrimage trail may be started at any point and refreshments are available along the route. The churches on the trail all welcome visitors and offer further information leaflets.

Suggested Devotion

1 Thessalonians 2.2–12: Courage to Declare the Gospel

The words David is believed to have said on his deathbed:

> Brothers and sisters, be cheerful and keep your faith and belief, and do the little things that you have heard and seen through me.

Nevern: St Brynach and the High Cross

Nevern is a delightful little village on the coast in the Pembrokeshire Coast National Park. Take the A487 towards Fishguard and the B4582 into Nevern (Nanhyfer in Welsh).

ST BRYNACH

Although he was born in Ireland some time in the sixth century, St Brynach is described in his *Life* as a 'Son of Israel', which seems to mean that he was of Jewish origin. Not a great deal is known of Brynach, although he is said to have been a friend of David, whose settlement is only about 25 miles to the south. His was a life of wandering, seeking somewhere to settle and worship God. As chaplain of the warlord Brychan, Brynach came to Brecknock in Wales, which the Irish warrior had occupied during the troubled times. After making a pilgrimage to the Holy Land, where he killed a monster, St Brynach returned to Wales. When he got back, the Welsh were in the process of expelling Irish settlers from Wales. Harassed as an Irishman, Brynach was attacked by would-be murderers, who wounded him seriously with a spear before he was rescued by friends. He was taken to a sacred source, the Redspring, where his friends washed his wound, and he was cured.

Escaping from the 'ethnic cleansing', Brynach and his companions travelled from place to place until they set up a cell at a bridge in Fishguard. Unfortunately, it was infested with evil spirits, and he was driven out. At the next place in which they tried to settle, they were persecuted by the

---

THE CELTIC KNOT is one of the most striking features of Celtic Christian art. The knots are generally endless, and thus cannot be untied. Here the symbolism is of the knots which bind the soul to the world. The knot seems to have developed from plaitwork. The idea of plaitwork comes from weaving, which itself has a profound symbolism. It is usually plain weave that is imitated. Like that of weaving, the basic symbolism is that of 'the great cosmic loom of the universe', but it is important also to note that there are no loose ends, and the symbol is also one of continuity of the spirit throughout existence.

inhabitants, who stole the trees they had felled to make a building. At their next stop, they lit a fire, and were summoned by the lord who owned the land. The lord had not given Brynach permission to stop, but he greeted him warmly. The *Life of Brynach* (stored in the British Museum) records that the lord concerned was Clechre or Clether. Subsequently, a further grant of land was made by Maelgwm Gwynedd, who died in the Yellow Plague of 547. The wandering was over; Brynach was given land at Nevern, close to the 'holy mountain of the angels', Carn Ingli, upon which he would go to commune with the inhabitants of heaven. Today his church stands in a venerable grove of yew trees (about 1,000–1,200 years old) that bear witness to the ancient sanctity of Brynach's settlement.

Interestingly, one of the trees has a unique feature – it 'bleeds'. Is the steady oozing of blood-red sap tears for the crucifixion, tears for the dead in the churchyard – or is it scientific?

THE CHURCH

Nevern church is strategically situated near the River Nyfer. Some have thought this area to be part of an ancient pilgrimage route that connected the north and south – particularly St Winifrede's Well with St David's. If that is the case this would have been one of the last stops for the pilgrims before arriving at St David's.

Pilgrims probably arrived here from Holywell and Strata Florida, from Brecon and Gloucester; ordinary people, but kings too – for William the Conqueror and Henry II (probably as penance for the murder of Thomas Becket in Canterbury Cathedral in 1170) are both known to have made the pilgrimage to St David's. Here in Nevern they rested; then in their groups they crossed the Pilgrim's Bridge behind the church at Pontgarreg and joined the path, marked first by the Pilgrim's Cross carved into the rock and then by their own footsteps.

At least one section of the church is Norman with its typical squat tower, but most of the walls are later, and date from the fifteenth and sixteenth centuries. As is the case in many churches in Britain the interior was greatly altered during the Victorian period. However, there are several older stones in and around the church that clearly indicate a very early foundation, most likely from the Celtic period:

- The Maglocunus Stone, set in the window ledge of the Trewern-Henllys (south) Chapel, is probably even earlier than Brynach himself, for the carving is bilingual, in both Latin and Ogham, which suggests a date of about 450 to 500. The inscription indicates a memorial to Maelgwm, son of Clutorius, about whom nothing is known.

- In the companion window of the same chapel is the Cross Stone, which is of uncertain date but generally accepted to be pre-Norman, perhaps Celtic. Incised in this stone is a Celtic Cross, about 5 feet long but with arms only a foot wide. It has unusual features. It seems to be made of rope strands that intersect in such a way that a Celtic Cross is formed from a Celtic knot. Variations on this knot-rope-cross are

  often seen in modern Celtic decoration and art, but there seem to be no other similar crosses from this early period, either in Wales or anywhere else, making it all the more unusual.
- Outside the church near the entrance is the Vitalianus Stone, also thought to be fifth-century. This, too, is a bilingual memorial stone, with an inscription in Latin as well as in Ogham. Many think it is dedicated to a Roman soldier as the inscription reads *Vitaliani discharged with honour*. Caerleon, the huge Roman fortress, is only 100 miles away. It may have been put up by grateful villagers in memory of a Roman friend and protector.
- On the north wall of the church there is a faintly lettered fragment of stone in the west corner of the sill of the second chancel window. In 1860 this was noted as being in the south wall when there were three more letters. Apparently the stone was recut to fit its present position. It is thought to be a remnant of a vertical Latin inscription and to date from about the last years of the Roman occupation.
- Outside the east wall of the Glasdir Chapel is an incised cross, obviously of great antiquity: there is little doubt that it is a Consecration Cross. The consecration of churches is an elaborate ceremony dating back to the ancient Church. An important part of the ceremony is the placing of crosses on the walls, both inside and outside. Robanus Maurus (788–856) observes that the crosses on the walls of the church, with their lighted tapers, recall the walls of the heavenly Jerusalem, on whose foundations were inscribed the names of the Twelve Apostles of the Lamb

who were sent to enlighten the world.
- There is also a missing stone. Before the restoration of 1864 there was a stone slab, about 10 feet by 3 feet, embedded in the pavement on the north of the chancel. On it was inscribed a Greek Cross, an early relic of British Christianity. The cross has disappeared but a full description of it exists as well as a sketch. A photograph of it hangs today on the vestry screen.

There are two interesting walks from the churchyard:

- A walk behind the church leads up to the remains of an early Norman castle.
- A few hundred yards from the church is a section reputed to be the original pilgrim walkway, perhaps two miles long, still in good condition and maintained as a signposted footpath.

THE CELTIC HIGH CROSS

Pembrokeshire has several notable crosses, of which four are exceptional by any standard: the two in the church at Penally, near Tenby; that in the ruins of Carew Castle; and the impressive High Cross at Nevern.

Dating from around the turn of the first millennium, the Nevern churchyard cross stands 3.96m (13ft) high. The head of the cross was carved from a separate stone, being fixed to the shaft by means of mortise-and-tenon joints in the manner of Stonehenge. There are two short inscriptions, one of which reads *DNS*, an abbreviation of the Latin word *Dominus* (master or lord). The second inscription is a jumble of half-uncial letters on the east face having an unknown meaning – maybe *halleluia*.

Viewed from any side the green-hued panels have a variegated effect but in fact the carvings on the bottom are variations of the T-shaped

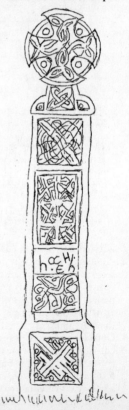

motif. The next four up are based on the knot as are the south and north faces of the next row, while the east and west faces have fret patterns. The top four panels combine degrees of complexity of knot-work. The carving on the sandstone cross-head is more intricate but still based on a limited number of motifs of linked oval rings, triquetra knots (consisting of three interlaced arcs), and the double-beaded two-cord twists that form the central cross. These abstract sculpted panels and totally decorated cross-head show the mastery of Celtic religious art that was practised here by the tenth century.

In the church, a stained-glass window representing the founder, St Brynach, has an anachronistic representation of the Nevern cross behind him, above which flies a dove.

PRACTICAL INFORMATION

- Contact number: 01239 820855
- Ordnance Survey Map: Landranger Series no. 145

Suggested Devotion

1 Corinthians 1.18–25: The Saving Power of the Cross

From Cintra Pemberton, *Soulfaring: Celtic Pilgrimage Then and Now* (SPCK, 1999, p. 177:

> The Cross was not hard to find . . . The message it conveyed to me in the rapidly descending darkness was one of welcome, stability, comfort and peace and I threw my arms around the shaft, embracing it as though it was alive.

Patrisio

St Issui

From Abergavenny take the A465 north to Llanfihangel Crucorney, then follow the signs up a steep and winding road to Patrisio (also spelt Patricio, Patrishow, Patrisiw, Patrisw, Parttrissw). It's best to walk up to the church as the road is very narrow and tricky – there's a very narrow bridge called Pontyresgob (the Bishop's Bridge), after Baldwin, Archbishop of Canterbury, who came here with Giraldus Cambrensis during the twelfth century to preach the Third Crusade.

Similarly, the patron saint's name has various spellings: St Issui, Ishow, Ishaw or Isho. Despite these various spellings, it is generally held that Patrisio is a very early church on an important Celtic foundation dedicated to St Issui the Martyr.

St Issui is not amongst the best known of Celtic saints. He's usually described as a holy man living a solitary life in the secluded valley who had a small cell beside a stream, Nant Mair. Nearby was his well, lined with stone and containing small niches where gifts could be left. Tradition states that an ungrateful traveller who had received welcome and hospitality from St Issui turned on the monk, murdering him and stealing the offerings that

had been left in the well. Because St Issui had a reputation for great sanctity, soon after his murder his hermit cell became a place of pilgrimage.

Over many years pilgrims have come to Patrisio. A story is told of a French pilgrim who came seeking healing for leprosy. In gratitude for the healing he received at the well he left a sack of gold which was used to build the earliest part of the church – which still stands today. The little niches in the walls of the well continue to hold gifts of coins and flowers from modern-day pilgrims. This chapel can be fairly accurately dated to the eleventh century, because the *Book of Llandaff*, compiled about 1150, tells us that Herewald, Bishop of Llandaff, consecrated the church of *Merthyr Issui* (Issui the Martyr) between 1056 and 1103.

The church has a deep peace and many unusual features, including a pre-Norman font, wall paintings, texts and dyed memorials, side altars in the nave, and a rood-loft and screen of Irish oak, decorated with winged dragons and minute details of a dragon, the symbol of evil, trying to consume the vine, the symbol of good (John 15.5). St Issui may be buried, under a stone altar bearing six

Consecration Crosses (instead of the usual five), in a chapel on the site of the original church at the west end of the nave. Behind the screen is a loft which can be reached by climbing the fifteenth-century stone steps set in the north wall of the church. All across the rail in the loft above the screen are sockets for candles.

The font is also noteworthy. Inscribed in Latin around its rim are the words in translation: *Menhir made me in the time of Genillin*. Genillin was Prince of Powys and Lord of Ystrad Yw just prior to the Norman Conquest (1066), so the font can be accurately dated to the eleventh century, when no doubt it stood in the tiny original chapel. It is one of the oldest surviving fonts in Wales.

Outside the church on the south side stands a tall preaching cross. Tradition has it that Archbishop Baldwin and Giraldus Cambrensis preached the Third Crusade from this spot in 1188. A relatively modern section of the cross shows carvings of the crucifixion, St Mary, St Issui and Archbishop Baldwin.

Just below the church is St Issui's Holy Well and the place where St Issui probably had his cell. At the entrance to the well area, set in the ground, is a flat stone, which has inscribed on it a Maltese Cross. The holiness of the well comes from its history, location and association with sanctity.

PRACTICAL INFORMATION

- Contact number: 01873 810348
- Ordnance Survey Map: Landranger Series no. 161.

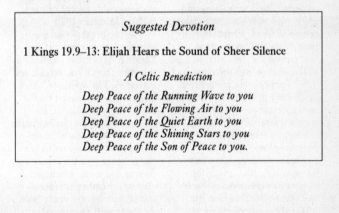

Suggested Devotion

1 Kings 19.9–13: Elijah Hears the Sound of Sheer Silence

A Celtic Benediction

Deep Peace of the Running Wave to you
Deep Peace of the Flowing Air to you
Deep Peace of the Quiet Earth to you
Deep Peace of the Shining Stars to you
Deep Peace of the Son of Peace to you.

Llantwit Major

St Illtud and St Samson

Llantwit Major is a town on the extreme south coast of Wales in the Vale of Glamorgan. Leave the M4 at junction 33 and, travelling south past St Fagan's Welsh National Folk Museum (which is well worth a visit), take the A48 to Cowbridge and then the B4270 to Llantwit Major. The church of St Illtud's is in the centre of the town. The first church at Llantwit Major (*Llanilltud Fawr* in Welsh, 'the big church of St Illtud') was established about 500 by St Illtud on the banks of a small stream in a fertile meadow, near the coast but not visible from the sea. The church enclosure or *llan* included also a monastery and a school, and it became a major centre of Celtic Christianity, though the only remains of this period are the Celtic stones in the west part of the church. This was probably the earliest monastery in Wales. It was an important missionary centre, with a school internationally famous for its Christian knowledge and teaching. Students were divided into 24 groups to enable worship to continue throughout the day and night. Tradition has it that there were only three centres in early Britain which practised this unceasing praise: Old Sarum (Salisbury),

Glastonbury and Llantwit Major.

Towards the end of the eleventh century, Glamorgan was conquered by the Normans. The Lord of Glamorgan, Robert Fitzhamon, had his base in Cardiff, but he kept Llantwit Major in his own hands to supply his garrison with grain. Fitzhamon founded the Abbey at Tewkesbury, and in 1102 he gave the church at Llantwit Major, with its tithes, to Tewkesbury. After the Dissolution of the Monasteries, the revenues of the church and the appointment of the priest passed to Gloucester Cathedral, and these did not return until the Disestablishment of the Welsh Church in 1920.

The medieval period was one of relative prosperity in Llantwit Major, and during this time the church was rebuilt and extended. The original Celtic church probably stood on the site of the west church, and this was rebuilt by the Normans around 1100, though the only existing Norman remains are the archway over the south door and some fragments of masonry. Further alterations and additions were made from the thirteenth century right up to the Victorian period. The medieval church would have been very different from the present-day one. The west church was probably the parish church, while the canons of the medieval monastery worshipped in the east church. The floor was of beaten earth and there were no pews; the elderly sat on stone benches. The church had its wall paintings and its rood over the chancel arch, though the paintings were covered over after the Reformation, and the Puritans removed the altars, statues and ornaments.

ST ILLTUD

Illtud (Elltud, Iltut and other forms) was a Celtic saint and an outstanding figure in the fifth–sixth centuries. He seems to have concentrated his efforts in south-east Wales, around the estuary of the River Severn. The earliest reference to St Illtud is found in the *Life of St Samson* written at Dol, near St Malo in Brittany, about 610. This *Life* tells how St Samson was taken by his parents to the school of an 'illustrious master of the Britons' named Illtud. It goes on to say that Illtud was the most learned of the Britons in knowledge of Scripture and philosophy. The school that St Illtud formed at Llantwit Major was part of the monastery he had established there and he was certainly one of the major founders of monasticism in Britain.

Illtud was probably born in Brittany of British parents and became a disciple of St Germanus of Auxerre. In his youth he was ordained a priest

by St Germanus (*c.* 445). Germanus had been sent to Britain by Pope Celestine I in 429 and again in 447 to check the spread of Pelagianism. In a later *Life* (*c.* 1140) he is said to have received the tonsure from St Dyfrig, bishop of Llandaff. That *Life of Illtud* speaks of him founding a quadrangular church of stone at Llantwit Major and living there as a hermit. It also records that many pupils soon began to pour in, to be instructed by him in the seven arts. It is believed that Gildas (who wrote the first book on Welsh history and founded the monastery at Rouel in Brittany), St Samson, St Paul Aurelian (Paulinus of Wales who also founded the monastery at St Pol de Leon in Brittany), and St David himself were among his pupils. Tradition states that he died between 527 and 537.

THE CELTIC STONES AT LLANTWIT MAJOR

Llantwit Major has a number of important early monuments:

- The Houelt Cross is a typical Celtic Cross, 1.9m high, with a disc head and shaft carved from one piece of gritstone. The disc has a cross with square ends and a central square, with diagonal patterning, and a ring whose arcs have a twist decoration. The inscription is in Latin, in half-uncial script with no punctuation or letter spacing. In translation the inscription reads: *In the name of God*

THE CELTIC CROSS may be considered as a continuation and refinement of a number of aspects of traditional spiritual culture. One of its most important features is that it contains symbolic elements that express the relationship of human beings to God. These elements are mainly transcendent of religious dogma and often belong to the perennial philosophy which underlies all religions. By Celtic Cross is usually meant crosses which show characteristic types of Celtic ornament, whether they are inscribed on rough blocks of stone, on recumbent or erect stone slabs, or are shaped into Celtic Crosses as commonly understood. The most characteristic of the Celtic shaped crosses have a vertical ornamented axis with a wheel-cross on top, and a square base. The symbolism is powerful: a square earth linked to a round heaven by a shaft symbolizing the world-axis.

the Father and of the Son and of the Holy Spirit, Houelt prepared this cross for the soul of Res his father.

Houelt, son of Res, was probably Hywel ap Rhys, who was king of Glywysing (the land between the Tawe and the Usk) in the ninth century.

• In the foreground is the St Illtud's Cross or St Samson's Cross, 2.15m high. It was probably capped by a wheel-cross, but this is missing. All the surfaces are decorated in patterns of squares and plaitwork. In translation the inscriptions read:

– (on the left side) *Samson placed his cross*
– (on the right side) *for his soul*
– (on the reverse side) *for the soul of Illtud, Samson the king, Samuel, Ebisar*

This stone originally lay by the path on the north side of the church. When it was raised to bring it indoors two skeletons were found beneath it.

- Behind the Houelt Cross is a smaller sandstone slab, each face carved with panels of double-beaded plaitwork.
- A pillar, known as the Pillar of Samson, 2.75m tall, carries a Latin inscription, which in translation reads: *In the name of the most high God begins the cross of the saviour which Samson the Abbot prepared for his soul, and for the soul of Iuthahelo the king and of Artmail and of Tecan.*

  Iuthahelo is thought to be Ithel, a king of Gwent who died in 846. A smaller pillar has a long, V-shaped groove cut down it. The purpose is not known, but it may have been one of a pair, carrying a screen.

These stones date from the late ninth and early tenth centuries and suggest that the monastery at Llantwit Major contained a flourishing and artistic school of sculpture at that time. They also indicate the significance of Llantwit Major as a school, monastery and mission centre.

Contact number: 01446 795551

Suggested Devotion

1 Peter 2.4–10: Living Stones

A Prayer

This ancient house of God was built and furnished by other hands than ours. Let not their work decay, or the spirit that inspired them. Give us rather to have such gratitude in our hearts for their example that we fail not to do all that in us lies to the glory of God and the preservation of this church for his worship and the preaching of the Holy Gospel of Christ Jesus.

Caldey Island
St Dyfrig

St Illtud, along with St Dyfrig, has also been credited with founding the first monastic community on Caldey Island, three miles south of Tenby, off the Pembrokeshire coast. Certainly he had close links with the island: one of his pupils, St Samson, who went on to found the monastery at

personal
prayer
8:00

sleep

grande
silenzio

dinner

evening
prayer
6:30

THE MONK'S DAY would

manual
work
2:00-5:00

lunch

Eucharist
12:00

Dol in Brittany, was a monk at Caldey and was appointed by Dyfrig as the second abbot. The pre–Norse name of Caldey was Ynys Pur – the Island of Piro – and a *Life* of St Samson claims that this Piro was the first abbot, describing his unseemly death by falling one night into a deep well when drunk.

Restored remains of the medieval priory include the gatehouse and St Illtud's Church, with its western tower. Inside the church is an Ogham slab of about 500 with a cross and Latin inscription; various attempts at translation have included the names of Dyfrig, Illtud, Cadwgan and Jesus.

morning bell

the day begins

lectio divina

morning prayer 6:00

roughly follow this pattern

chapter

personal prayer

manual work 8:00-12:00

intellectual work 8:00-12:00

ST DYFRIG

Dyfrig (also Dubricius, died *c.* 550) was the son of a Welsh chieftain's daughter from the small territory of Erging in Herefordshire. His chief monastery was at Hentland, near Ross on Wye. Its name, *Hen Llan*, means 'the old, or former church', suggesting that it fell into disuse and was later rededicated. There is a cluster of churches named after Dyfrig, some on Roman sites. One at Whitchurch is built beside the river Wye, with an ancient landing stage in the churchyard to provide access by boat. The early *Life of Samson* describes Dyfrig as having authority over Illtud's great monastery at Llantwit Major. Dyfrig's *Life* relates how Dyfrig visited Illtud's community on a Sunday to ordain Samson as deacon and two other men as priests. Early manuscripts describing the event call Dyfrig *papa* or *episcopa*, so he seems to have been regarded as a Romano–British bishop.

Dyfrig had jurisdiction over a community on Caldey Island; the monastery was a daughter house of Llantwit Major in the Vale of Glamorgan, 40 miles in the south-east direction. At this time, Caldey Island was named Ynys Pur after its first abbot, Pyr or Piro. Dyfrig appointed Samson its second abbot, under whom the community had a peaceful existence, and Dyfrig used to come to Caldey each Lent, for forty days of solitude. There are many caves around the island's coastline; the monks

probably lived in these, and in wattle huts clustered around a chapel, near the spring which still supplies the island with abundant fresh water. A grave slab found near the well is inscribed in Ogham *Magl Dubr*, '(the stone of) the tonsured servant of Dubricius'.

Caldey was a foundation of some significance: a sixth-century fragment of red glazed pottery from the eastern Mediterranean was found here, and the base of a seventh-century jar from Gaul. The tiny parish church of St David on Caldey may be built on a sixth-century foundation; in earliest times this site was just above the high water mark. Linked with the monastery was a community of nuns on St Margaret's Island, which adjoins Caldey. At that time it was possible to walk across low-lying marsh to St Margaret's Island from the mainland at Panally.

In old age, Dyfrig retired to Bardsey Island in North Wales, off the tip of the Llŷn Peninsula, where he died and was buried. The followers of Dyfrig played a part in the migration southwards of Welsh missionaries, for Porlock Church on the Somerset coast is dedicated to Dyfrig.

THE ISLAND

Monks of one sort or another have lived and worked on Caldey for more than 1,500 years. The early history of the island dates back to 8,000 BC. Human remains, early flint tools and the bones of animals long

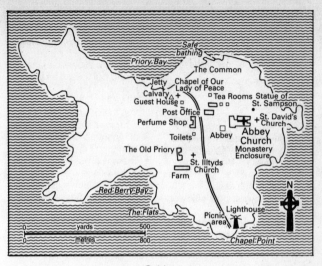

Caldey

since extinct in Britain have been excavated on the island. In 1113 Henry I made a gift of the island to Robert Fitzmartin, a Norman nobleman, who promptly gave it to the Benedictine monks of the Abbey of Tiron in France, who had already founded an abbey at St Dogmael's near Cardigan. Their new priory was built on Piro's earlier, primitive, monastic settlement. It was a building of great strength, and is still intact today. In 1536 Henry VIII dissolved the monasteries, and the Benedictines were expelled from Caldey.

PRACTICAL INFORMATION

A fleet of boats runs to the island from Tenby Harbour from about the Spring bank holiday to late September. These boats, which are strictly supervised by the Ministry of Transport, are owned by local boatmen, many of whom are members of the crew of Tenby Lifeboat. Tickets are obtained from the booking kiosk in Castle Square above the harbour. This ticket includes a charge for landing on Caldey and there are no further costs involved. Having purchased a ticket one can travel and return on any boat as they are all part of the same 'pool'. The crossing takes approximately 30 minutes and the boats run every 15 minutes between 9.30am and 4pm Monday to Friday. At high tide all boats leave from the harbour and at low water from the temporary landing stage on the Castle Beach. The island is closed to visitors on Saturday and Sunday. Landing on Caldey takes place directly on to the island's small concrete jetty. At extreme low water, passengers may be off-loaded on to an amphibious landing craft for the final few yards to the slip.

There are a number of facilities on the island:

- The village tea gardens, run by the monastery, provide a comprehensive selection of light refreshments throughout the day.
- There is a gift shop, perfumery and post office on the island.
- There are toilets near the village post office.

- Tours of the monastery are available for men only. Details are listed in the post office.
- Dogs are allowed on the island but must be kept on a lead at all times.
- All visitors should remember that the weather can change with great rapidity, and bring an anorak or waterproof with them.
- There is a public telephone in the village.
- Ordnance Survey Map: Landranger Series, no. 158.
- Contact number: 01834 844453 or 01834 842296.

Suggested Devotion

Jeremiah 17.7–10: **Trusting in God**

From 'The Transistor' by Fr Pascal, in the Caldey Island Guide Book:

> *. . . Music and song,*
> *I have it, all day long! . . .*
>
> *. . . My transistor is divine,*
> *In the voice of the birds,*
> *My Beloved speaks to me!*
> *From day-break to sunset,*
> *The song of birds is my radio-set!*

England

Introduction to England

It is a mistake to think that Celtic Christianity only existed in Wales, Ireland and Scotland. During the first millennium (the period I would regard as the Celtic era) there was a great deal of significant religious activity in England. My choice of sites to illustrate that point is, of necessity, selective. They are the main places of Celtic Christian religious activity which show both the places and the saints associated with the very foundations of Christian England.

During the period of Roman occupation Christianity had on the whole failed to emerge in Britain generally as the predominant religion, and we may assume that the vast majority of the native British population was totally unaffected by it. There is no evidence for the existence of a parochial system and few if any indications that Christianity was making any progress towards becoming the religion of the general mass of Romano-Britons. It is undoubtedly the case that the British churches left no lasting mark on the countryside in physical terms and little or no impact in terms of a native tradition of learning.

In the late sixth and seventh centuries, however, Christianity came to the Anglo-Saxons from several sources. The central impulse of mission came from Rome in 597 when Pope Gregory the Great sent Augustine as Archbishop of Canterbury. Missionaries also came to Northumbria from Iona, to the west of England

BRITISH: the inhabitants of the island of Britain which was occupied by the Romans between 43 and 410 AD (most had left Britain during the 380s). When the Angles and the Saxons invaded Britain in the late 440s, the British were pushed to the west and to Gaul.

ANGLES: members of a tribe from Schleswig (now in North Germany). Angul was a district in Schleswig. *Anglus* (Angle) is the Latinized root of the Germanic form *Engle* (English). The Angles settled in Britain during the fifth century.

SAXONS: members of the Germanic people that conquered parts of Britain in the fifth and sixth centuries. Saxony was an area in what is today called Germany.

ENGLISH: the title later given to the amalgamation of the Angle and the Saxon peoples (Anglo-Saxons). The actual word derives from *Engle*, a form of Angle.

from Wales, and to the south from France (Gaul). By the eighth to the tenth centuries England was sending missionaries to Europe and throughout the whole period of Anglo-Saxon Christian culture connections with the European church were close.

The emerging church in England was seriously challenged by the Viking invasions of the ninth century. Much of the north-east was destroyed as well as the south. But by the middle of the tenth century a united kingdom of the English was created. At this time church structures developed greatly and monastic life and culture were renewed on a large scale.

Canterbury

St Augustine

POPE GREGORY THE GREAT (590–604)

It was Pope Gregory above all others who initiated the conversion of the Anglo-Saxons to Christianity. In 597 he sent Augustine to establish the church in England, an establishment which was eventually centred at Canterbury. The letters that passed between Augustine and Gregory show the latter's deep humanity and concern for the spiritual well-being of both missionaries and converts.

He recommends Augustine to be aware of the habits of the people, and to use them in spiritual formation: if the people are used to sacrifices at sacred places, let these places be consecrated to God, and Christian feasts take the place of heathen rituals.

Gregory himself never visited England. The earliest biography of him was written at Whitby, and it is there, as well as in the writings of Bede, that the story of Gregory seeing Anglo-Saxon slaves in the market places is told. When Gregory puns, calling the slave boys *not Angles but Angels*, not from *Deira* (part of Northumbria), but to be rescued from God's wrath (*de ira* in Latin), and says that *Aella* (the name of their king)

echoes the *Alleluia* to God in the future, he shows not only wit, but also a profound optimism about the mission of the Church and the potential of the people. Gregory never lost that vision.

AUGUSTINE (DIED 605)

The sending of St Augustine by Pope Gregory the Great to convert the Anglo-Saxons was an event of great importance in the history of the English church. It brought the Anglo-Saxons, still heathen, in touch with the old, Greco-Roman Christianity of the Mediterranean: in touch with what was, at the end of the sixth century, the modern church practice of Latin Christendom and into a filial relationship with the apostolic see of the West. The Anglo-Saxon church took its place among the provinces of the Roman patriarchate.

Gregory's choice of Augustine, provost of St Andrew's Monastery on the Caelin (where Gregory himself had trained), with a band of monks, to be missionaries to England may seem strange, for monastic tradition stressed the enclosure of the monk within his monastery; but it was recognized that a bishop might take a monk out of his monastery and remove him from the monastic to the clerical service at need, and Augustine was already designated to be bishop of the English before the party set out.

Augustine arrived in Britain, taking with him the necessary Frankish interpreters, who spoke a language and followed ecclesiastical customs with which the kingdom of Kent was familiar. He landed in Thanet and sent an envoy to Aethelberht, a most powerful king in Kent, whose dominions stretched up to the Humber. Bede tells us that he was the third of the Bretwaldas (over-kings of the Anglo-Saxons). As such, he had the right to summon the other kings to battle and to lead their forces.

However, Aethelberht was not unacquainted with Christianity. His wife Bertha, a Frankish Christian princess, had brought with her as her chaplain Liuthard, Bishop of Senlis, and the Christian faith was practised in the ancient church of St Martin at Canterbury. Bede says that this church was dedicated to St Martin of Tours and built while the Romans were still in Britain. While no part of the extant structure can be shown to be of Roman work, it incorporates Roman material. We know from Gregory's own letter to Bertha in 601 that this Christian presence in Kent was not unknown in Rome.

The king is said to have received them in the open air, and the monks approached him

with a processional silver cross and an icon of Christ painted on wood, in the contemporary Byzantine manner then used at Rome. Aethelberht sent them to Canterbury, the seat of his government, there to live and to begin the conversion of England.

Parts of Britain had already been converted. It's interesting to note that Augustine arrived in Canterbury in the same year as Columba died (597) after a fruitful and long ministry. It is also important to remember that according to the records there were three British bishops present at the Council of Arles back in 314 (London, York and Lincoln or Colchester) – over 200 years before the arrival of Augustine to convert the English!

The subsequent encounter between Augustine and the existing British bishops is interesting: Augustine organized a meeting at a place called Augustine's Oak, where he encouraged them to join in the work of conversion upon which he was engaged. The only condition attached to this was that the British bishops should adopt the Roman method of calculating Easter, that same issue which was to divide Roman from Celt in 664 at the Synod of Whitby. Bede describes this encounter as a long and wearisome struggle, which Augustine attempted to resolve; a blind man was brought to the meeting and was healed by Augustine. The British bishops subsequently went away to consult and a second meeting was arranged. This was to prove even more ill-fated than the first.

Before coming to the second meeting the British bishops consulted a hermit who gave them a simple test to apply to Augustine, to see whether he was of God or of men. It was believed to be the test of humility, and was based upon whether Augustine would rise at the arrival of the bishops or remain seated, thereby not acknowledging their authority. Bede tells us that Augustine did not rise and the British bishops contradicted him at every occasion and stated that they would not accept him as archbishop and would continue to practise in the manner of their own tradition. The issue regarding the relationship between the British bishops and Augustine and his followers was left to others to deal with. Augustine died in 605, before the monastery of SS Peter and Paul was built.

CANTERBURY CATHEDRAL

The uniquely important position Canterbury had in relation to the other cathedrals of England is due in mainly to the sacrifice of Thomas Becket in 1170. Pilgrims responded favourably to his death and his canonization as a saint in 1173 and the fire that devastated the cathedral in 1174 provided the monks with a marvellous opportunity to reconstruct a magnificent setting for a shrine of Thomas of Canterbury, Saint and Martyr, whose fame was spreading throughout Christendom.

The church at Canterbury existed long before Becket's time. Augustine had arrived there in 597 and Bede informs us that there was nearby, on the east of the city, a church built in ancient times in honour of St Martin, while the Romans were still in Britain, in which the Queen (Bertha, wife of Aethelberht) used to pray. In this church they first began to meet, to chant the psalms, to pray, to say mass, to preach and to baptize until, when the king had been converted to the faith, they received greater liberty to preach everywhere and to build and restore churches.

Augustine was consecrated Archbishop of the English in 602. He had already founded the Benedictine monastery dedicated to SS Peter and Paul, which was later called St Augustine's, but a cathedral was called for. Again Bede tells us that after Augustine had received his episcopal see in the royal city (Canterbury) he, with the help of the king (Aethelberht), restored the church in it which, as he had been informed, had been built in ancient times by the hands of Roman believers; he dedicated it in the name of the Holy Saviour. Only the name, Christ Church, remains, but the present cathedral stands on the ancient site.

Following the Norman

Conquest, the first Norman archbishop, Lanfranc, who influenced William the Conqueror and the supremacy of Canterbury over York, was secured with the Accord of Winchester in 1072. Very little even of the Norman work done by Archbishop Lanfranc (1070–89), who rebuilt the Saxon cathedral, remains today. It was his successor, Archbishop Anselm, who was responsible for the great crypt and the little staircase towers abutting on the two eastern transepts. There are still traces of contemporary wall painting in St Gabriel's Chapel. Above the crypt he built a magnificent quire which was to last barely four decades before being destroyed by the great fire of 1174.

In the medieval period the monks were determined to rebuild. They arranged the construction of the transepts, Trinity Chapel, Corona and crypt. And on 7 July 1220, in the presence of Henry III, St Thomas Becket's relics were carried in a chest up the successive stages of the cathedral – one of the features of Canterbury – until they reached the shrine. That was the beginning of the major pilgrimage tradition to Canterbury, one of Christendom's chief places of pilgrimage, surpassed perhaps only by Jerusalem and Rome.

PILGRIM ROUTES

There are two well-known routes to Canterbury. The one from Winchester to Canterbury is known as the Pilgrim's Way (Southern Route); the second is the Westminster to Canterbury Route (Northern Route).

THE PILGRIM'S WAY (SOUTHERN ROUTE)

From St Swithin at Winchester to St Thomas at Canterbury.

Main route: Winchester, Farnham, Compton, Guildford, Newlands Corner, Albury, Shere, Chaldon, Kemsing, Aylesford, Harbledown, Canterbury.

Winchester

- St Catherine's Hill: south-east of Winchester between the river and the Twyford Down by-pass of the M3, by exit 10 – the remains of a turf maze. Mazes were Christian symbols of the soul caught up and confused by the intricacies of the material world, yet always seeking to escape.
- St Martin's Well and monastery site: near the cathedral, by the old Roman wall – fourth-century foundations of the original Christian community.
- Castle Hall and the Round Table: off the High Street – links with King Arthur and the Romano–Celtic ruler of Britain, Ambrosius Aurelianus (c. 480), who tried to rally a last stand against the invading Angles.
- Winchester Cathedral and St Swithin (Bishop of Winchester c. 852): in the city centre – in the cathedral there are so many signs of the importance of pilgrimage.
- Hyde Abbey: Hyde Abbey Road, just north of city centre – burial place of King Alfred.
- The route to Farnham passes close to Alresford, which is worth a detour. The site was one of the original pieces of land given to the new church at Winchester while St Birinus (c. 650) was still there.
- Winchester to Farnham (29 miles): follow signs to Alton out of Winchester and take A31 to Farnham. Alresford is *en route*, just north of A31 on B3046.

Farnham

- Farnham's economic success as a medieval village was to a great extent built upon the revenue of the pilgrims passing through.
- To the south-east, on the B3001, are the ruins of Waverley Abbey, an established pilgrimage place.
- Farnham to Compton (9 miles): continue on A31 to Guildford. Compton is south of A31 on B3000.

Compton

- St Nicholas' Church contains the oldest wooden screen in England (Norman).
- Compton to Guildford (3 miles): return to A31 and continue to Guildford.

Guildford

- Famous for its inns; originally built to handle the pilgrim trade.
- Guildford to Albury (5 miles): follow A281 (signposted Horsham) then at Shalford take A248 going east; continue to Albury.

Newlands Corner

- One of the most religiously dominated and shaped landscapes in England. It seems that the Christian Pilgrim's Way at this point follows an even older pre-Christian pilgrim's way.

Albury

- The church has two octagonal pillars thought to have come from a Roman temple which stood on nearby Blackheath, which still displays the remains of earthworks.
- Albury to Kemsing (3 miles): from Albury continue on A248 and go east on A25 through Dorking to Reigate. From here take A217 north to join M25. Go as far as junction 5 and take A25 east to Seal, then follow local signs to Kemsing (detours to Shere on the A25 and Chaldon on B2031).

Kemsing (961–84)

- St Edith's Well: this well is first mentioned in 926, making it the earliest recorded Christian well.
- Kemsing to Aylesford (14 miles): return to A25 and follow signs for M26 (becomes M20). Aylesford is just north of junction 5.

At Aylesford the Southern Route is joined by the Northern Route.

THE WESTMINSTER TO CANTERBURY ROUTE (NORTHERN ROUTE)

From St Edward the Confessor at Westminster to St Thomas at Canterbury.

Main route: Greenwich, Dartford, Gravesend, Rochester, Aylesford, Harbledown, Canterbury.

Greenwich

- This settlement was a popular stop because of its church dedicated to another martyred Archbishop of Canterbury, St Alphage (953–1012).
- Greenwich to Dartford (10 miles): take the A207 to Dartford.

Dartford

- This was a major pilgrimage centre, with a nunnery where women travellers could stay in safety. Here pilgrims could follow an old Roman road (Watling Street) to Canterbury.
- Dartford to Rochester (22 miles): from Dartford join A2, which joins M2 just before Rochester.

Rochester

- This small city is dominated by two buildings: the castle, built on a site fortified since Roman times; and the nearby cathedral, founded in 604 by St Justus, one of the early missionaries sent to England by Pope Gregory.
- Rochester to Aylesford (8 miles): go south on A229 to Maidstone and follow local signs for Aylesford (just north of Maidstone and west of A229).

At Aylesford the Southern and Northern Routes meet.

Aylesford

- The site of one of King Alfred's major victories over the Danes in 893. It witnessed one of the first great defeats of the Saxons by the British.

- Aylesford Priory: a place of pilgrim welcome.
- Neolithic stones: some 4 miles north of Aylesford, west of A229 going towards Rochester. Follow local signs. The most famous of these five Neolithic remains are the burial mounds known as Kit's Coty House and Little Kit's Coty House. Local legend claims that they were built to contain the bodies of Horsa and Certigorn, killed at the famous battle of 455.
- Aylesford to Canterbury (33 miles): return to A229, head north towards Rochester and join M2 going east to Canterbury.

Harbledown

- Here the hospital of St Nicholas was founded by Archbishop Lanfranc in 1084 to care for the outcast, aged and infirm. It was probably chosen for the well nearby.

CANTERBURY THE CATHEDRAL
(see also p. 85)

PRACTICAL INFORMATION

- The mission of the cathedral is to encourage a living faith in God by interpreting the Christian gospel through the cathedral building itself, its history, its saints, its worship, preaching and teaching, and through its work in the wider community.
- *Visiting Times:*
  Weekdays:
    summer 9am – 7pm
    winter 9am – 5pm
    the Crypt 10am – 5 / 7pm
  Sundays:
    All year 12.30 – 2.30pm
    including the Crypt 4.30 – 5.30pm
- *Service Times:*
    Sundays: 8am / 9.30am / 11am / 3.15pm / 6.30pm
    Weekdays: 7.30am (Sat 9.30am) / 8am / 5.30pm (Sat 3.15pm)
- Arrangements for advance bookings by groups and organizations are made with the Visits Office (adults), Schools Office (school parties) or Education Centre Administrator (conference facilities): 01227 762862, fax 01227 865222.
- There are guided tours in several languages throughout the day.
- Audio-tours in 7 languages, lasting 40 minutes, are available inside the main entrance.
- Audio-visual presentations in several languages, lasting 15 minutes, are available in two theatres in the Education Centre which each seat up to 60 people.
- Facilities for the disabled include toilets, ramps, wheelchairs, a touch and hearing system and a lift. A leaflet giving full details is available at the Welcome Centre or from staff.
- The cathedral shop offers a large range of publications and gifts.

England

- The Archives and Library are open to the public for research by appointment: Mon – Thurs 9am – 5pm. Groups may visit the Archives and Library by appointment: 01227 762862, fax: 01227 865222 / 865250.
- Parking is not possible within the precincts except for a certain very limited provision for disabled drivers, by prior arrangement.
- The recently completed Education Centre offers a unique venue for a wide range of activities including conferences, lectures and performances.
- Eating facilities are not available in the cathedral, but the cathedral is centrally situated and there are ample eating places within easy walking distance.
- A small charge is made for the use of the toilets in the cathedral precincts.
- There is a charge made for entry and for some other services to the cathedral (a price list is available).

- Canterbury Tourist Information: 01227 766567, fax: 01227 459840.
- *Travel details:*
  By road – the M20 (M25/M26) and M2 (A2) motorways are close by.
  By rail – there are two mainline stations: 08457 303030.
  By air – Gatwick airport is about an hour's journey.
- The Park and Ride service: every 8 minutes, Mon – Sat 7.30am – 6.30pm: Sturry Road on the A28 between Canterbury and Sturry village.
- *Other Useful Telephone Numbers:*
  St Martin's Church: 01227 259482
  St Augustine's Abbey: 01227 767345
  The Cathedral: 01227 762862
  Roman Museum: 01227 785575
  Canterbury Heritage Museum: 01227 452747
  Eastbridge Hospital: 01227 471688
  Canterbury Festival of Music: 01227 452853

Suggested Devotion

John 17.11–23: The Unity of the Church

From 'Good Counseil of Chaucer', by Geoffrey Chaucer (*c.* 1340–1400).

> *Forth pilgrime! Forth best out of thy stalle!*
> *Loke up on hye, and thonke God for alle;*
> *Weyve thy lust, and let thy goste the lede,*
> *And trouthe shal thy delyver, hit is no drede.*

Lullingstone Roman Villa and Faversham Stone Chapel

The main reason for choosing these two places is that they offer important glimpses in appreciating and understanding more about structures in the early part of the first millennium and particularly places associated with Roman Britain.

LULLINGSTONE ROMAN VILLA, KENT

Lullingstone Roman Villa is one of England's most exciting archaeological finds. It was occupied during much of the Roman period. Its remains include fine mosaic floors, painted wall-plaster and a unique private Christian chapel. It offers an excellent introduction to Roman domestic life and to the methods of archaeology.

Lullingstone was a large country house occupied during much of the Roman period. The Roman occupation at Lullingstone began in 80–90 AD with a modest timber-framed house on flint foundations. This was transformed in the late second century into a much more luxurious dwelling with a tiled roof, a bath suite and a pagan shrine. The owners at this period were people of substance who used high quality pottery and glassware. The bath suite had hot, tepid and cold rooms, the latter being plastered and painted. The room used for cult worship was also painted with frescoes of water goddesses.

These paintings, though much decayed, still show a high level of skill and are one of the most notable features of Lullingstone, giving a rare glimpse of Roman interior decoration.

Around 200 the house was suddenly deserted. The reasons for this are unclear but may have been due to political disruption. The inhabitants left the house in such haste that they abandoned some marble family portrait busts. The busts are of eastern Mediterranean origin and depict bearded men, apparently related, wearing Roman dress. For 60 years or so the house was unoccupied but then it came back into continuous occupation until the fifth century when it was finally destroyed by fire. Most of the remains that can be seen today date from the fourth-century rebuilding, including two fine mosaic floors. One of these shows a panel of Europa and the Bull and the other shows Bellerophan riding Pegasus. There is also a wall painting of three water goddesses in the niche of a blocked doorway. The central nymph has greenery in her hair and blue water streaming from her breasts.

Around 370 the owners of Lullingstone converted to Christianity and installed a chapel above the old cult room. This is a unique find in Britain and one for which Lullingstone is famous. Strangely enough the pagan shrine in the room below it still continued in use. A family might have been hedging its bets, or maybe pagan and Christian worship were practised simultaneously by different groups in the household. Similar ambivalence is displayed by earlier burials in a deep vault of the pagan temple–mausoleum on a terrace above the villa. A young man and young woman, in lead coffins embossed with scallop shells, were accompanied by pagan grave goods, but the coffins were packed with gypsum – a practice of people expecting bodily resurrection.

Painted wall decoration in the chapel and adjacent rooms incorporated Christian symbols, such as *Chi-Rho* monograms (the opening letters of the Greek *Christos*), and male figures with arms outstretched in the ancient attitude of Christian prayer, called *orantes*. These painted panels have been conserved and are on display in the British Museum but copies can be seen at Lullingstone. Other finds from the site include a lead coffin with scallop shell decoration peculiar to the Thames Valley, and grave goods from the late third-century mausoleum of a young couple that was discovered behind the villa.

PRACTICAL INFORMATION

- Location: 1 mile south-west of Eynsford off the A225, midway between Dartford and Sevenoaks. Ordnance Survey Map: Landranger Series no. 177. The villa is signposted off the A225 opposite the church. The A20 is about two miles to the north.

By train: Eynsford 1 mile.

- Opening times:
  1 April – 30 Sept: daily
  10am – 6pm
  1 Oct – 31 March: daily
  10am – 4pm
- Facilities:
  Access for the disabled is limited at present to the ground floor.
  Touch maps for the visually impaired may be borrowed on site.
  There is a small exhibition of some of the finds.
  A shop sells books, postcards, etc.
  There is a toilet on site.
- Free educational visits – pre-booked at least 14 days before. Limited party number – 100 max; required staff–pupil ratio – at least 1 to 15
- Free audio tour
- Admission charges: adults £2.50, concessions: £1.90, children: £1.30, under 5s: free, 15% discount on groups of 11 or more
- Booking and site information: 01322 863467 / 01732 778000

FAVERSHAM STONE CHAPEL

The ruined church of Our Lady of Elwarton lies just north off the A2 two miles west of Faversham. The remains lie at the bottom of Syndale Valley, beneath Judd Hill and Beacon Hill, close to where a stream once ran. From the road, or from the railway to the north, there appears to be just a group of crumbling remains set at the edge of a small copse in the middle of a field, and of no particular significance.

The church has not been in use since some time in the sixteenth century. The date at which it was abandoned is uncertain, but the records of a visitation in 1511 indicate that it was in a state of disrepair at that time, and bequests during the early years of the sixteenth century indicate that repairs to the fabric continued to be necessary. It is most likely that the church was not used at all after the Reformation.

Excavation reports of the site record that buttresses were added to the north wall of the nave during the thirteenth century because wooden beams had rotted; this suggests that the building was based on an earlier structure already old by that time. Saxon and Roman remains found during the 1967 excavation indicate a long period of use at the site, spanning more than a thousand years.

The remains consist of walls standing about a metre above ground level, somewhat higher at the east end. The walls enclose three distinct areas: the nave to the west, the sanctuary to the east and a section linking the two. The walls of the nave and the sanctuary are mainly of flint, bonded with a mortar rich with broken seashells. The construction of the centre section is quite different; the walls here rest on a foundation of flint and consist of layers of tufa blocks, each around 30cm square, separated by a double layer of red brick 3cm thick. This construction is typically Roman and the discovery of Roman coins dating from the third and fourth centuries confirms this section as Roman in origin. The size and nature of the foundations revealed during the excavation suggest that this was a mausoleum. The building was windowless, with a barrel vaulted roof and a stout door with a megalithic stone frame. Stones which formed the door-frame can still be seen, reused in the thirteenth-century buttresses. The sill of the door is still *in situ*.

The site is now somewhat remote from habitation, though a road ran to the north of the church until the early part of the nineteenth century. In Roman times, however, the area was quite heavily populated. There was probably a Roman camp on Judd Hill, and a cemetery of substantial size has been found a few hundred yards to the east of the church.

A number of Roman artefacts have also been found in the field in which the church stands. The *Itinerary* of Antonius places the Roman station Durolevum 16 miles from Rochester and 9 or 12 miles from Canterbury. It is quite possible, but unproved, that the site on Judd Hill is this station.

In 601 Pope Gregory the Great directed St Augustine not to destroy pagan buildings, but to adapt them for Christian use. King Aethelburht of Kent allowed St Augustine to build and repair churches in the area. It is tempting to think that this little church at Stone is one of the churches St Augustine converted, but there is no proof that the fabric is of this early date. As it is, the remains are a unique record of the adaptation of a pagan Roman building for Christian use, and are preserved for that reason.

Contact number: 01795 534542

Suggested Devotion

Matthew 7.21–29: Building the House on Firm Foundations

From Mary Batchelor (ed.), *The Lion Prayer Collection* (Lion, 1992), p. 139:

God of the nomad and the pilgrim, may we find our security in you and not in our possessions. May our homes be open to guests and our hearts to one another so that all our travelling is lighter and together we reach the goal.

Lindisfarne and Holy Island

St Aidan

INTRODUCTION TO NORTHUMBRIA

Northumbria is rich in Christian heritage. During the early part of the first century the Romans marched in and set up camp, bringing with them their own pagan religions. However, it was not long before visitors from Rome brought the people of Northumbria tales of a new faith, Christianity. So even before Aidan arrived on Holy Island in the seventh century, Roman Christians had been worshipping and living in the fertile Tyne valley. Their legacy lives on at sites such as Vindolanda where, within the grounds of the Roman fort, are the remains of a fourth-century church. In fact Paulinus, one of the group sent to England by Pope Gregory the Great in 601 to assist Augustine, came to Northumbria in 625 as chaplain to the Christian Princess Ethelberga of Kent, bride of King Edwin of Northumbria.

The very word 'Northumbria' conveys how hard it would have been for Romans posted to the furthest corners of the Empire. Hadrian's Wall is a huge rampart, spanning some of the most remote countryside in England. Impressive stretches of the wall still stand on bleak bluffs and outcrops across Northumberland; and frontier life is vividly revived in forts and museums along the banks of the Tyne – for example at Vindolanda, Chesters, Corbridge and Arbeia Fort at South Shields.

In the seventh century St Aidan (died 651) brought the Christian message to Northern England from Iona; he founded the monastery of Lindisfarne in 635. Three centuries later St Cuthbert became the focus of the Christian Church, as wandering monks journeyed with his remains for over a century. They finally found sanctuary in Durham, and around Cuthbert's tomb grew up the castle and cathedral of Durham city.

So how is all this known?

Northumbria was also the home of the first English historian, Bede, a monk whose work is now celebrated in the Bede's World museum in Jarrow.

Out of the chaos of the Northumbrian wars during the early seventh century emerges Oswald. He was the son of King Aethelfrith, who fled to the monastery at Iona because of the habit kings had of killing off any possible contenders for the throne. There Oswald became a Christian, and, returning to Northumbria with a small band

in 633, he defeated Caedwalla, the Welsh king who had seen off kings Edwin, Eanfrith and Osric, and who had devastated the land.

During most of the Celtic period when churches were developing, Northumbria was governed by the Angles. These were pagan Germanic tribes from Denmark who began raiding Britain's east coast during the late Roman period. One of their chiefs, Ida, fought his way north and became the first king of Northumbria. He established himself in the fortress of Bamburgh, on a rocky outcrop beside the shore, 15 miles south-east of Berwick-upon-Tweed.

In 634 Oswald (604–42) became king and sent to Iona for a missionary bishop. In that same year Aidan and a company of monks arrived to preach in Northumbria. They made their base on Lindisfarne, and their influence made for a rapid and effective growth of Christianity. Bede tells memorable stories of

Aidan and Oswald travelling the country, Aidan preaching and Oswald translating.

Despite plague and war the progress of the conversion was relentless. Provinces were founded, bishops consecrated, and monasteries grew and some even emerged into fame: Bede's twin monasteries of Monkwearmouth and Jarrow; the 'double' monastery of Whitby, housing both men and women separately, under Hilda. Many more have been lost, and we know some only by name, and not by location; others have in all probability disappeared from the record altogether. One thing that needs to be stressed firmly is that it was monasticism above all else that effected conversion to Christianity in this early period. Monks provided preaching, teaching, hospital, hotel and orphanage facilities, as well as counsel for kings. Monasteries were not cut off from the world: Augustine, Wilfrid, Hilda and Aidan were politicians, whether they liked it or not, and, indeed, whether they were suited to it or not.

LINDISFARNE AND HOLY ISLAND: ST AIDAN

Aidan came to Northumbria in 635 at the request of the recently converted King Oswald, who was keen to evangelize the area. Aidan chose Lindisfarne as his base and established there both a church and a monastery. Lindisfarne was close to the capital, Bebbanburgh (today's Bamburgh) and secure in its island position. From here Aidan preached the gospel throughout Northumbria, with King Oswald sometimes acting as his interpreter.

The meaning of the Celtic word *Lindisfarne* is 'the land by the Lindis'; Lindis being a small stream, now called the Low, which is visible only at low tide. The monastery that Aidan constructed probably consisted of small, simple huts with room for just one or two monks and they would have surrounded the church. This area was perhaps divided off from the guest house and the other more public buildings. The whole complex would have been enclosed by a bank and ditch.

As in other Celtic monastic communities, there would have been hermitages outside the boundary walls. There are two good examples in this area:

- 400 metres south-west of Lindisfarne, St Cuthbert's Isle contains the remains of a seventh-century cell and a later medieval chapel. At low tide, it can be reached on foot from Lindisfarne.
- Seven miles south-east, Aidan and his successors found a more isolated retreat on the island of Inner Farne.

Lindisfarne's monks undoubtedly evangelized much of north-east Britain; they travelled northwards into Scotland and south into Mercia, East Anglia and Wessex. Monastic craftsmen and artists developed new styles of sculpture and illumination,

which they took with them on their missionary journeys.

The mission flourished. People gave lands for churches and monasteries to be founded. Children were often sent to Lindisfarne to be educated by the Scottish monks. Four brothers who arrived there, Cynebil, Caelin, Cedd and Chad, became priests, the last two of these being made bishops. Cedd founded churches and monasteries in Essex and North Yorkshire. Chad was sent to Ireland by Aidan and, having completed his studies, returned to Northumbria. He was a devout and gentle man, similar to Aidan in his devotion to work. After his death in 672, he was venerated as a saint. Pilgrims visited his tomb in the belief that it held powers of healing.

Aidan's mission on Lindisfarne changed the Northumbrian people. According to Bede, many Northumbrians, both noble and simple, laid aside their weapons, preferring to follow the way of the cross rather than study the art of war. Missionaries trained by Aidan travelled throughout Britain, some even journeying to the Netherlands.

During Aidan's lifetime, communities of nuns were founded in Northumbria. Hilda, the first Northumbrian woman to take the veil, was appointed Abbess of Hartlepool. After Aidan there was a bishop at Lindisfarne for almost 250 years. During this time nine saints and 16 bishops were associated with Lindisfarne. The sixth bishop, Cuthbert, was to earn the greatest fame.

Today about 200 people live on Holy Island, most of them making a living either from fishing or through some aspect of the tourist trade, which every year brings thousands of visitors and pilgrims to their village.

THE LINDISFARNE GOSPELS

The sixth and seventh centuries were a period of outstanding brilliance for Northumbrian arts. The Priory museum contains much from this 'golden age' including sculptured stone crosses and intricate figure carvings with vine-scroll ornamentation intertwined with birds and beasts. However, without doubt the crowning achievement of the ancient Northumbrians was the magnificently illuminated manuscripts known as the Lindisfarne Gospels, one of the finest surviving examples of Celtic art. They were written in honour of St Cuthbert by Eadfrith, Bishop of Lindisfarne, between 698 and 721.

Around 130 calf-hides were scraped and cured to produce the vellum sheets on which the Gospels were written, mainly in Latin. Pens were made from feathers while the black ink was a combination of soot and egg whites. Plants and mineral pigments provided the colours for the illuminations. The binding was richly adorned with jewels and gold.

When the monks fled from the Danes in 875, they took the Gospels with them. Legend has it that the book was lost at sea but miraculously recovered during an attempt to remove the body of St Cuthbert to the safety of Ireland. In the twelfth century the Gospels were in Durham, but their history after that date is uncertain. It is unlikely that the rich adornment of jewels and gold was left untouched during the Dissolution of the Monasteries in 1537, but there is no record of what happened to the Gospels until the seventeenth century, when it was noted that they were in the hands of the Clerk of Parliaments. The Gospels are now in the British Museum.

LINDISFARNE TODAY

The parish church of St Mary was built between 1120 and 1145. Today, original Norman architecture remains in the form of three arches on the eastern side of the north aisle. The chancel is thirteenth-century and there is a medieval tombstone, decorated with a cross and a sword, on the north wall. A small belfry was added to the church at the beginning of the eighteenth century.

In addition to the parish church, there are a number of organizations and establishments that offer a 'ministry of welcome' to modern-day pilgrims. Also, a carefully produced programme of retreats – either conducted or 'free' – has been designed for people to make full use of this sacred place. Five particularly stand out:

- Marygate House and Cambridge House – accommodation for groups, and also for those wishing to come alone on retreat (01289 389246)
- The Society of St Vincent de Paul – hostel accommodation for young people (0141 3327752)
- The Lindisfarne Mustard Seed Project – facilities for private, group and public retreats
- The St Cuthbert's Holy Island Project – open to visitors, and hosts informal Saturday night worship and occasional day retreats (01289 389254)
- The Open Gate, Community of Aidan and Hilda House – small family accommodation. This organization is a scattered community of Christians who seek to cradle a Christian spirituality for today inspired by Celtic saints. Its members look after this house and the wardens welcome guests for personal retreats, study and quiet holidays (01289 389222).

PRACTICAL INFORMATION

- Lindisfarne Priory: open all year 10am – 5pm; admission charges vary and there are parking facilities, gift shops and toilets on Holy Island as well as exhibitions and a museum (01289 389200)
- How to get there: reached only at low tide by car across the causeway, tide tables at each end or details from the Berwick Tourist Information Centre (01289 330733). Trains to Berwick-upon-Tweed (14 miles); bus information (01670 533128)
- The Lindisfarne Gospels Exhibition: information on museum, workshops and events (01670 856968)
- Maps: Holy Island Map ref. B5; Ordnance Survey Map: Landranger Series no. 75
- Tourist Information: Berwick-upon-Tweed 01289 330733

Suggested Devotion

Exodus 40.36–38: God Guides His Pilgrim People

A Prayer for Holy Island, based on 'St Aidan's Prayer', from Ray Simpson's *Give Yourself a Retreat on Holy Island* (St Aidan's Press, 1998), p. 5:

> *Here be the peace of water lapping shore,*
> *Here be the peace of praise by night and day;*
> *Here be the peace of those who do your will,*
> *Here be the peace of people serving others.*

Whitby

St Hilda

ST HILDA AND THE SYNOD OF WHITBY

One of Aidan's most influential missionary companions was St Hilda (614–80). Hilda was of royal lineage and related to the royal families of Northumbria and East Anglia. She was baptized by Paulinus at the age of 13 and at the age of 33 she decided to become a nun in Gaul. However, Aidan managed to persuade her to stay in Northumbria and she subsequently led the monastery at Hartlepool on the coast which admitted men and women, 75 miles south of Lindisfarne. She left this community to become the Abbess of Streanaeshalch (which was later called Whitby by the Danes), on the cliffs above a harbour settlement, 20 miles south of Hartlepool, and she stayed there until her death at the age of 66.

Hilda's mixed monastery at Whitby quickly gained a reputation as a centre of learning and the arts. It was here that she encouraged Caedmon, an Anglo-Saxon lay brother, to write songs and stories to illustrate the Scriptures. He composed a 'Hymn of Creation', and possibly 'The Dream of the Rood', and is considered to be the first English religious poet. Hilda trained at least five bishops, and hosted the Synod of Whitby in 664, at which she supported the Irish party in the debate over the date of Easter, but accepted the council's decision in favour of Rome.

What led to the Synod of Whitby in 664 was the fact that the church of Iona had a method of calculating Easter which was different from that employed by the church in the south of England and on the continent, and which it passed on to Northumbria.

A particular circumstance was the marriage of Oswald's successor Oswiu to Edwin's daughter, who had been brought up in Kent and whose household adhered to the southern method, whereas Oswiu followed that of Iona. The result, Bede tells us, was that the king might be celebrating Easter Sunday while the queen was still observing Palm Sunday, such were the variations produced by the use of two methods for fixing the date of Easter. Further, Alhfrith had been taught by Wilfrid, future Bishop of York, who had by this time studied the teachings of the church in Rome and at Lyons in what was then Gaul, and who therefore opposed the Easter calculation

THE DATING OF EASTER: The question of Easter was the main item on the agenda of the Synod of Whitby in 664. The technicalities of the Easter debate were those which the Church had wrestled with since the third century. The difficulty was rooted in the origins of the faith. Easter was tied to the Jewish Passover (the Last Supper in the Gospels). The Jewish Passover was a festival determined by the lunar rather than the solar calendar. According to the story of the first passover in the Book of Exodus, Passover was to be celebrated at the first full moon of the Hebrew month Nisan, the first month of the Jewish year. Christian dating experts regarded this as the first full moon after the spring equinox and as Easter had to be celebrated on a Sunday, the rules were clear: Easter must be the first Sunday after the first full moon after the spring equinox. The next question was: when was the spring equinox? Some Christians said 25 March, the date fixed by the Julian calendar in 46 BC. The Council of Nicaea (325) said 21 March to take into account solar changes to the length of the year. Still others said 22 March. At the Synod of Whitby, Wilfrid, the Abbot of Ripon and the representative of the Roman Church, followed the Alexandrian tradition and favoured Easter between the 15th and the 21st of the lunar month. Bede also adopted this line. Colman, the Irish Bishop of Lindisfarne and the representative of the Celtic Church, favoured Easter between the 14th and the 20th. Eventually the construction of Easter tables was deemed necessary. Colman and his followers adopted an 84–year cycle and Wilfrid a 19–year cycle, after which the same Easter dates would recur. Wilfrid won the day. Bede, in adopting this method and applying *Anno Domini* dates to it, not only defined for the future the Church's method for the calculation of Easter, but also played a major part in establishing *Anno Domini* dating as the normal system of dating in Western Europe.

of the clergy from Iona, to which Oswiu adhered.

So the synod was called, and Oswiu himself presided over it, with Alhfrith also present. On the one side were Colman, the Irish bishop of Lindisfarne, and his Irish clergy, supported by the saintly Abbess Hilda of Whitby and the equally saintly Cedd, who was at this time Bishop of the East Saxons, but was another product of Lindisfarne.

The other side was led by a visitor from the south, Agilbert, who was Bishop of the West Saxons, although he came from Gaul. With him were Wilfrid, whom Alhfrith had made Abbot of Ripon; a Kentish priest, Romanus, who had come to Northumbria with Oswiu's queen; and James, a deacon who had come to Northumbria with the ill-fated mission of Paulinus in the late 620s.

Bede gives a full account of the debate. Oswiu stressed the importance of unity and Colman spoke about how he and his group were following the pattern laid down by St John. Wilfrid then said that he and his party observed Easter in the same way as Christians in Rome, Italy, Gaul, Africa, Asia, Egypt and Greece.

Clearly there was a huge disagreement. Wilfrid supported the Eastern and European tradition and Colman the Celtic custom seemingly based on the tradition of the apostle John. Wilfrid won the debate and was soon made Bishop of York (which now replaced Lindisfarne as the Northumbrian episcopal see). There were to be no more bishops of Northumbria from Iona, or indeed from Ireland; so the relationship inaugurated by Aidan was ended.

The Synod of Whitby was thus a turning-point in the history of the Church, not because it broke the links between England and Ireland, not because it resolved some great clash between 'Celtic' and 'Roman', but because it began the process by which one of the greatest scholars of the Middle Ages at last established the rules for fixing the date of the Church's greatest festival – and did so from a remote monastery in the valley of the River Tyne.

It is important to remember that the Synod of Whitby had three items on the agenda:

- to determine the date of Easter;
- to decide whether monks should shave their heads according to the continental form of tonsure (symbolizing the circular crown of thorns) or, according to the Celtic style (to shave the front part of the head and allow the back part of their hair to grow into a pony-tail, adopting the form of marking out holy men that was current amongst the Druids of the time);
- to determine whether at baptism new converts should be dipped once or thrice in the water. The Celtic tradition stipulated three dippings.

WHITBY TODAY

Whitby, with its quaint cobbled streets and picturesque houses, stands on the steep slopes of the River Esk and is dominated by its cliff-top abbey. The first monastery, founded by Hilda, was destroyed by the Vikings in 867 but substantial ruins survive from the thirteenth-century rebuilding.

Access to this site is on the

cliff top east of Whitby town centre. It has standard opening times with a small entrance fee.

Tourist information: 01947 602674

Suggested Devotion

Philippians 4.4–9: Rejoice in the Lord Always

A Prayer

Almighty God, who has established your church through the love and devotion of your saints: we give thanks for your servant Hilda whom we commemorate in this place. Inspire us to follow her example, that we in our generation may rejoice with her in the vision of your glory; through Jesus Christ our Lord. Amen.

St Cuthbert's Way: Melrose Abbey to Holy Island

ST CUTHBERT

While working as a shepherd in southern Scotland, a young man named Cuthbert (634–87) beheld a column of light descending from heaven to earth and, within it, a band of angels carrying the soul of a holy person to heaven. Inspired by this vision, he gave up sheep-herding and enrolled as a monk at the nearby Melrose Abbey. When St Aidan died, Cuthbert heard about Lindisfarne, and transferred himself there. After a period in Ripon, in 661 St Cuthbert became Abbot of the Lindisfarne monastery, though he spent much of his time in solitary isolation on St Cuthbert's Isle nearby. While here, he became famous for his healing powers. He was appointed Bishop of Lindisfarne, and for several years travelled widely, preaching the gospel.

He spent the last part of his life in retreat on the island of Inner Farne. After his death, Cuthbert's body was buried at the monastery on Holy Island. In 875, following a number of Viking raids, the community left the island carrying the saint's relics, and were said to have rested in the spot now known as St Cuthbert's Cave. Then they transferred them to Durham Cathedral. It was the Community of St Cuthbert that was responsible for the Lindisfarne Gospels, perhaps the greatest work of art of the Anglo-Saxon period.

The route of St Cuthbert's Way thus links a number of places associated with his story. A fuller account is provided in the trail guide, and books about the saint can be purchased at the church, or at shops on Holy Island.

ST CUTHBERT'S WAY

The route includes Melrose Abbey, the Eildon Hills, the River Tweed, Dere Street Roman road, the Cheviot Hills, the Northumberland Fell sandstone moors and the Lindisfarne National Nature Reserve.

The route starts at the superb Melrose Abbey, a twelfth-century Cistercian foundation. From here St Cuthbert's Way crosses the Eildon Hills to Bowden, and continues through Newtown St Boswells, and along the River Tweed to Maxton.

Dere Street, the Roman road, is followed to the Harestanes Countryside Visitor Centre. A detour will allow travellers to visit the Waterloo Monument. The route continues to Cessford, where the formidable

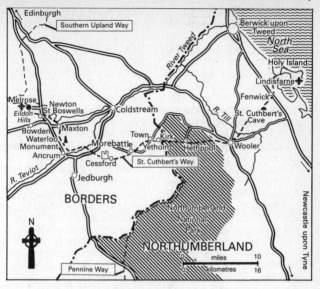

St Cuthbert's Way

remains of Cessford Castle can be seen.

The route continues through Morebattle and then climbs on to the 1000ft Grubbit Law. From here a ridge walk with splendid views leads to the twin villages of Town and Kirk Yetholm. The route crosses the border fence below Eccles Cairn and enters the Northumberland National Park.

From Hethpool in the College Valley, a high level route crosses a moorland area rich in prehistoric remains before dropping down into the market town of Wooler.

St Cuthbert's Way then crosses Weetwood Moor and the river Till, reaching St Cuthbert's Cave and soon gaining the first view of Lindisfarne. The final section leads on to the coast at the edge of the Holy Island sands. Take the causeway on to the island, or follow the posts of the historic Pilgrims' Path across the sands (for which a far shorter safe crossing time applies).

PRACTICAL INFORMATION

- Overnight accommodation and refreshments are available in the following places on or near the route: Bowden; Newtown St Boswell's; St Boswell's; Ancrum; Jedburgh; Crailing; Morebattle; Town Yetholm; Kirk Yetholm; Wooler; Lowick; Fenwick; Holy Island.
- Equipment and safety: the

route includes low level stretches along riverside paths and in the Northumberland coastal area as well as more strenuous stretches through the Cheviot Hills between Morebattle and Wooler. Although the route is waymarked throughout in both directions with the St Cuthbert's Cross symbol, a reasonable level of fitness and navigational skill are needed, especially in poor weather conditions. Suitable footwear, warm and waterproof clothing, food and drink, maps and compasses are all necessities.

- The causeway to Holy Island is closed twice a day at high tide, so you need to plan your crossing carefully. Times are available at the Harestanes Visitor Centre (01835 830306) to enable you to plan ahead. You can also check at the tourist information centre in Wooler (01668 282123) and Berwick (01289 330733) for safe crossing times, which are shown on the door when the office is closed.

- A selection of leaflets on accommodation and facilities is available from tourist information centres or by post from the Scottish Tourist Board (01835 863435); details are also available on the website at www.scot-borders.co.uk – follow the links to the walking section.

- Access: the route follows rights of way or routes where access has been agreed with landowners, as well as public roads, within Scotland; and public footpaths, bridleways, permissive paths agreed with landowners and public roads within England. The

---

Suggested Devotion

Matthew 28.16–20: The Great Commission of Jesus

A Prayer

O God, by whose grace the holy father Cuthbert, enkindled by the fire of your love, became a shining light in your church: Grant that we may be inspired with the same spirit of discipline, love and prayer, and so walk before you as children of light; through Jesus Christ our Lord. Amen.

Some words attributed to Cuthbert, in Douglas Dales, *Called to be Angels* (Canterbury Press Norwich, 1998), p. 29:

Even if I could possibly hide myself in a tiny dwelling on a rock, where the waves of the swelling ocean surrounded me on all sides, and shut me in equally from the sight and knowledge of men, not even thus should I consider myself to be free from the snares of a deceptive world: but even there I should fear lest the love of wealth should tempt me and somehow or other should snatch me away.

route is a footpath only and is not intended for use by cyclists. Dogs are not allowed for a short section of the route near Bowden and camping is very limited – check with the tourist office.

- Tourist information:
    Melrose – 01896 822555
    Jedburgh – 01835 863170/ 01835 868435 / 863688
    Wooler – 01668 282123
    Berwick-upon-Tweed – 01289 330733
- Public transport along the route – 01835 823301

- Baggage transfer – 01665 575767
- Organized walking holidays – 01522 684104 / 01896 830515
    Perth: 01738 624194
    Sterling: 01786 445703
    Falkirk: 01324 714132
- One book that I found particularly useful is Mary Low's *St Cuthbert's Way: A Pilgrim's Companion* (Wild Goose Publications, 2000). It is extremely comprehensive and has much valuable information.

St Paul's Monastery and Bede's World Museum

THE VENERABLE BEDE

Bede's *History of the English Church and Nation*, which was completed in 731, is one of the most important English history books. The enthusiasm shown for his writings in the eighth century by English missionaries on the Continent, such as Boniface, Lul and others, led to the spread of the knowledge of his works throughout Europe.

So deeply are we indebted to Bede for our knowledge of the history of England before the eighth century that it comes as something of a shock to us to realize that if Bede had not written, the names of Chad, Cedd, Hilda, Aethelrhryth, Edwin, Oswald, Caedmon and Benedict Biscop would be either completely unknown or known only to scholars, around which to spin webs of conjecture; and our knowledge of the greatest of his themes, St Augustine's mission and the conversion of the English, would be fragmentary.

Ironically, we know very little about Bede's own personal life, except what he himself tells us at the end of his book. He tells us that he was 59 when his *History* was completed in 731. He was therefore born in 672/673 and he describes his birth place as being in the territory of the monastery of Wearmouth and Jarrow. In 680 Bede, at the age of seven, was given into the care of Benedict Biscop, the ex-soldier who had become a monk and had founded the new monastery at Wearmouth in 674. About 681 Jarrow, the sister-house, was founded and though the two monasteries had separate rulers, they continued all through Bede's life to be considered as one monastery. He remained at Jarrow engaged in his studies all through his youth. At the age of 19, six years before the canonical age, he was ordained deacon. Age exceptions were occasionally made in the case of men of outstanding learning and devotion. He was ordained priest in 703, and the rest of his life was that of a typical scholar-monk.

Bede was particularly good at describing the passing of the saints; so it was only fitting that his own death should have been most movingly described by his disciple Cuthbert who later became abbot of the monastery of Wearmouth-Jarrow. Bede died on the eve of Ascension, 735.

As well as offering us some clues as to who Bede was, his work also offers a fairly clear picture of the monastic life which he lived. The rule observed at the Wearmouth-Jarrow monastery was not exactly that of St Benedict, though Benedict Biscop the founder used it in composing the conflate rule which was observed there. It is unlikely that, as in many Gaulish monasteries, they used the Columban rule in addition to that of St Benedict. This is what probably happened at Lindisfarne, but that monastery was much more influenced by the Irish tradition than Wearmouth-Jarrow. Benedict Biscop was one of the champions of the Roman cause and Columban had been a notorious upholder of the Celtic Easter and tonsure against the Gaulish clergy. As the Benedictine rule was strongly opposed to anything in the nature of competition in ascetic feats, it is unlikely that the violent ascetic practices of the Irish and British monasteries would find favour there.

ST PETER'S CHURCH, MONKWEARMOUTH

St Peter's Church is one of the oldest churches in Britain, where Christians have gathered to worship for more than 1,300 years. It was built in 674 by Benedict Biscop, the pioneering monk, who was given a grant by the Northumbrian king, Egfrith. Benedict built an important complex of church and monastic buildings in the Roman style, probably on the site of a settlement founded by Hilda of Whitby. Glaziers from Gaul created the windows for Benedict's church, establishing Monkwearmouth as one of the birthplaces of British stained glass.

Benedict's work was continued and expanded by his successor Ceolfrid, the second abbot. Ceolfrid expanded the library and supervised the making of three copies of the Latin Bible, one of which, the Codex Amiatinus, survives today in Florence. Ceolfrid's pupil Bede began his monastic life here at the age of seven. Later in life Bede recounted the early history of St Peter's and its sister church of St Paul at Jarrow in his *Lives of the Abbots of Wearmouth and Jarrow*.

Though much has changed at this site since the seventh century, the porch at the base of the tower and the west wall remain from Benedict's time. The carved animals on the stones either side of the west doorway are badly weathered and fragile, but still recognizable as serpents with birds' heads. High on the inside of the west wall are two small windows with ballusters (lathe-turned columns). The windows are original, but the glass is modern. The small door high in the wall leads into an upper chamber of the porch which may have been a private chapel or the sacristan's room. In the exhibition area is the Herebericht Stone; a Saxon grave marker from the eighth century. And by the medieval north-west door is the figure of a monk, probably a Master of Wearmouth put in charge of the monastery when it was a cell of Durham between 1083 and 1545.

- The church is normally open to visitors on Tues – Sun, 2 – 4-30pm, from Easter to the end of October, or at other times by arrangement.
- Contact number: 0191 5160135

BEDE'S WORLD, JARROW

The extraordinary life of the Venerable Bede created a rich legacy that is celebrated today at Bede's World, Jarrow, where he lived and worked 1,300 years ago. Now there are new dimensions to Bede's World including a fascinating permanent exhibition. This opens up the life and times of Bede, and explores his remarkable contribution to the world. We find out what daily life was like for Bede and his fellow monks, and how much of Bede's work is of continuing importance to us today. Visitors and pilgrims can experience life at an Anglo-Saxon farm, relax at Jarrow Hall and enter the holy surroundings of St Paul's Church and monastic site.

THE MUSEUM

The stunning new museum building houses 'The Age of Bede', an exciting major exhibition which takes visitors through the makings of Bede's Northumbria, his many achievements and the legacy which lives on 1,300 years later. There will also be a programme of temporary exhibitions.

ST PAUL'S CHURCH AND MONASTIC SITE

Those who visit this place can also experience the unique atmosphere of the place at which Bede lived and worked. The chancel survives from the original monastery founded in 681/2. Visitors are invited to walk around the Anglo-Saxon monastic site and the ruins of the later medieval monastery.

GYRWE – THE ANGLO-SAXON FARM

The experimental farm called Gyrwe (pronounced 'Jeerwe'), after the Old English name for Jarrow, includes a full-size early Northumbrian timber hall, a Grubenhaus (sunken-featured building) and a monastic workshop, all built using only traditional tools and techniques. Rare breeds of cattle, wild boar, sheep and geese can be seen (and fed). Ancient strains of cereal and vegetable crops are grown and harvested, and regular Living History demonstrations show how Anglo-Saxon people dressed and lived.

PRACTICAL INFORMATION

- Bede's World is located 2 minutes from the A19 Tyne Tunnel south entrance (it is a toll tunnel) and about a 20-minute walk from the Bede Metro Station on the Newcastle–South Shields line. Bus services 526 and 527 stop close to the museum and usually run every half hour. Buses and taxis run from next to Jarrow Metro Station – a 5-minute drive from the museum.

- Opening times: April – October: 10am – 5.30pm (Sun 12)
Nov – March: 10am – 4.30pm (Sun 12)
St Paul's Church is usually open 10am – 4pm (Sun 12)
- Facilities:
shop selling a wide range of souvenirs and gifts
Education Department – e-mail: education @bedesworld.co.uk
access for disabled and toilets
no dogs (except dogs for the blind)
- Further details: 0191 4892106 / website: www.bedesworld.co.uk

---

Suggested Devotion

John 16.13–14: The Spirit of Truth

The spirit in which Bede studied and wrote is best captured in the little prayer with which he closes his *History*, quoted in Douglas Dales, *Called to be Angels* (Canterbury Press Norwich, 1998), p. 39:

I pray thee, merciful Jesus, that as thou hast graciously granted me sweet draughts from the Word which tells of thee, so wilt thou of thy goodness grant that I may come at length to thee, the fountain of all wisdom, and stand before thy face for ever.

A Prayer of the Venerable Bede

*I pray you good Jesus
That as you have given me the grace
To drink in with joy
The word that gives knowledge of you,
So in your goodness you will grant me
To come at length to yourself,
The source of all wisdom,
to stand before your face for ever. Amen.*

Durham Cathedral

THE RELICS OF CUTHBERT AND BEDE

In the year 875, when the Danes descended on the east coast sacking and pillaging towns and monasteries alike, the 'congregation of St Cuthbert' at Lindisfarne took the coffin of St Cuthbert out of its shrine, opened it up and added to its contents the remaining bones of St Aidan and the head of St Oswald. Bearing these relics in a wooden coffin, together with other treasures offered at the shrine such as the Lindisfarne Gospels, they wandered about Northumbria and Galloway for eight years before settling down at Chester-le-Street. For 112 years the saint's relics and his former see remained based there. But the Danes drove the successors of the Lindisfarne community further south, to Durham, where in 995 these monks built a church to shelter the relics upon the rocky plateau in a loop of the River Wear where the massive Norman cathedral now stands.

In 1091 the second Norman Bishop of Durham, William of St Carileph, laid the foundations of a great abbey church for the Benedictine order and the bones of St Cuthbert were translated into an incomplete building in 1104. The whole structure, finished in 1133, retains its massive Norman character today despite later additions and modifications. Prior Melsanby added in 1242 the Chapel of the Nine Altars beyond the high altar and the bones of St Cuthbert were subsequently translated into a famous shrine at its entrance.

Throughout the Middle Ages the annual feast of St Cuthbert attracted thousands of pilgrims and the miraculous powers of the relics grew in fame. Grateful or hopeful pilgrims adorned the shrine with their gifts; it became the cathedral's great glory and a chief centre of pilgrimage. Kings and prelates came there and multitudes of lesser people, bringing their offerings and their prayers.

There are three separate lists of the treasures which accumulated at St Cuthbert's shrine. Among them are some very extraordinary claims: part of the rod of Moses, a piece of Christ's manger, a piece of the tree under which were the three angels with Abraham, a piece of the throne of the twelve apostles. The shrine itself, says the *Rites of Durham*, was 'estimated to be one of the most sumptuous monuments in all England'. Today the bones of St Cuthbert and the head of St Oswald lie under a grey stone slab inscribed simply: *Cuthbertus*.

In addition to the bones of St Cuthbert, the monastic building

at Durham also possessed the bones of the Venerable Bede. Bede died and was buried at Jarrow in 735, but about the year 1022 a monk called Aelfred stole the remains and brought them to Durham, where he was a sacrist, adding them to the collection of relics of northern saints which he had already accumulated. Bede's shrine once stood encased in gold and silver in the twelfth–century Galilee Chapel at the west end of the cathedral. Now Bede's bones lie beneath a plain table tomb in the same place.

THE CATHEDRAL

The cathedral is a fine example of Early Norman architecture. After the conquest in 1066 the Normans concentrated on the north. The castle at Durham was begun in 1071, at a time when most of the north of England was beyond the rule of law. A Norman settlement needed to be established that could withstand the savage attacks of the Scots and the fiercely independent borderers. There was already a religious community in Durham dating back to 998, when the 'White

Church' was dedicated by Saxon Benedictine monks as a burial place for St Cuthbert. The second Norman Bishop, William of St Calais (1081-96), was the founder, in 1093, of the present cathedral.

The Cathedral Treasury is a display of valuable and beautiful objects that are a guide through the 900 years of the cathedral's history. Here are to be found the relics of St Cuthbert (including the coffin that brought his body to Durham in 995), fine altar plate, richly illustrated manuscripts, bishops' rings and seals, embroidered copes. All have played their part in the life of the cathedral.

The Monks' Dormitory, situated above the treasury, is now a library. It is regularly open to the public between Easter and the end of September.

PRACTICAL INFORMATION

- Durham Tourist Information: 0191 3843720
- Cathedral Contact: 0191 3864266 or e-mail:
  Maureen.Dempster@ durhamcathedral.co.uk
  Enquiries@ durhamcathedral.co.uk
- Access for coaches to the cathedral is prohibited (minibus from coach park)
- Audio-visual display in the Prior's Hall Undercroft
- Undercroft Restaurant in the cathedral (former monks' wine cellar)
- Mostly wheelchair friendly / help available
- Cathedral worship:
  open for quiet prayer
  Mon–Sat: 7.30am – 9.30am / Sun: 7.45am – 12.30pm
  The cathedral closes at 6.15pm Mon–Sat / 5pm Sunday
  Services:
  Sunday: 8am / 10am / 11.15am / 3.30pm
  Mon – Sat: 7.30am / 8.45am / 12.30pm (Wed, Thurs and Fri) / 5.15pm

---

Suggested Devotion

Luke 23.50–56: The Burial of Jesus

Part of 'Cuthbert's Letter on the Death of Bede', in Bede's *Ecclesiastical History of the English People*, ed. and trans. B. Colgrave and R. A. B. Mynors (Oxford, 1969):

Christ is the morning star who when the night of this world is past promises and reveals to his saints the light of life and of everlasting day.

Ripon Minster

St Wilfrid

ST WILFRID

Wilfrid (died 709), then Abbot of Ripon, was the successful protagonist at the Synod of Whitby (664). He is often regarded as a representative of the traditions of the Roman Church in the seventh century, and indeed credited with introducing them into Northumbria in opposition to the 'Celtic' traditions represented by the church of Lindisfarne and its founder Aidan.

After becoming a monk at Lindisfarne in his youth, Wilfrid had indeed travelled to Rome, which impressed him greatly, and where he learned about the calculation of Easter. And it was to Rome that he repeatedly appealed when his later career brought him into conflict with the Northumbrian kings.

Wilfrid was unquestionably a very ambitious churchman, becoming Bishop of York soon after the Synod of Whitby.

He had himself consecrated in Gaul at Compiègne. Jealous for the landed possessions of his churches, he also patronized at least one Gospel book written in gold on purple parchment, and he built churches at his two most important monasteries of Hexham and Ripon, the magnificence of which still finds some echo in their crypts, which are all that survive of the architecture that he patronized.

But to categorize Wilfrid as 'Roman' is to ignore the influence of the Church of Gaul on him. He spent three years in Lyons after his first visit to Rome, and his consecration in Gaul was, Bede says, according to Gaulish traditions. In this sense, the term 'Roman' applied to Wilfrid is an over-simplification.

Some aspects of Wilfrid's career even look rather Irish in character. Although he became Bishop of York, he seems mostly to have worked through a network – a confederation – of monasteries, of which he was the head. Their abbots and abbesses even willed their possessions to him, and his biographer Eddius (sometimes called Stephanus, who was the singing master who Wilfrid brought to Ripon) calls them his 'kingdom of churches'. That 'kingdom' transcended political boundaries. We find Wilfrid active not only in Northumbria, but also in Mercia, Sussex and Kent. Such confederations of monasteries were characteristic of Irish church organization, a notable example being the

confederation centred on Iona itself, so that in this respect Wilfrid looks more Irish than 'Roman'. His career in the church had, after all, begun at Lindisfarne, the monastery founded from Iona; and in Gaul, too, he had probably been exposed to Irish influence, for the Irish missionary Columbanus, who had founded highly influential monasteries there and in northern Italy, had had a major impact on the Gaulish Church, including Jouarre, the monastery with which Wilfrid's partner at the Synod of Whitby, Agilbert, was associated.

Wilfrid died at Oundle, aged 76. The monks of Ripon carried his body to their abbey for burial. It may possibly have rested under the present Ripon Minster in the Saxon crypt where Wilfrid had displayed the relics he had brought from Rome. His shrine stood in the north choir aisle.

HEXHAM

The spirit of Wilfrid can perhaps be sensed best at Hexham. Here he had built the predecessor of the present abbey church in the days of his episcopate. His master masons began work in 674, bringing stone from the Roman camp at Corstopitum (Corbridge). The plan of the church of St Andrew at Hexham, as shown by the crypt, recalls that of the church built by Constantine's architects over the traditional burial place of St Peter, which Wilfrid must have regarded with particular awe. Wilfrid built at Hexham a similar church: colonnaded, with two aisles, short transepts and a small apse in the centre of the transepts. The church, like that at Ripon, is described by Eddius, Wilfrid's priest and biographer, sometimes called Stephanus.

The crypt designed by them is probably the finest early crypt extant in north-west Europe. It consists of an innermost chamber, where the relics would have been kept, and two antechambers. Pilgrims made their way from the nave down a narrow stair into the first antechamber, from which they could see the shrine. Then they departed through the other antechamber and ascended a stairway to the north-east. A similar stair on the south side of the choir, no doubt for the clergy alone, led directly to the relic chamber. This 'holy of holies' – which according to tradition housed a relic of St Andrew brought from Rome by St Acca, Wilfrid's successor at Hexham – was lit by three cresset lamps, small stone bowls set in the walls, which would be filled with oil and the wick set floating in it.

In the much restored church above, some part of the early floor remains, as well as a fifteenth-century rood screen with 16 painted panels depicting various saints and prelates, and part of a retable, or altar-back, of similar date and subject. The apse at the end of St Wilfrid's original church probably curved just beyond the site of the screen in the present choir. His bishop's seat or *cathedra*, known as 'St Wilfrid's Chair' or the 'Frith Stool', may be standing in the same position as it occupied more than 12 centuries ago, facing down into the body of the church. This remarkable low seat, scooped from a single stone and incised with restrained ornamentation, may have been in the centre of the clergy bench around the apse. According to tradition, it served as the coronation throne of the kings of Northumbria, and it was also connected with the privilege of sanctuary (*frith* in Old English means 'peace'), whereby anyone taking refuge in a church could claim freedom from the law.

RIPON

The first reference to the early illuminated manuscripts of Northumbria comes from Eddius' *Life of St Wilfrid*. He says that Wilfrid built a great church at Ripon (671–78), 'adorning the bridal chamber of the true Bridegroom and Bride with gold and silver and varied purples', and that he also 'provided for the adornment of the house of God a marvel of beauty hitherto unheard of in our times'; these were some illuminated Gospel manuscripts. Bede too describes how in 655 a small monastery was founded in this area and how by 672 Abbot Wilfrid had dedicated his stone church, one of the first in England.

Ripon, today a quiet, historic

town, looks as if nothing much has happened there over the centuries. But until the early 1300s it was one of the most regularly destroyed cities in England, often at the hands of Scottish raiders.

Around 650, the local king invited monks from the famous monastery at Melrose in the Borders, founded by St Aidan, to come and establish a monastery. The founder abbot was St Eata, a pupil of St Aidan. Possibly using the site of a holy well, now known as St Wilfrid's Well, the monks founded their monastery. Here the great St Cuthbert was guest master.

The earliest church (minster) was destroyed in 950, the first of many disasters to befall it. Only the crypt, formerly beneath the high altar, remains to give a tangible link with Wilfrid's church. It is the oldest complete crypt in England. A second minster was built on the site, but it too perished – this time at the hands of William the Conqueror. A new church soon rose, however, dedicated to St Wilfrid and St Peter and instigated by Thomas of Bayeux, first Norman Archbishop of York. The legacy of Thomas' building can best be seen in the vaulted undercroft. Part of this was recently restored and is now the Chapel of the Resurrection. During the twelfth century there were further substantial developments, and more in the fifteenth and sixteenth centuries.

THE PILGRIM'S WAY BETWEEN RIPON AND JARROW

This pilgrimage takes us deep into Anglo–Saxon Christianity and the struggles between Celtic Christianity and Catholic, Roman, Christianity. From cities now at peace, but which were once scenes of terrible warfare, to an ancient monastery built in the wilderness and now lost in the debris of post–industrial Britain, this route encourages the modern pilgrim to look into the uncomfortable face of violence and destruction and to seek the divine spark within.

Main route:

From St Wilfrid at Ripon to the Venerable Bede at Jarrow. (98 miles/159km)

- Ripon to Sockburn (11 miles): take A61 north-east from Ripon, then turn north on A167 through Northallerton towards Darlington. At High Entercommon take B1264 going east and follow local signs on left to Girsby, Neasham and Sockburn.
- Sockburn to Bishop Auckland (18 miles): return to Neasham, turn left to Hurworth-on-Tees and at Croft-on-Tees take A167 north. Pick up A68 out of Darlington, then turn right on to A688 at West Auckland.
- Bishop Auckland to Durham (11 miles): take A688, then A167.
- Durham to Monkwearmouth (15 miles): take A690 to

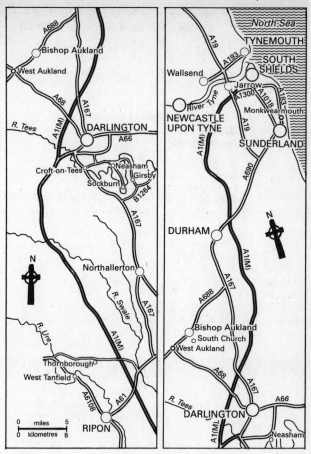

Ripon–Tynemouth

Sunderland, then A1018 towards South Shields and turn on to A183 to Monkwearmouth.
- Monkwearmouth to Jarrow (10 miles): take A1018 towards South Shields, then left on to A300 and right on to A19.
- Jarrow to Tynemouth (8 miles): take A19 north to River Tyne, then turn right on to A193.

PRACTICAL INFORMATION

- Ripon Cathedral Contact: 01765 603462
- Ripon Tourist Information: 01765 604625

Suggested Devotion

Deuteronomy 1.19–25: The Promise of God in the Exodus

A poem in Martin and Nigel Palmer's *Sacred Britain* (ICOREC Piatkus Press, 1997), p. 152:

> *Start here (or anywhere you are): seeing*
> *That to call this journey pilgrimage*
> *Means an echoing in your heart*
> *That changes it.*
>
> *Meaning who you are, too,*
> *Suddenly in your innermost unnamed self*
> *That has always called itself you –*
> *Being who you were always meant to be.*

Lichfield

St Chad

CHAD AND CEDD

Among those who were schooled in Christianity on Holy Island were two brothers, Chad and Cedd. The brothers were made bishops and Cedd was sent to Mercia where Paeda, son of Penda, had been converted to Christianity and allowed monks from Holy Island to evangelize among his people. Cedd then became bishop to the Saxons in Anglia, where he established churches and monasteries; the tiny church at Bradwell-on-Sea in Essex remains as a testimony to his work. His brother Chad was sent to Ireland to study, and on his return became Bishop of Mercia, establishing his episcopal centre at Lichfield, whose cathedral bears his name. Like Aidan, he travelled widely on foot, with miracles accompanying his proclamation of the gospel.

Born in Northumberland in the very early seventh century, Chad was known then by his Celtic name Caedda. After studying under Aidan at Lindisfarne, he spent his life as a missionary in the Saxon kingdom of Mercia. He became Archbishop of York in about 668, but St Theodore, the Greek Archbishop of Canterbury, removed him in order to restore a degree of

harmony following the Synod of Whitby. Even after his demotion (which he took in good spirit and went quietly and humbly for the sake of the Church) and appointment as the first Bishop of Lichfield in 669 he continued to wander around his vast diocese, preaching and baptizing the inhabitants. The numerous wells named after him in the bounds of Mercia and beyond are testimony of his restless Celtic travels. At Lichfield itself Chad prayed in an oratory beside his well, and on winter days stood naked in the cold water to mortify his flesh. The well still exists in a small garden next to St Chad's church. At one time church leaders and flocks of children visited it on Maundy Thursday and dressed it with boughs and flowers, an ancient pagan custom introduced to Christianity which continues in some places today, notably at Tissington in Derbyshire.

Chad died in 672 and his remains rested first in a plain wooden shrine in the churchyard of St Mary's at Lichfield. Bede described it as 'a wooden monument, made like a little house covered, having a hole in the wall, through which those that go thither for devotion usually put in their hand and take out some of the dust, which they put into water and give to sick cattle or men to taste, upon which they are presently eased of their infirmity and restored to health'. When Bishop Walter Langton completed the rebuilding of the cathedral of St Peter with the splendid Lady Chapel early in the fourteenth century he installed there a new shrine. After the Dissolution of the Monasteries various people preserved and passed down the relics of the saint, and some of his bones are believed to lie today in the Roman Catholic cathedral at Birmingham, dedicated to St Chad.

At some stage the separated head of the saint, placed in a head reliquary, stood in the Chapel of the Head of St Chad, south of the quire in Lichfield Cathedral. From the Sacrist's Roll it is clear that this painted wooden *chef* lived in an iron-bound coffer enclosed in another chest. In the chapel today the pilgrim can still see an aumbry used for storing relics. A fourteenth-century stone gallery separates the chapel from the south choir aisle.

LICHFIELD

The three mighty spires of Lichfield, known as the 'Three Ladies of the Vale', make the cathedral of St Chad highly visible to all who travel past the city. But long before this cathedral or its two predecessors stood here, Christians gave their lives for the faith, if an ancient tradition

is to be believed. The name 'Lichfield' is said to mean 'the field of the dead'. During the last and worst period of persecution under the Roman Empire, up to a thousand Christians may have perished here. In 303 the Emperor Diocletian launched a savage campaign against Christianity, which by this time was probably, in terms of numbers, the main religion of the Empire. Persecutions of staggering brutality and scale are recorded from Syria, Africa, Germany and France. The site of the original Lichfield lay just outside the Roman fort and settlement of Letocetum. The Romans rarely killed people within the city boundaries and never buried them within the walls. So if a massacre of local Christians did take place, it is possible that this was where they died.

The first cathedral built to house the shrine of St Chad was replaced by the Norman cathedral and was started in 1085. The present Gothic building was built between 1195 and 1330. The Reformation saw the destruction of the shrine of St Chad and, during the sieges of the Civil War, the fabric of the cathedral was badly damaged. Restoration, begun in 1660, has continued ever since.

The cathedral houses a number of treasures which include: the Lichfield Gospels, an eighth-century illuminated manuscript; the Herkenrode windows of the Lady Chapel; sculptures by Francis Chantrey

> **HOLY WELLS:** the veneration of healing and holy waters was crucial in the Celtic period. Holy wells remain plentiful in all the Celtic lands, and most of the Celtic saints have holy wells dedicated to them. Generally, the wells are not deep stone-lined shafts but rather, natural springs, marked and protected by stone structures or buildings. Many resemble smaller versions of the great Celtic/Roman sanctuaries. They often have provision for drinking, bathing, contemplation, and worship. It is probable that the vast majority of these holy wells were venerated before the introduction of the Christian tradition. They were rededicated by the Celtic saints whose name they bear. The attributes of the indwelling spirits of the holy wells were transferred to the actual saints. Most of these wells have waters reputed to heal specific ills.

and Sir Jacob Epstein; and the Lang Lichfield collection of modern silver.

Lichfield is also rich in holy wells. Just outside the city, in the village of Stowe, is St Chad's Well, a Roman well which appears to have been taken over as a Christian well at an early stage. It is even possible that there was a Celtic monastery here before the arrival of St Chad – it might explain why he chose this area as his centre. Another ancient holy well can be seen at St Mary's Church, while under the Chapel of St Peter in the cathedral there is evidence of yet another.

PRACTICAL INFORMATION

- The Visitor Study Centre: 01543 306240
- Guided tours: 10am – 12 noon and 2pm – 4pm (evening by arrangement) standard tours: £2.75; special tours: £3.50 (more in-depth) several all-inclusive tour packages – contact Visitor Study Centre
- Catering available in the Refectory: 01543 306100
- Audio-visual presentation: group charges – contact Visitor Study Centre
- Parking available: contact Visitor Study Centre for useful maps
- Lichfield Tourist Information: 01543 308209
- Worship:
  Weekdays: 9.30am and 5.30pm
  Sundays: 8am / 10.30am / 3.30pm
  The cathedral choir sings daily at Evensong (except Wednesdays and choir holidays) and at the 10.30am and 3.30pm services on Sundays.

Suggested Devotion

Luke 18. 9–14: On Humility

George Fox (1624–90), the founder of the Quakers, experienced a vision in Lichfield. Sydney Carter expresses Fox's beliefs in his hymn 'George Fox':

> *There's a light that is shining in the heart of a man,*
> *It's the light that was shining when the world began,*
> *There's a light that is shining in the Turk and the Jew,*
> *And a light that is shining, friend, in me and in you.*

Glastonbury Abbey: the Marian Cult

The ruins of Glastonbury Abbey, set among noble trees and well kept lawns, are all that remain today of one of the greatest monasteries of medieval England. When the abbey was dissolved in 1539 the buildings were stripped and the walls left to the neglect of 350 years. Much of the town is built of stone from the ruins.

Throughout antiquity the Glastonbury area was a focus of mythology, much of it associated with Avalon and King Arthur. The unique 150m landmark of Glastonbury Tor (an Old English word for hill) was the inspiration for much of it. The transition of much of the mythology to Christianity is interesting.

Tales of a miraculous chalice or grail were part of such pre-Christian mythology. It appears that over time this concept of a special vessel became interwoven with Christ and the Last Supper. Legend has it that Joseph of Arimathea, who placed Christ's body in the tomb, obtained the chalice (Holy Grail) as a memento. After many years he brought it to Glastonbury, burying it near the Tor on Chalice Hill, perhaps by Chalice Well. An important pagan sanctuary developed here which would explain the coming of the earliest Christian missionaries. Today the Tor is crowned by the fourteenth-century Chapel of St Michael, but this is probably the successor to many shrines.

The church was probably founded by missionaries who accompanied King Lucius, an early British ruler, back to Glastonbury from Rome in the second century. They converted the local inhabitants and built a church on the site of the present Lady Chapel. It was simply constructed of wattle and daub: interwoven branches packed with clay applied by hand. The church was dedicated to the Virgin Mary, and Glastonbury became the first home (*c.* 500) of the Marian cult in Britain. The grail became Mary's emblem. Indeed, the title Our Lady of St Mary of Glastonbury has survived to this day.

The core of Glastonbury's first monastery was the ancient cemetery which had grown around the old church of St Mary, to the south where the Lady Chapel stands today. Very early graves are packed together here – an eager attempt by the great men of the neighbourhood to obtain burial as near as possible to the oratories and tombs of the saints which studded the area.

In the seventh century

Somerset was conquered by the Saxons, who by then were converts to Christianity. They re-endowed the monastery and their king, Ine of Wessex, erected a new principal church of stone at what is now the west end of the nave. This was enlarged once in the eighth century and again by St Dunstan who was Abbot of Glastonbury (940–56) and later Archbishop of Canterbury.

When the Saxons occupied the area soon after 658 they found a Celtic monastery below the Tor at Glastonbury, established by monks either from Wales or Ireland. Indeed, in the fifth century St Patrick is said to have arrived at Glastonbury and organised the hermit monks who worshipped in the two churches into a community with himself as the first head. In later times a monk of Glastonbury had a vision informing him that St Patrick's body lay buried to the right of the altar, and so his tomb augmented the wonders awaiting the pilgrims to this hallowed place.

St David is also believed to have settled here for a time with seven companions, and it was claimed that he lay buried at Glastonbury. There is also a tradition that northern monks brought the relics of St Aidan and St Paulinus (appointed Bishop of York by St Augustine) to Glastonbury for safekeeping when the Danes ravaged the north.

Perhaps the most important figure in the abbey's history,

Dunstan, was born nearby, becoming abbot at a time when both the fabric and the religious life of the abbey were at a very low ebb. His main work lay in the monastic buildings which he erected to the south of the church, the earliest example of the cloistered layout in England. Dunstan lengthened Ine's church, adding a tower and aisles. The result resembled the monastery at Cluny in Burgandy, and was truly a huge church. Little remains of it today.

In 960 Dunstan was appointed Archbishop of Canterbury by King Edgar. There he ruled as primate for 28 years, and oversaw many developments in both church and state. Foremost among these was the widespread proliferation of Benedictine monasteries throughout England. In this he was much assisted by friends such as Ethelwold, Bishop of Winchester, and Oswald, Bishop of Worcester. Dunstan also maintained his own scholarly, artistic and musical activities and was remembered at Glastonbury for his sanctity. In many ways the life and example of Dunstan bring into focus the manifold features of Anglo-Saxon Christianity as it had developed over the previous 400 years.

The Norman churches were built east of the Lady Chapel or old church, which continued in existence. This removal was designed to preserve the ancient cemetery, still the sacred centre of the abbey. In 1184 a fire destroyed the monastery and the treasures. Excavations show that the ruined twelfth-century church was patched up and continued to serve until the eastern part of the new church was ready. The first part of the new building was the existing Lady Chapel, which was erected, completed and dedicated within a few years of the fire. It owed its unusual position at the west of the church to the fact that it replaced the old church of St Mary. Further developments took place during the twelfth century and the monks took possession of the new monastery on Christmas Day 1213.

GLASTONBURY PILGRIMS

Glastonbury has been a pilgrims' magnet for generations. They came to venerate the relics preserved in the abbey, the bones of saints and other objects of religious importance, placed in ornate shrines. Outside the abbey a small town serving its secular needs grew up in the course of centuries. Inside the precincts a set route, marked by stations, would be followed. As part of their pilgrimage, many people would also climb the Tor to St Michael's Chapel. This marked what was probably the oldest sacred place in the area, rebuilt in the fourteenth and fifteenth centuries with the help of the offerings of pilgrims.

Today the high point of the calendar is the weekend of the Glastonbury Pilgrimages. These commence on the first Saturday in July. Usually the Anglican celebration takes place on the Saturday with a noon Eucharist in the ruined nave; on the same day the Orthodox celebration takes place in the undercroft; the Roman Catholics meet on the Sunday afternoon. They begin on the slopes of the Tor and celebrate mass in the ruins.

Today Glastonbury remains its enigmatic self. Here pilgrims find the highest concentration of religious fervour in England. Many people come to make sense of an insensitive world and find here a place of great spiritual power, discovering the sacredness of this landscape – a sacredness which is a quintessential fusion between the old Celtic and earliest Christian traditions.

PRACTICAL INFORMATION

- Custodian of the Abbey: 01458 832267
- Opening hours: 9.30am – 6pm (or dusk if earlier)
- Every Tuesday services are held in the undercroft or St Patrick's Chapel
- Entrance fees vary: group and age concessions
- Good disabled facilities
- Toilets on site (inc. disabled toilet and nappy changing)
- Audio tapes (inc. for visually impaired and in various languages)
- Gift shop
- Abbey entrance approx 50 yards from town centre
- Contact abbey for good directions and details of parking nearby
- An award-winning museum and display
- Glastonbury Tourist Information: 01458 832954
- Good English Heritage map and details of other attractions: 0171 9733399

Suggested Devotion

Luke 1.26–38: The Annunciation

William Blake's 'Jerusalem' is associated with the idea that Christ visited Glastonbury:

> *And did those feet in ancient times*
> *Walk upon England's mountains green?*
> *And was the holy lamb of God*
> *On England's pleasant pastures seen?*
> *And did the Countenance Divine*
> *Shine forth upon our clouded hills?*
> *And was Jerusalem builded here*
> *Among those dark Satanic mills?*

From an address given by Max Thurian, a monk of Taizé:

Instead of being a cause of division amongst us, Christian reflections on the role of the Virgin Mary should be a cause of rejoicing and a source of prayer.

Cornwall

St Michael, St Petroc and St Perran

INTRODUCTION TO CORNWALL

To look at a map of Cornwall is like looking at a geographical list of saints. So many churches, parishes and settlements bear the names of Cornish saints: St Austell, St Germans, St Ives, St Michael's Mount. Many other places, though lacking the prefix 'St', are called after people who came to be thought of as saints – Advent, Ladock, Probus – or contain a saint's name in a compound form, like Egloskerry (church of Keri). Churches and chapels have been built in honour of the early saints and are furnished with their shrines, images and pictures. They have also been linked with chairs, wells, rocks, walls, paths, trees, harbours and islands, and have prompted written *Lives*, liturgical observances, calendar customs and Christian names.

In the sixth and seventh centuries, Devon, Somerset and the south-west were criss-crossed by monks travelling to and from Ireland, Wales and Brittany, before the Saxons drove the Celts westward into Cornwall, and obliterated much of their culture.

Christianity reached south-west Britain quite early, and a number of Romano–Celtic cemeteries have been found in Somerset (for example, Fosse Way at Shepton Mallet and Cannington). However, Roman remains in Cornwall are few and evidence of Roman Christianity is scanty, although there are examples of Roman milestones there, particularly on routes leading to Cornish harbours (examples at Breage; north end of the Lizard Peninsula; Tintagel).

Cornwall could not boast major monasteries like those founded by Illtud and Cadog in south-east Wales; the earliest Cornish communities, like that of Landocco, were probably founded from Welsh monasteries. Many of Cornwall's nine or ten monasteries may have grown up around earlier churches with their cemeteries, as happened in Ireland and Wales, where monks enclosed a larger tract of land around the graveyard, in order to grow their food.

In the fifth and sixth centuries, Cornwall may have been influenced by Christians arriving from Ireland, Wales, Gaul and the Mediterranean. At small monastic sites around the Cornish coast there is a scattering of Near Eastern pottery and fragments of wine vessels dating from this period. From the fifth century, Christian grave markers were erected in churchyards and beside tracks and fords; their Irish, British and Latin names indicate a range of cultural influences.

We only have a sketchy knowledge of the history of Cornwall in Celtic times. Devon, Cornwall and Somerset formed the kingdom of Dumnonia, and the names of some of its kings are known. We also know that there was considerable migration to and from Armorica, which from the mid–sixth century was named Brittany, after its British inhabitants. During this time there were perhaps 600 Cornish villages with small Christian cemeteries, some with a chapel attached. Little is recorded of the Celtic missionaries who worked among the people. However, the dedications of villages, churches and holy wells indicate a strong Christian presence. Clusters of dedications provide clues about the various groups of missionaries who preached in different parts of Cornwall. Three saints in particular are commemorated in Cornwall: Michael the Archangel, Petroc and Perran.

What speaks to us most in Cornwall are the primitive origins of medieval pilgrimage: sacred springs and wells of fresh water and the holy hill of St Michael's Mount, so mysteriously joined and separated from the mainland, which drew to them religious men and women in joy or need long before the Celtic saints colonized the peninsula with the Christian faith and the memory of their heroic lives.

The following selection of places traces some of those clues.

PRACTICAL INFORMATION

- Cornwall Tourist Board: 01872 322900
- North Cornwall Visitor Information: 01208 265644
- The Royal Cornwall Museum: 01872 272205
- Cornwall County Records Office: 01872 323127
- Cornwall Archaeological Unit: 01872 323603
- Cornish Studies Library: 01209 216760
- Institute of Cornish Studies: 01872 263457
- Cornwall Heritage Trust: 01208 873039
- One particular book that I have found valuable on the saints of Cornwall and on Cornish religious history is Nicholas Orme, *The Saints of Cornwall* (Oxford, 2000).
- *Festivals*
  Information sheets are available from the Cornwall Tourist Board.
  The following are associated with the Celtic Saints:
  St Piran's Tide: 1 March, procession to the site of the Oratory of the Lost Church; evensong in Cornish at St Piran's Church on nearest Sunday
  Helson flora or *Furry*: 8 May, a St Michael's Feast – famous dance
  Bodmin Riding: early July, carnival mixed with commemoration of the return of St Petroc's relics in 1177

St Michael's Mount, Penzance

This is one of the wonders of Britain: the church and the castle perched upon their dramatic rocky outcrop seem to come from some fairy tale or children's picture book. The dedication of this rock to St Michael is a classic example of the Christianizing of an older site. St Michael and St Catherine are the customary dedications for churches on hills. The local legend behind this particular dedication is that in 495 some hermit monks or local fishermen saw a vision of St Michael standing on a ledge of rock on the island.

There is no evidence of any ritual or religious use of the island before the arrival of Christianity. Many claim that it was the island Ixtis, spoken of by the first-century BC Greek geographer and historian Diodorus Siculus. He describes how the Phoenicians from the eastern Mediterranean traded with the Cornish from an island reached only by an isthmus, dry at low tide; this exactly describes St Michael's link to the old town of Marazion. It seems that the Cornish tin miners brought their ore to be purchased by the Phoenicians from perhaps as long ago as 1000 BC.

The earliest record of any religious body here is in 1044, when Edward the Confessor gave the Benedictines both St Michael's Mount and Mont St-Michel in Brittany. Because of its exposed situation, the church and the monastery appear to have been fortified from the earliest days. But the wars with France in the fourteenth and fifteenth centuries, combined with the Black Death in the mid-fourteenth century, left the Mount badly understaffed and the monastery struggling to cope. The king took responsibility for the fortifications and in 1410 tried to suppress the monastery on the grounds of its being run from France. It limped on until 1425, when it finally closed. From then on, the Mount was primarily secular, though pilgrims still came.

The buildings which pilgrims see today date largely from the nineteenth century, but they include the carefully restored church of the monastery. There the pilgrims of old made their first stop, to pray and make their offerings at three altars. The high altar, which stood between the altars of St Michael and the Crucified Saviour, bore a tabernacle and a box full of relics. Many pilgrims came for healing. Before crossing to the Mount, pilgrims may well have visited the Chapel of St Catherine. This small medieval building did not survive the Civil War and all that is left is the name Chapel Rock. Pilgrims today

---

Suggested Devotion

Revelation 12.7–12: St Michael and his Angels Attack the Dragon

In 1602 the poet Richard Carew was impressed by the pilgrims and wrote:

> *Who knows not St Michael's Mount and Chair*
> *The Pilgrims' Holy Vaunt?*
> *Both land and island twice a day*
> *Both fort and port of haunt.*

---

can see on the left of the causeway a rock pierced by a socket: medieval pilgrims would have knelt briefly at the wooden cross which stood in this hole.

Opposite St Michael's Mount is the town of Marazion. It is said that the name commemorates the Jewish traders who came here to hold fairs at which they bought tin, and Marazion is supposed to mean Bitter Zion, as a reminder to them of the Sweet Zion – Jerusalem – which they had left behind.

PRACTICAL INFORMATION

- St Michael's Mount is owned by the National Trust
- Contact number: 01736 710265
- Opening times:
  1 April – 29 Oct:
  Mon – Fri 10.30am – 5.30pm
  last admission 4.45pm
  Nov – end March: guided tours as tide, weather, circumstances permit
  Castle/grounds open most weekends during the season

BODMIN

ST PETROC

Petroc (also referred to as Petrox, Pedrog and Perreux) was born during the last part of the fifth century, the son of Glywys, a Welsh prince in mid Wales. He ministered as an important missionary during the first half of the sixth century and received his early education in Ireland. He returned to Britain about 518 and made his way to Cornwall, landing in Trebetherick. He was probably followed by a group of Irish Christians. He settled initially at the monastery in Padstow (lit. Petroc Stow) which had been established by St Wethinoc, and where Petroc spent about 30 years exercising a preaching, praying and teaching ministry. In about 540, after a seven-year missionary journey and pilgrimage, possibly to Rome and Palestine, he moved to Bodmin where a hermit named Guron lived. Here he built a large religious community and it is said that the monastery was active for

1,000 years after his death in 564. He was buried at Bodmin. His remains were venerated and in 963 King Edgar gave a gilded shrine to store them.

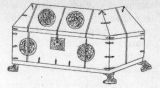

By the eleventh century Bodmin had become an important centre for the Petroc cult. The Augustinian Canons even claimed to have possession of Petroc's relics. In 1177 a distinguished canon stole the relics and took them to the Abbey of St Meven (or Meen) in Brittany. It took the intervention of King Henry II to get them back to Bodmin with an apology. They came back in a casket made of ivory shell with brass, decorated with medallions constructed by Arab craftsmen in Sicily in the twelfth century. The relics returned in style, led in triumphal procession to Bodmin, and remained in the monastery until its dissolution in 1539, when the casket was hidden and not found until restoration work during the eighteenth century.

THE CHURCH OF ST PETROC

The building outside the west end of the present church covers the well of St Guron, who established the first Christian cell here just after 500. The present church building stands on a site

---

Suggested Devotion

John 4.5–14: A Meeting of Different Traditions: Jesus at the Well

An anonymous hymn commemorating Petroc:

> *Godly and prudent*
> *Was our holy Petroc,*
> *Peaceful and learned.*
> *To his faithful preaching,*
> *Constantine hearkens:*
> *Even beasts draw near him*
> *Enticed by his kindness.*
>
> *Now dwelleth Petroc*
> *With Saints in glory,*
> *But ever mindful of*
> *The soil he planted.*
> *Though parted from us,*
> *Poureth supplications*
> *Pleading for Llanbedrog.*

occupied by many earlier constructions. Part of the tower contains masonry from the Norman period. The present church was built in 1469–72 and is the largest parish church in Cornwall. The shrine of Petroc lies in the south wall of the church. Over the centuries thousands of Irish and Welsh pilgrims have come here, often on their way to Spain or Palestine.

AN ANCIENT RITUAL IN PADSTOW

Today it is the Padstow Hobby Horse Festival on May Day which draws most visitors to Padstow. It seems to be a rare survival of pre-Christian or pre-Celtic ritual dance. The Hobby Horse, or *Oss* as it is known locally, dances through the streets – a strange mixture of horse and pantomime. No one knows where it comes from or what it is supposed to be. It is possibly connected with fertility or to the horse cult of early Britain. Whatever the background, the tradition that this is the oldest dance festival in Europe ensures its popularity and continuity.

Perhaps on this note it is worth reflecting on how diverse the traditions which shape our faith – or lack of faith – are. Christianity in Britain is a mixture of pre-Christian and Christian ideas and practices.

PRACTICAL INFORMATION

- Contact number: 01208 73867

- Opening times: Easter – end of Sept, 2pm – 4pm (other times by appointment)

THE ORATORY OF THE LOST CHURCH AND THE CROSS, PERRAN SANDS

Piran or Perran is the third most important saint of Cornwall. According to legend he came across the sea as a missionary from Ireland to Cornwall during the sixth century. We know almost nothing else about his life, but his importance is shown by the many place names based on his name.

The remains of his ancient church, overtaken by the sand; his holy well on the edge of Penhale Point; and St Perran's Round, an ancient amphitheatre on the downs, all bear witness to the sacred landscape which Piran entered and then added to in his own way.

One of Cornwall's chief medieval shrines was that of Piran at Perranporth, seven miles north-west of Truro. Piran was the patron saint of Cornish tin-miners, who flocked to his oratory by the sea. His monastery is now lost and buried beneath the sand dunes at Perranporth on the north Cornish coast. The outline of the churchyard probably delineates the boundary wall of his monastery, which was called Lanpiran. A fine Celtic Cross still marks the site.

Piran's chapel was excavated several times, and finally reburied in 1981. Now safely cocooned, its walls are of unhewn, uncemented stones, leaning inwards to minimise roof stress. The chapel's east wall perhaps dates from Piran's time; the remainder is early Norman. Before the dunes encroached, Piran's church stood at the head of a small valley. Converts were baptized in a spring which rose beside the chapel and flowed down to the sea. In the ninth century, sand engulfed the buildings, but the Penwortha stream prevented it from encroaching further. The monks built a new monastery and a second church on the landward side of the stream.

In the eleventh or twelfth century, a north door was constructed in Piran's first church, to ease the flow of pilgrims, so that they could pass through the chapel to venerate Piran's relics, and leave by the door on the opposite side. A thirteenth-century document describes a reliquary containing Piran's skull, which was placed in a niche above the altar, and a shrine containing his body, which rested on the chancel floor. Piran's small copper bell and his pectoral cross carved out of bone were also preserved, together with his pastoral staff, which was decorated with gold, silver and precious stones. At the same time, mining caused the Penwortha stream to go underground, and the monks' second church was gradually lost and engulfed in sand; it survives as a ruin.

Perranzabuloe Folk Museum and Information: 01872 572121

Suggested Devotion

Matthew 7.24–27: The Man who Built his House on Sand

Piran influenced his country greatly. The *Tao Te Ching*, the classic Chinese text of the fourth century BC, describes the way in which the sage or wise one affects the world around him:

> *Heaven and Earth are enduring.*
>
> *The universe can live for ever,*
> *because it does not live for itself.*
>
> *And so both last — outliving themselves.*
>
> *The sage guides his people*
> *by putting himself last.*
>
> *Desiring nothing for himself,*
> *he knows how to channel desires.*
>
> *And is it not because he wants nothing*
> *that he is able to achieve everything?*

Ireland

Introduction to Ireland

The written historical record for the history of Christianity in Ireland begins with the entry for the year 431 in the *Chronicle* of Prosper of Aquitaine to the effect that 'Palladius was ordained by Pope Celestine and sent to the Irish believers in Christ as their first bishop'. Who these Christians were and how they came to Ireland is a question that has excited much debate, but it is entirely reasonable to suppose that just such a community existed, evolving through contact with the Celtic Christians of Western Britain, prior to the missionary activity of Patrick.

Prosper was apparently in Rome when he published his *Chronicle* and his statements must therefore be regarded with the greatest respect. What, then, can we deduce from them? The entry for 431 leaves no doubt that there were Christians in Ireland already by that date. These Christians were sufficient in number, and apparently far enough advanced in their beliefs, to warrant the despatch of a bishop to oversee their activities and to ensure their adherence to orthodoxy. The bishop sent to them was Palladius, who had been ordained by no less a figure than the Pope. It is notable that the foundations that are linked with the name of Palladius by tradition are all in Leinster, in the eastern part of Ireland, and thus a short sea journey away from the western coast of Britain.

But Irish tradition knows of a different bishop whose missionary efforts are indelibly linked with the foundation period of the Irish Church, and that man was not Palladius but Patrick the Briton. Patrick is likely to have been a Brythonic Celt from a Christian family in north-west Britain (possibly Carlisle), from where he was snatched by an Irish raiding party and taken into slavery. He then escaped and made his way back to Britain, but returned later to Ireland with a strong commitment to work as missionary there. It is likely that he worked mainly in the north of Ireland around the middle of the fifth century. Muirchu's *Life of Patrick* was written in Ireland in the seventh century and marks an upsurge of interest in the figure of Patrick after some 200 years of silence. This trend culminates in the *Book of Armagh*, written in the north of Ireland in 807.

A second important, though less well attested, area of influence was Gaul and the Gaulish Church. Patrick probably had Gaulish helpers and he himself may well have visited Gaul. The Irish monks, who from the sixth century travelled across the continent of Europe, were following in the footsteps of ancient Irish traders, and the great monastic foundations of Southern Gaul, such as Marmoutier and Lérins, were seedbeds of monasticism that undoubtedly left their mark on the early Irish Church.

It is to the canons of the church that we should turn, however, for the earliest and most reliable evidence concerning the initial development of Christianity in Ireland. The earliest group of canons attributed to 'The First Synod of St Patrick' may date from the late sixth century, and these depict a church that is neither in the first flush of mission nor yet fully integrated into the host society. These canons also abound in references to pagan practices and depict a church governed by bishops operating within territorial dioceses, based on the territory of the indigenous tribe.

Later canons show a church that has become more fully part of Irish society and has taken on features that serve to distinguish it from the continental model that we see in the earlier canons. By the seventh and eighth centuries the power of the bishop was equalled by that of the abbot, especially in major monastic foundations, and the territorial diocese had been partly superseded by the monastic 'parishes', which were the conglomeration of different foundations, all of which traced a common lineage.

The second half of the sixth century was a period of great monastic leaders and founders. Throughout Ireland individual men and women, such as Comgall of Bangor, Ciaran of Clonmacnois, Columba of Iona and Brigid of Kildare, came to embody the values of the new religion in a special way, some stressing the role of learning and others the place of asceticism in the Christian life.

In the late sixth century Columba established the community on Iona. The island became a greatly influential centre of Irish Christianity from where the religion of the Irish passed to Northumbria, where it took root at Lindisfarne and elsewhere, and even extended down into parts of East Anglia. The happy coalescence of Irish and early English culture and Christianity during this period, which led to what is termed the 'Insular' tradition, suffered a blow with the Synod of Whitby (664) and its associated controversy over the calculation of Easter.

Another major Irish figure of this period was Columbanus (543–615) who in 587 left Ireland for Gaul. Quite a lot of writings attributed to him convey the picture of an active, able Christian leader. He was the founder of monasteries such as Luxeuil in south-east France and Bobbio in northern Italy. The life-long and voluntary commitment of Columbanus to exile from his homeland is a good example of the tradition of 'Wandering for Christ' (*Peregrinatio*), whereby a monk would cut himself off from his own land or family to bring Christianity to others. It is these wandering monks in exile who were responsible for bringing Christianity to large areas of Europe.

The religious vocation of these early monks, with its combination of learning and asceticism, was an ideal that was to reappear time and again in the history of the Irish Church.

PRACTICAL INFORMATION

- Irish Tourist Board: 003531 679 1977
- Northern Ireland Tourist Board: 01232 327888
- Irish Tourist Board in London: 08701 555 250
- Belfast International Airport: 01849 422888
- Dublin Airport 003531 705 2222
- Dublin Central Bus Station: 003531 836 6111

Armagh
St Patrick

Armagh can claim to be – after Rome – one of the oldest ecclesiastical capitals in Europe. It was here that St Patrick founded his first bishopric in about 444. It still remains the primatial see of both the Roman Catholic and Anglican communities in Ireland. Like Rome it is a city of hills. On two of these hills the cathedrals stand; the Anglican cathedral is the older of the two and it stands on the site of St Patrick's foundation.

ST PATRICK

Ireland's patron saint, Patrick, was born in north-west Britain in about 390. He was the son of a church deacon and grandson of a Christian priest. At the age of 16 he was taken captive by pirates and sold into slavery in Ireland, where he began to explore for himself the mysteries of the Christian faith. After six years in slavery, God instructed Patrick in a dream to leave Ireland and return to his home. Escaping from his master, Patrick was guided some 200 miles to a ship which took him back to Britain. Eventually he returned to his home where he was trained and ordained a priest. Patrick had a series of dreams which called on him to return once again to Ireland as a missionary

and, against the wishes of his family, he made his way through Britain, possibly *via* Auxerre in Gaul, and on to Armagh in about 433.

There was already some Christian missionary activity in Ireland, and Patrick worked tirelessly baptizing and confirming Christians, and ordaining those with education and a calling to the priesthood. Although not a monk himself, he encouraged men and women to embrace the monastic life and his deep love and pastoral care for the people of Ireland led him to travel through the land bringing the gospel to those who followed the ancient Druidic cults.

Legend has it that Patrick lit a fire in celebration of Easter on the very night that Loegaire, High King of Ireland, was lighting his own fire to celebrate the rebirth of spring. Angered, the king called his Druid priests to him, and was further enraged when they prophesied that the fire Patrick had lit would burn for ever, overcoming the king's own fire. Loegaire led an army forward from Tara, and as they challenged Patrick, they saw him lift his arms in prayer before escaping into the night with his disciples. Further trials of strength ensued, but the God of Patrick always proved to be superior to that of the Druid priests. Eventually the High King allowed Patrick to preach Christianity in his realms, although he himself remained resolutely pagan.

In his old age, Patrick wrote two letters to the soldiers of Coroticus, the second of which survives. Coroticus may have been a Dumbarton chieftain; his forces had raided Ireland, captured some of Patrick's converts and sold them to the Picts. Patrick wrote demanding their release. His writings are amongst the first to survive from the early British Church, and they give us a glimpse of the experience of a Celtic missionary. Patrick died in about 461 and it is possible that his own handbell is preserved in a beautiful jewel-studded shrine, dating from about 1100, in the National Museum of Ireland in Dublin.

THE CATHEDRAL

A church has probably stood on this site for about 1,500 years, but in the course of Ireland's troubled history it has been destroyed and rebuilt on at least 17 occasions.

The story of the cathedral begins as far back as 445 when St Patrick himself, according to tradition, built a stone church on a hill then called Druimsailech granted to him by a local chieftain named Daire. So rare were stone buildings at that time that St Patrick's Church was known as *Damhliag Mor* or Great Stone Church. According to the *Book of*

Armagh, it was an oblong building 140 feet in length, divided into nave and choir. In 447 St Patrick ordained that Armagh should have the pre-eminence over all the churches in Ireland, a position which, in the Anglican and Roman Catholic traditions, it still holds today.

Around the cathedral sprang up one of the most celebrated of the great Irish schools and the one which lasted the longest. During the centuries that followed St Patrick, students came in great numbers from England and from Europe which at that time was being inundated by barbarian hordes.

Of the original building probably nothing remains except, perhaps, the bases of the tower piers, rebuilt in 1834. From 832 when the peace Armagh had enjoyed for almost 300 years was broken by Danish invaders, the history of the cathedral is one long record of burnings and plunderings. Partially burned by a fire caused by lightning in 995, the cathedral lay for the most part unroofed for some 130 years until Archbishop Celsus roofed it with shingles. This is recorded in the twelfth-century *Annals of the Four Masters*. After further burnings Primate O'Scanlon, in 1261, had almost to rebuild it and it is from his time that the history of the existing building may be said to begin.

143

PRACTICAL INFORMATION

- Armagh Tourist Information: 01861 521800
- Cathedrals well signposted and have daily services
- *Anglican Cathedral opening times*:
  April – Oct: 10.30am / 5pm
  Oct – March: 10.30am / 4pm

Conducted tours June – August, 11.30am and 2.30pm or by arrangement
- *Catholic Cathedral opening times*:
  Daily 9am – 6.30pm
- Contact numbers:
  Anglican Cathedral: 02837 523142
  Catholic Cathedral: 02837 522802

Suggested Devotion

Revelation 22.1–5: A Vision of the River of Life

Part of 'St Patrick's Breastplate', in George Simms, *Christ Within Me* (Christian Journals Limited, Belfast, 1975), p. 62:

> *I bind unto myself to-day*
> *The power of God to hold and lead . . .*

Monasterboice: the High Crosses

Monasterboice, Co. Louth, gets its name from a monastery founded by a little-known saint named Buite, who died in 521. Its main attraction today is as the site of two of the most important Old Irish High Crosses, probably of the ninth century. The crosses show a crucifixion scene, the Last Judgement, and other Old and New Testament scenes, as well as scenes from the lives of the desert fathers Paul of Thebes and Antony. There are also other remains which consist of an old graveyard, two churches, two early grave slabs and an ancient sundial.

The south church is the older of the two and still has the remains of the chancel arch. The smaller church is situated beside the Round Tower and has no trace of a chancel. The Round Tower is about 100ft high. It is now missing its upper part and conical cap. The door is six feet above ground level and is approached by a modern flight of steps. The cross nearest the graveyard entrance is Muirdeach's Cross, an outstanding example of the High Crosses of the early Christian period in Ireland.

THE WEST CROSS AND MUIRDEACH'S CROSS

The two famous Celtic Crosses at Monasterboice are both intact and on their original sites. The West Cross, which measures 22ft, is the highest ancient cross remaining in Ireland. The cross-shaft is carved with panels that represent scenes from the biblical tradition. The wheel-head of the West Cross, which contains a number of bosses, is in a better state of preservation than the shaft or cap. It is likely that the cross was repaired in antiquity with new stone that replaced the original, for the depiction of the crucified Christ, whose head leans to one side, is in the manner of later styles.

The other, more famous, cross at Monasterboice is that of Muirdeach, named after an abbot who died in the year 922. He is commemorated by an inscription at the base of the shaft on the west side. The cross measures 18ft, though some of the lower part of the shaft is missing now, the cross having been re-erected on its original pyramidal base. This cross is a remarkable synopsis of syncretic religion. Its east and west faces are sculpted with biblical scenes, while the sides have spirals, bosses with

interlace, and intertwining beasts. The outer part of the wheel-head is carved with bands of interlace between which are intertwining serpents. At the centre of the east face is an image of Christ, based on the iconography of the resurrected Egyptian god, Osiris. Christ is holding a cross and staff in the Osirian position, and on his head is an eagle that resembles the crown of Egyptian gods and pharaohs. On the left of Christ is the great god Pan with his pipes, while on the right is a harp-playing figure, King David or Apollo. The tension between the emotional left side and the rational right side is resolved in the figure of Christ, the perfect man.

THE HILL OF SLANE

The Hill of Slane is one of the most historic sites in Co. Meath, and is associated with St Patrick. It is believed that he lit the first Paschal Fire here in 433. The first monastery here was founded by St Erc, the first Bishop of Slane. Various parts of the existing building were erected at different times, the oldest parts probably at some time in the fifth century. St Patrick is said to have consecrated the little church and for a while he lived there. From the top of the hill one can get good views of the river Boyne and directly south is the Hill of Tara.

THE HILL OF TARA

Though best known as the seat of the High Kings of Ireland, the Hill of Tara has been an important site since the late Stone Age when a passage-tomb was constructed there. Tara was at the height of its power as a political and religious centre in the early Christian centuries. Attractions here include audio-visual presentations and guided tours. Exciting new research and excavations by the Discovery Programme team continue to add to our understanding of the site.

PRACTICAL INFORMATION

- Drogheda Tourist Office: 00353 41 37070
- Drogheda bus station: 00353 41 35023
- Drogheda train station: 00353 41 38749

- Newgrange Neolithic Monuments and Centre: 00353 41 9880300 / 9824488
- No admission charge to Monasterboice
- Access all year round, guides available
- *The Hill of Tara:* Much of the tour is outdoors

– good clothing and shoes needed

Restricted disabled access

Contact number: 00353 46 25903 / 00353 41 982 4488

Parking spaces and toilets available as well as restaurant

Suggested Devotion

John 3.12–16: The Sacrifice on the Cross

From Brendan O'Malley, *Celtic Blessings* (Canterbury Press Norwich, 1998), p. 167:

Bless O Lord Jesus Christ this cross, through which you have freed the world from the power of evil.

Glendalough

St Kevin

Kevin or *Coemhghein*, meaning 'fair begotten', a descendant of one of the ruling families in Leinster, studied as a boy under the care of three holy men, Eoghan, Lochan and Eanna. During this time he went to Glendalough (which means 'the Valley of Two Lakes') and lived, we are told, 'in the hollow of a tree'. He was to return later with a small group of monks to found a monastery where, as the earliest version of his life tells us, 'the two clear rivers form a confluence'. His fame as a holy man spread and he attracted numerous followers. He died in about 618. For six centuries afterwards Glendalough flourished and the Irish Annals have references to the deaths of abbots and raids on the settlement.

The present remains in Glendalough tell only a small part of the story. The monastery in its heyday would have included workshops, areas for manuscript writing and copying, guest houses, an infirmary, farm buildings and dwellings for both the monks and a large lay population. The buildings which survive probably date from between the tenth and twelfth centuries.

PILGRIMAGES TO GLENDALOUGH

Local tradition has it that Kevin came to Glendalough 'over the mountains'. After his death it is likely that the old road through the Wicklow Gap became a pilgrim road, when Glendalough became famous as a pilgrimage centre in the sixth and seventh centuries. Pilgrims came to Glendalough in their thousands with a popular belief that, 'for obtaining remission of their sins from God, it is the same for anyone to visit Rome, and to visit the relics and beds of Coemgen'.

The old St Kevin's Road is marked by crosses and stones and early Christian church sites at Dunboyke and Templeteenawn. Near Templeteenown Church there is a stone known as the Piper's Rock, where people on pilgrimage would rest and share music and dancing. A few miles away, on top of a hill at Togher, there is a seventeenth-century cross, cut in a granite boulder, known as the Wooden Cross. There is another cross on a granite pillar a few miles further on at Granabeg.

The best known stone from the old pilgrim road was located near Hollywood. It is a Labyrinth stone (a stone left by pilgrims in a labyrinth to denote particular prayers), known locally as 'the Walls of Troy'. It is now in the National Museum in Dublin. This stone probably marked a spot where the pilgrim entered a toilsome journey through desolate mountainous country, where prayer and religious fervour would be needed to help him on his way.

At the top of the Wicklow Gap it is possible to stand on a remnant of the old St Kevin's Road. It is about ten feet wide and made up of large rough granite stones, laid down across the bog. There is a wonderful view in all directions, westwards towards the great plains of Ireland and eastwards towards the sea, shining and glistening on the horizon on a bright day. One can imagine pilgrims standing there in times past, looking back along the rough way they had travelled and giving thanks to God for bringing them safely to this point in their journey. We can imagine also the sense of expectancy and excitement as they looked down the valley to the east, knowing that the end of the road was almost in sight. Already, part of the purpose of their pilgrimage had been realized in telling their story and sharing their problems with those who accompanied them on the way.

At the crossroads, where the Wicklow Gap road meets the Laragh to Glendalough road, another old stone can be found with two crosses on it. Pilgrims would have gathered here for a prayer before entering

Glendalough, no doubt feeling relief after making a hazardous journey and looking forward to completing their pilgrimage in the holy places of the valley.

ST KEVIN

Kevin was born in the middle of the sixth century to the noble family of Dal Mesincorb. From an early age he was renowned for his special gifts. At the age of twelve he was sent to Kilnamanagh Monastery in Co. Dublin where he studied under three holy men, Eogan, Lochan and Erna.

Kevin founded his first monastery at Cluainduach and was joined by several companions. But Glendalough was his special place. He founded his original monastery there in the Lower Valley. After a while he decided to become a hermit and set out alone to the Upper Valley where he built a small cell between the mountain and the lake.

But what was the vision that drew him to Glendalough? He was born into a time and a land that was alive with conversion to Christianity. Holy wells and places such as Lough Derg and Croagh Patrick were already vibrant places of pilgrimage for Christians.

Kevin was at heart a hermit and a Christian mystic. He was a determined ascetic whose great strength and endurance sprang from his extraordinary faith and commitment to monastic celibacy and the teachings of the desert spiritual tradition. As well as being a hermit and founder of monasteries, he wrote poetry and prose, including a Rule for monks in Irish verse. Tradition has it that he was a gentle, loving and kind person, with an extraordinary and unusual affinity to nature, especially the animals and birds. He was deeply attracted to the poetic experience of the hermit life, and courageous in his desire to draw out to the edge to test his strength and endurance. He chose hardship quite deliberately; his cell was on the dark side of the lake which remained in shadow for six months of the year. This was probably out of a desire to feel very exposed – to test himself to the limit, and through that test find his own deepest strength – but perhaps most of all it was through an ascetic way of life that he found the poetry of his own soul.

The Annals of Ulster records the date of Kevin's death as 618 and his life story is found in six important books. Three of these are in Latin and three in Irish, the earliest being the Latin *Life*, Codex Kilkenniensis in Marsh's Library in Dublin.

There are many fascinating and inspiring stories and myths about St Kevin. They are in one sense archetypal stories: we all fight the 'monsters of the deep'; we all struggle with conflicts and contradictory longings that pull us at times in different directions. Perhaps as we touch into his experience and walk in his footsteps, Kevin's story may help us to understand more of our own story, his struggles illuminate our own struggles, the peace he found become our peace. May his dream give us hope and courage to follow our own dreams, as we make our pilgrimage through the valley.

MONUMENTS IN THE LOWER VALLEY

THE GATEWAY

The Gateway to the monastic city of Glendalough is one of the most important monuments, now unique in

Ireland. It was originally two-storeyed with two fine, granite arches. The *antae* or projecting walls at each end suggest that it had a timber roof. Inside the gateway, in the west wall, is a cross-inscribed stone. This denoted sanctuary, the boundary of the area of refuge. The paving of the causeway in the monastic city is still preserved in part but very little remains of the enclosure wall.

THE ROUND TOWER

This fine tower, built of mica-slate interspersed with granite, is about 30m high, with an entrance 3.5m from the base. The conical roof was rebuilt in 1876 using the original stones. The tower originally had six timber floors, connected by ladders. The four storeys above entrance level are each lit by a small window, while the top storey has four windows facing the cardinal compass points. Round Towers, landmarks for approaching visitors, were built as bell-towers, but also served on occasion as store-houses and as places of refuge in times of attack.

THE CATHEDRAL

The largest and most imposing of the buildings at Glendalough, the cathedral had several phases of construction, the earliest consisting of the present nave with its *antae*. The large mica-schist stones which can be seen up to the height of the square-headed west doorway were reused from an earlier, smaller church. The chancel and sacristy date from the late twelfth and thirteenth centuries. The chancel arch and east window were finely decorated, though many of the stones are now missing. The north doorway to the nave also dates from this period. Under the southern window of the chancel is an aumbry or wall cupboard and a piscina, a basin used for washing the sacred vessels.

A few metres south of the cathedral an early cross of local granite, with an unpierced ring, is commonly known as St Kevin's Cross.

THE PRIEST'S HOUSE

Almost totally reconstructed from original stones, based on a 1779 sketch made by Beranger, the Priest's House is a small Romanesque building, with a decorative arch at the east end. It gets its name from the practice of interring priests there in the eighteenth and nineteenth centuries. Its original purpose is unknown although it may have been used to house relics of St Kevin.

ST KEVIN'S CHURCH OR 'KITCHEN'

This stone-roofed building originally had a nave only, with an entrance at the west end and a small round-headed window in the east gable. The upper part of the window can be seen above what became the chancel

arch, when the chancel, now missing, and the sacristy were added later. The steep roof, formed of overlapping stones, is supported internally by a semicircular vault. Access to the croft or roof chamber was through a rectangular opening towards the western end of the vault. The church also had a timber first floor. The belfry with its conical cap and four small windows rises from the west end of the stone roof in the form of a miniature round tower.

ST CIARAN'S CHURCH

The remains of this nave and chancel church were uncovered in 1875. The church probably commemorates St Ciaran, the founder of Clonmacnois, a monastic settlement that had associations with Glendalough during the tenth century.

ST MARY'S OR OUR LADY'S CHURCH

One of the earliest and best constructed of the churches, St Mary's Church consists of a nave with a later chancel. Its granite west doorway, with an architrave, has inclined jambs and a massive lintel. The underside of the lintel is inscribed with an unusual saltire (X-shaped) cross. The east window is round-headed, with a hood moulding and two worn carved heads on the outside.

TRINITY CHURCH

A simple nave and chancel church, with a fine chancel arch, Trinity Church is beside the main road. A square-headed doorway in the west gable leads into a later annexe, possibly a sacristy. A Round Tower or belfry was constructed over a vault in this chamber. This fell in a storm in 1818. The doorway inserted in the south wall of the nave also dates from this period. Projecting corbels at the gables would have carried the verge timbers to the roof.

ST SAVIOUR'S CHURCH

The most recent of the Glendalough churches, St Saviour's was built in the twelfth century, probably at the time of St Laurence O'Toole. The nave and chancel with their fine decorated stones were restored in the 1870s using stones found on the site. The Romanesque chancel arch has three orders, with highly ornamented capitals.

The east window has two round-headed lights. Its decorated features include a serpent, a lion and two birds holding a human head between their beaks. A staircase in the eastern wall leading from an adjoining domestic building would have given access to a room over the chancel.

MONUMENTS NEAR THE UPPER LAKE

REEFERT CHURCH

Situated in a grove of trees, this nave and chancel church dates from around 1100. Most of the surrounding walls are modern. The name derives from *Righ Fearta*, 'the burial place of the kings'. The church, built in simple style, has a granite doorway with sloping jambs and flat lintel and a granite chancel arch. The projecting corbels at each gable carried verge timbers for the roof. East of the church are two crosses of note, one with an elaborate interlace pattern. On the other side of the Poulanass River, close to Reefert, are the remains of another small church.

ST KEVIN'S CELL

Built on a rocky spur over the lake, this stone structure was 3.6m in diameter with walls 0.9m thick and a doorway on the east side. Only the foundations survive today but it is possible that the cell had a stone-corbelled roof, similar to the 'beehive' huts on Skellig Michael, Co. Kerry.

THE 'CAHAR'

This stone-walled circular enclosure on the level ground between the two lakes is 20m in diameter and is of unknown date. Close by are several crosses, apparently used as stations on the Pilgrims' Route.

TEMPLE-NA-SKELLIG AND ST KEVIN'S BED

This small rectangular church on the southern shore of the Upper Lake is accessible only by boat, *via* a series of steps from the landing stage. West of the church is a raised platform with stone enclosure walls, where dwelling huts probably stood. The church, partly rebuilt in the twelfth century, has a granite doorway with inclined jambs. At the east gable is an inscribed Latin Cross together with several plain grave slabs and three small crosses. Close by is St Kevin's Bed, a cave in the rock face about 8 metres above the level of the Upper Lake and reputedly a retreat for St Kevin and later for St Laurence O'Toole. Partly man-made, it runs back 2 metres into the rock.

PRACTICAL INFORMATION:

- Access – direct and well-signposted
- *Visitor Centre Opening Times:*
  Mid Oct – mid March: daily 9.30am – 5pm
  Mid March – mid Oct: daily 9.30am – 6pm

Last admission 45 mins before closing

- Contact number: 00353 404 45325 / 45352
- Admission free / guided tour on request (charges)
- The Visitor Centre is fully accessible for visitors with disabilities
- Wheelchair users may have difficulties in the monuments
- Car/coach park close to site
- Toilets / picnic tables / extensive lawns

Suggested Devotion

Jeremiah 6.16: Walking with God

An ancient Irish blessing taken from Alexander Carmichael, *Carmina Gadelica* **(Floris Books, Edinburgh, 1992), p. 244:**

> *Bless to me, O God*
> *The earth beneath my feet;*
> *Bless to me, O God*
> *The path whereon I go;*
> *Bless to me, O God*
> *The thing of my desire;*
> *Thou evermore of evermore,*
> *Bless Thou to me my rest.*

Kells: the Book of Kells

The town of Kells in Co. Meath is famous for the Book of Kells, now stored at Trinity College, Dublin, which bears the name of this place and is said to have been kept here for some time. Surviving from an old monastery here are a Round Tower and three High Crosses (with characteristic carvings on them) in the grounds of the church. Another cross, the Market's Cross, was at a street junction in the town and is presently being restored. A notable feature is St Columba's House, which in reality is a stone-roofed church building. Kells (20 miles west of Drogheda) was known in days as early as St Patrick's in the Latinized form of *Cenondae*, bearing at a somewhat later date the name of Cenannus and Kenlis. *Kennaansa* was its old Irish appellation. Of the monastery of Cenannus or Kells no trace remains, but persistent tradition has ascribed the founding of this vanished monastic institution to St Columba in about the year 550.

THE BOOK OF KELLS AND OTHER EARLY CHRISTIAN MANUSCRIPTS

Seven biblical manuscripts, dating from between the sixth and the ninth centuries, form a famous family among the treasures of the Library at Trinity College, Dublin.

Through these early centuries, a spirit of discipline and reverence marked the pages of all the books in this collection; yet each one has its distinctive features. Some in the group are world-famous; some are *de luxe* Gospel books, famed for their beauty and colourful dignity; some are large, others are pocket-size; some are plainer than others; a few are fragmentary. Yet all share a great tradition of fine writing and dedicated copying. Their 'house-style' script, nurtured variously in the monastic foundations of Iona, Ireland and Northumbria as well as continental Europe, is quickly recognizable. High standards for these scribes were set by St Columcille (St Columba, 521–97).

The seven surviving manuscripts are:

- The Book of Kells
- The Book of Durrow
- Codex Usserianus I
- Codex Usserianus II or 'The Garland of Howth'
- The Book of Armagh
- The Book of Dimma
- The Book of Mulling

The seven manuscripts from the libraries and writing rooms (*scriptoria*) of Irish monastic foundations, in Ireland, neighbouring islands or the 'greater Ireland' of Europe, where books written in an 'Irish hand' (*libri scottice scripti*) still abound, help to illustrate the way of life in these ancient places of prayer and learning. The regular display of these manuscripts in the exhibition at Trinity College, Dublin points to a tradition which has done much to shape the history of Ireland.

THE BOOK OF KELLS

The Book of Kells is one of the most beautiful illuminated manuscripts in the world. It contains the Latin text of the four Gospels in insular majuscule script accompanied by magnificent and intricate whole illuminated pages, with smaller painted decorations everywhere within the text. The origins of the Book of Kells are uncertain. It was written and painted with outstanding expertise about the year 800 in a monastery scriptorium, but it is impossible to identify where this monastery was located. The first probable record of the existence of the Book of Kells is an account of the theft of 'the great Gospel of Columkille, the chief relic of the western world' from the great stone church of Kells in the year 1007. The book was found buried in the ground almost three months later, and presumably remained at Kells until it was brought to Dublin and presented to Trinity College by Henry Jones, Bishop of Meath, some time after the year 1661. It has been in the College Library ever since as its greatest treasure.

The Book of Kells has not survived the centuries complete

and has lost some folios at the beginning and end. It may also have lost some of its painted pages, or perhaps the plan for the illumination was never completed. It now has 680 pages, many of them richly illuminated with a flamboyant exuberance unique in Irish and Insular manuscript art. Each Gospel begins with a richly ornamented page in which the opening words of the text are submerged by the decoration. There are portraits and many representations of the four evangelists by their symbols: the man (Matthew), the lion (Mark), the calf (Luke) and the eagle (John). In addition almost every page has painted decoration in the text, with brightly coloured birds, animals, faces and figures often entwined into the capital letters at the beginning of lines.

Originally a single large volume, the Book of Kells was repaired and rebound in 1953 in four volumes. There are normally two volumes on display, one opened at a completely illuminated page and the other showing pages of the text. The openings are changed regularly.

TRINITY COLLEGE LIBRARY, DUBLIN

Trinity College Library, Dublin is one of the world's great research libraries, holding the largest collection of manuscripts and printed books in Ireland. There has been a library since Trinity College was founded by charter of Queen Elizabeth in 1592. The earliest surviving building, the Old Library, was built between 1712 and 1732 to the design of Thomas Burgh.

Today, three areas of the Old Library are open to visitors: the ground floor was originally an open colonnade divided longitudinally by a central wall, with the sunny south side reserved for Fellows of the College. In 1892, the arcades were filled in to form bookstacks. In 1992, the area was reconstructed internally to form an expanded library shop

and an excellent modern and educational exhibition area for the Book of Kells in the East Pavilion.

PRACTICAL INFORMATION

- Kells – Midlands/East Regional Tourism: 00353 44 48761
- Ordnance Survey Map: Ireland Discovery Series no. 42
- The Dublin Experience (and the Long Room) A major visitor attraction at Trinity College telling the story of Dublin – stunning visuals, light, music and voice. It is located in the Arts Building, across the square from the Long Room. Opening times: 22 May – 6 October, hourly 10am until 5pm (inc. Sundays) – charges
- Library opening times: Mon – Sat 9.30am – 5pm (Sun, Oct – May 12 – 4.30pm) – admission charges Contact number: (01) 6082320 (UK code: 003531)
- There is a good library shop
- Soundstik facilities
- Toilets are located under the forecourt of the library shop
- Kells contact: Church View House, Kells, Ireland

Suggested Devotion

John 21.24–25: Conclusion to the Gospel

From 'St Columba at Iona', early twelfth century, in Kenneth Jackson, *Studies in Early Celtic Poetry* (Llannerch, 1995), pp. 9–10:

> *That I may pore on one of my books,*
> *good for my soul,*
> *a while kneeling for beloved heaven,*
> *a while at psalms.*
> *A while meditating upon the Prince of Heaven.*

Kildare
St Brigid

ST BRIGID

Tradition records Brigid as co-founder of Kildare and gives her birth at about 454 and her death at 524. Brigid is also closely associated with Foughart and it has been a place of pilgrimage for many years. Known also as Muire na nGael, Brigid is much associated with works of charity, compassion and healing. She was venerated as the patron of pilgrims and travellers during the Middle Ages. *Feile Bride* on 2 February is a very important religious and cultural feast in Kildare and in Foughart.

The cult of St Brigid encapsulates every aspect of Celtic religion. There was an original pre-Christian Brigid, a three-fold goddess of Light, Fire and Healing who was worshipped at the annual fire festival called *Brigantia* or *Imbolc*. Bishop Cormac in his ninth-century *Glossary* describes Brigid as 'a goddess whom the bards worshipped, for very great and noble was her perfection. Her sisters were Brigid, the woman of healing, and Brigid, the smith-woman'. Thus when Christianity replaced polytheism, the attributes of the goddess were transferred to the saint of the same name.

Her festival falls on 1 February, close to the feast of Candlemas, which is also the old pagan festival day of *Brigantia*. Until 1220 a perpetual fire, tended by 19 nuns, burned in a shrine near Kildare – it was kept alive only by the breath of women. This was the old fire of the Celtic pre-Christian tradition. These nuns, like others, kept the best of the ancient Celtic traditions that they had inherited from the Druids.

St Brigid is the epitome of kindness and charity. There are many stories of her assisting the poor, freeing slaves and interceding on behalf of the unfortunate. She is the protectoress of women, kind to animals and famous for the ale she brewed. It is said that she supplied 17 churches in Co. Meath with ale from Maundy Thursday to Low Sunday.

It seems that Brigid held a unique position in the early Irish Church and society of her day. As abbess, she presided over the local church of Kildare and was later leader of a double monastery for men and women. Tradition suggests that she invited Conleth, a hermit from Old Connell near Newbridge, to assist her in Kildare. Her abbey was acclaimed as a centre of education, culture, worship and hospitality in Ireland, and far beyond, up until the suppression of the abbeys in the sixteenth century.

Nothing remains today of the original Brigidine church and abbey which were probably constructed of timber or of mud and wattle. They were pulled down, rebuilt and enlarged many times as numbers grew in the double monastery for men and women. Cogitosus (the seventh-century Brigidine monk who wrote her *Life*) describes a remarkable building in Kildare in the seventh century:

> The church contains the glorious bodies of Conleth and Brigid, resting in monuments which are placed on the right and left of the decorated altar, and which are adorned with various ornaments of silver and gold . . . One partition, decorated and painted with figures and covered with linen hangings, extended across the whole breadth of the eastern part of the church from one wall to the other . . . Through the door on the right hand side, the chief bishop entered the sanctuary, accompanied by his regular school . . . Through the other door . . . enters the abbess with her nuns . . .

SOLAS BHRIDE: A CHRISTIAN COMMUNITY CENTRE FOR CELTIC SPIRITUALITY IN THE SPIRIT OF BRIGID

The Brigidine Sisters, founded in 1807, are a restoration of the ancient order of Brigid. In 1922 they came to Kildare to re-connect with their roots and to reclaim Brigid in a new way for a new millennium. This led to the re-lighting of the Flame of Brigid in 1993.

Cairde Bhride (Friends of Brigid), in association with the Brigidine Sisters, is a group of men and women inspired by the values of Brigid to promote peace, justice and reconciliation. This group meets on the last Wednesday of every month for reflection, visioning and planning for action.

Solas Bhride claim that Brigid is relevant for today in a number of ways: her life inspires hope

- in those who yearn for the full equality of men and women in the church and in society today;
- in those who work to conserve our earth;
- in those who promote peace, justice and reconciliation.

Her warm compassionate heart crossed all divides and reached out to those in need.

In order to earth this hope the Solas Bhride Community stand for:

- exploration of Celtic spirituality

- action for peace, justice and reconciliation
- centre for prayer and hospitality
- celebration of Celtic feasts, especially *Feile Bride*
- reverence for the sacredness of all creation
- ecumenism
- spiritual direction and counselling
- pilgrimage

THE PILGRIMAGES

There are five important pilgrimages associated with Kildare and St Brigid:

- to St Brigid's Wells
- to St Brigid's Cathedral
- to the Fire Temple
- to the Peace Pole
- to the Labyrinth

Maps and guide books are available for these pilgrimages in Kildare.

ST BRIGID'S WELLS

The Wayside Well

Outside St Brigid's Parish Church is a roadside sign for the Irish National Stud, with Japanese Gardens, St Fiacra's Garden and St Brigid's Well; leaving the town behind, your pilgrimage continues with a 20-minute walk (less by car) towards the Wayside Well.

This well, with its newly landscaped entrance, has a particular appeal for the local people. It is embraced by an arc-shaped stone surrounded with an inscription in Irish which reads:

A Naoimh Bhrid, Muire na nGael, gui orainn
(St Brigid, Mary of the Gael, pray for us)

In pre-Christian times, wells were often associated with the presence of a goddess and were seen as the entrance to the womb of mother earth, the source of life. This wayside well is a spring well.

Retrace your steps back towards the Black Abbey (signposted) and take the first turn left, and left again, down a quiet lane to St Brigid's Well and Prayer Stones.

St Brigid's Well and Prayer Stones

For many years people have gathered at this second well to say the Rosary. In more recent times, people have also been gathering here to reflect ritually on the life and values of St Brigid.

There are five Prayer Stones standing in line and the practice is to stop at each stone in turn and dwell on an aspect or quality of Brigid. As one leaves each stone it is customary to say: *A Naoimh Bhrid, gui orainn* (St Brigid, pray for us).

- *The First Prayer Stone: Brigid; a Woman of the Land* The Celts cared for and respected the basic elements of life: earth, air, fire and water. Brigid was attuned to nature and the seasons. Her feast day, originally a pre-Christian festival called Imbolc, marks the beginning of Spring. It speaks of new beginnings as the ground is prepared for seed, and the first signs of new life appear on the landscape. *The Book of Lismore* describes Brigid as 'the dove among birds, the vine among trees, the sun among stars'.

- *The Second Prayer Stone: Brigid; the Peacemaker*
  Brigid's fame as a peacemaker was such that she became known as 'a woman who turns back the streams of war'. There was much domestic strife in Brigid's Ireland and clan feuds were commonplace. She is often depicted as one who intervened in disputes between rival factions, so as to bring healing and reconciliation.

- *The Third Prayer Stone: Brigid; the Friend of the Poor*
  Tradition speaks of Brigid's extraordinary compassion and concern for the poor people of her day.

- *The Fourth Prayer Stone: Brigid; the Hearthwoman*
  The whole idea of hospitality as an expression of love is central to Brigid. To welcome a stranger to your own fireside is to follow her example. She made her abbey a safe place of refuge and sanctuary.

- *The Fifth Prayer Stone: Brigid; Woman of Contemplation*
  Celtic spirituality has a deep sense of the mystery and presence of God in everything and everyone. It fosters a contemplative

approach to all creation. Brigid's life reflects this approach. This stone allows us an opportunity to remember, to awaken, to contemplate and to begin to integrate the pilgrim experience, so that it can reveal its meaning.

ST BRIGID'S CATHEDRAL

St Brigid's Cathedral stands on the original site of St Brigid's Church and Abbey. In the market square in Kildare one finds the entrance gates to St Brigid's Cathedral.

At the west end of the nave, the window over the Chapter Room depicts scenes from the lives of the three Patron Saints of Ireland, Patrick, Brigid and Colmcille (Columba). The lowest picture relates to the building of the abbey at her chosen site. Tradition has it that Brigid stood with her friend St Mel as a young sister, at Brigid's bidding, asked Prince Ailell for some of his 'peeled rods'. When he refused the horse went to his knees, unable to proceed because Brigid needed his load. According to the same tradition, Brigid got the wood for her abbey.

Walking around the grounds of the cathedral one notices two important features:

- *The High Cross of Kildare.* Facing east, it is an ancient cross of granite, with no carving on its surface.
- *The Round Tower.* Round Towers were built in

connection with monastic establishments. They usually had a two-fold use: as belfries and as places of safety to store monastic treasures. This Round Tower is eleventh-century or earlier and has a base made of beautifully cut granite, while the rest is made of local limestone. The tower has an especially fine Irish Romanesque doorway in red sandstone and the remains of a triangular hood can be seen above the entrance. It can still be climbed today. The Round Tower is a symbol of faith, determination, welcome and safety.

THE FIRE TEMPLE

Fire is a central image in the Brigidine tradition. On the north side of the cathedral are the restored foundations of an ancient fire temple. Research suggests that in pre-Christian times priestesses used to gather here to tend ritual fires invoking the goddess Brigid to protect the herds and provide a fruitful harvest. Giraldus Cambrensis, the twelfth-century Welsh cleric and historian, refers to the perpetual fire still burning in Kildare during his visit.

THE PEACE POLE

Between Kildare and the nearby town of Newbridge lies an extensive tract of flat unenclosed grassland called 'The Curragh'. This beautiful stretch of land is also known as Brigid's Pastures. The flat pasture of nearly 5,000 acres still retains the right of commonage for grazing sheep which originated with Brigid. It is a place to explore, containing large numbers of ancient earthworks.

Leaving Kildare town *via* the station road, travel north for 2km, passing Cill Dara golf club, until you come to Rathbride Crossroads. On your right there is a large stone known as the 'wart stone' and thought to be the base of a High Cross. If the weather has been wet, boots will be needed to cross the grass in search of the 'Fox Covert' which lies to the south-east. For a drier route, go by road back towards Kildare town, turning left up the unsurfaced road beside the thorn tree. The Fox Covert is easily recognized as it is enclosed in a large square of deciduous trees. Entering the Fox Covert, to the right you will see the Peace Pole.

Peace Poles are hand-crafted monuments erected the world over as an international sign of peace. The Peace Pole Project was started in Japan by the World Peace Prayer Society. The project was launched with a dedication to uplift humankind toward harmony rather than conflict. Peace Poles are a silent prayer and message for peace on earth. This was Brigid's prayer too.

THE LABYRINTH

Very close to the Peace Pole is the Labyrinth. The labyrinth is an archetype, a divine imprint, found in all religious traditions in various forms around the world. A labyrinth is a circular pathway that winds its way to the centre. It is not a maze where one can get lost or run into a dead end. The Curragh Labyrinth is based on the design on the Labyrinth stone found near Hollywood, Co. Wicklow, in 1908 (now housed in the National Museum in Dublin). It is in the classical seven-circuit form and was built by the Newbridge youth group and Cairde Bhride in 1997.

Walking the winding path of the Labyrinth can serve as a metaphor for one's spiritual journey. It can become a mirror for where we are in our lives. It has a way of touching sorrows and releasing joys, so it is best to walk it with an open mind and an open heart. It can calm people and help them see their lives in the context of a faith journey: a pilgrimage.

PRACTICAL INFORMATION

- Midlands/East Regional Tourism: 00353 44 48761
- Ordnance Survey Map: Ireland Discovery Series no. 55
- The Brigidine Sisters (Solas Bhride): 00353 45 22890

Suggested Devotion

Psalm 61.1–3: God is Our Rock

St Brigid's Blessing:

> *May Brigid bless the house wherein you dwell.*
> *Bless every fireside, every wall and door.*
> *Bless every heart that beats beneath its roof.*
> *Bless every hand that toils to bring it joy.*
> *Bless every foot that walks its portals through.*
> *May Brigid bless the house that shelters you.*

Clonmacnois

St Ciaran

Clonmacnois, the monastery founded by St Ciaran in the sixth century, is on the banks of the River Shannon. It has two Round Towers, one of which is incorporated into one of the six surviving churches. It also offers two complete and other fragmented High Crosses and a large collection of early Christian grave slabs. It is one of the most popular places of pilgrimage in Ireland. In medieval times, the centre of veneration was the tomb of St Ciaran. The original High Crosses and grave slabs are on display in the Visitor Centre. Buried here is the last High King of Ireland, Ruari O Connchabhair. There is an audio-visual show as well as a number of exhibitions.

ST. CIARAN

From early days Ciaran's community at Clonmacnois gained a good reputation as a place of learning – referred to sometimes as the first Celtic university. Ciaran was born in 515; his father was a chariot builder from Larne in Co. Antrim and his mother, Darera, a native of the south of Ireland. Ciaran was educated by a deacon called Justus and later studied at St Finnian's community at Clonard.

He founded a number of monasteries but in 549 came to Clonmacnois to establish a new religious community. Like other major centres such as Clonard and Durrow, Clonmacnois had a large number of students. The monastic cultivation of art and learning reached a peak here. Scribes recorded poems in both Latin and the Irish language, and music, astronomy and medicine were taught.

The monastic site of Clonmacnois is said to have occupied an area of approximately ten acres. Various *Annals* of Ireland give an insight into the history of such communities. Ciaran did not live to see his monastery reach its days of glory. He is said to have died of a fever seven years after the foundation of Clonmacnois and was buried in St Ciaran's Church. The glorious days of Clonmacnois lasted for several centuries, but it fell into a decline after numerous raids by Irish and Viking invaders.

THE ANCIENT MONUMENTS

Clonmacnois preserves a fine collection of Celtic carvings. It is renowned for its grave slabs, carved with Celtic Crosses, names and invocations in ancient script. There are also a number of ancient crosses

13. Detail of stonework, St Saviour's Church, Glendalough
(see pp. 150–4)

14. Decorated initials of St Luke's Gospel, The Book of Kells, Dublin (see pp. 155–7)

15. Ruins at Clonmacnois (see pp. 164–6)

16. Skellig Michael, off the Kerry coast (see pp. 167–70)

17. Round tower at Clonmacnois

18. Main hut, Skellig Michael

19. Celtic Cross at Kilfenora (see pp. 178–9)

20. Part of Iona Abbey, the 'street of the dead' and St Martin's Cross
(see pp. 192–6)

21. The Ruthwell Cross (see pp. 204–5)

at Clonmacnois. A fragment of headless cross-shaft that exists to the north of the old church bears a carving of the horned god of the forest, Cernunnos, who in Brittany was worshipped as St Hoeirnin. Often, far from being destroyed by Christian priests, images of the old gods were maintained at the shrines where once they were the chief deities. This cross dates from around the year 800. The South Cross at Clonmacnois is a little more recent, dating from around 825. It is mostly carved with interlace and bosses, with a crucifixion on the westward side.

Considered to be one of the finest Celtic Crosses in Ireland is Flann's Cross. Named after King Flann, it is also called the Cross of the Scriptures. It stands to the west of the enclosure at Clonmacnois. A mutilated inscription at the bottom of the cross-shaft commemorates Flann, who died in the year 916, and Abbot Colman, who died in 921. Above the inscription is a

carving of the king and abbot setting up a post, which may represent a cross. The centre of the wheel-cross has an image of Christ. The ring of this cross is emphasized. Instead of the usual method of construction, in which the stonemasons made a cross and attached four arcs of stone to make the wheel, the designer of this cross emphasized the wheel in the form of a continuous stone ring linking four roundels. Thus, the centre cross with Christ in majesty is separated from the arms of the cross outside the ring. On top of the cross is a carving of a house-shrine.

Excavation has revealed intensive settlement outside the monastery, with traces of circular houses and evidence of trades and crafts: metalworking in iron and bronze, gold and silver, and either antler-working or comb-making. Stonemasons worked here too, for there are remains of 700 carved stone slabs, mostly grave markers dating from the eighth to the twelfth centuries. Today, the large monastic site contains six ruined churches including Ciaran's shrine. The Clonmacnois Crozier in the National Museum, Dublin, is said to have come from the shrine.

PRACTICAL INFORMATION

- Access is direct and signposted
- Some steep gradients
- All coach tours must be pre-booked

Ireland

- It is a very busy site and visitors may have delays during the summer
- Location: 21km from Athlone signposted from the N62. Or 20km from Ballinasloe from R357
- Opening times:
  Sept – mid May: 10am – 6pm
  Mid May – early Sept: 9am – 7pm
- For service times contact: 00353 506 31406
- Admission charges vary (concessions)

- Guided tours
- Contact number: 00353 905 74195
- A good, well-equipped Visitor Centre with audio-visual (seats 55 and lasts 23 mins) and exhibitions
- Access for the disabled to the Visitor Centre
- Many facilities: toilets (incl. disabled), car and coach park, tearooms, shop

---

Suggested Devotion

Matthew 13. 51–52: Learning for the Kingdom

Some words by the poet T. W. Rolleston on 'The Dead of Clonmacnois':

> In a quiet watered land
> A land of Roses
> Stands St Ciaran's city fair . . .

Dingle Peninsula and Skellig Michael

THE DINGLE PENINSULA

Within its small compass, the Dingle Peninsula has more interesting antiquities, historic sites and varied mountain scenery than any other part of Ireland. The pilgrim can complete a round trip of the peninsula, starting at Castlemaine – the Castle of the River Maine, which lies directly south of Tralee. Moving into the peninsula will take the pilgrim through Inch and Annascaul and on to Dingle, the most westerly town in Europe and the chief town of the peninsula. It is an excellent centre for those visiting this part of Ireland and though a progressive town today, it still retains much of the old-world atmosphere of a fishing village.

Ventry, the scene in which the ancient romantic tale *Cath Fionntragha* is set, is on the way to Slea Head where viewing points afford an excellent panorama of the Blasket Islands. Travelling along the west coast of the peninsula takes in villages such as Dunquin, Ballyferriter and Ballydavid, where there are some of the best known archaeological sites in the area. Between Ballydavid and Feothanach is Teach Siamsa, a centre of cultural activity at all times of the year.

The pilgrim returns to Dingle town and takes the northern drive over the Conor Pass towards Castlegregory and Tralee. The golden beaches at this end of the peninsula are quite beautiful and can be found all along the coast of Tralee Bay. This *Gealtacht* (Irish speaking) area attracts many people every year, wishing to learn the Irish language. The language, folk customs, crafts and lore all add to the many attractions of this area. There are a great many antiquities and historic sites to see on the Dingle Peninsula and a local map of the area is available with details of their location and history. There are also many walks including the Dingle Way, a long distance walking route covering the peninsula.

SKELLIG MICHAEL

The great pinnacle of rock, *Sceilg Mhichil*, the larger of the two Skellig rocks 8 miles off the south-west Kerry coast, is the location of the finest preserved early Christian monastery in Western Europe.

It was founded relatively early – a small enclosure of stone huts and oratories which, though long since unoccupied, still stands to this day near the island's northern pinnacle, some 182m above the sea. The founder of the monastery is not named. Tradition attributes it to one of two St Fionans, and the influence of Fionan is certainly strong in local place names. However, another, seldom-mentioned, possible founder member of the monastic community is St Suibhne of Skellig, who is listed in the *Martyrology of Tallaght* written at the end of the eighth century. The exact date of the foundation is also unknown, but the style of building suggests the sixth century onwards.

In 795 the first Viking attacks from Scandinavia were launched on the Irish coast. Three important early Irish manuscripts provide information about the raids (*Annals of Innisfallen*, *Annals of Ulster*, *Annals of the Four Masters*). The first two of these manuscripts report that Skellig Michael was sacked by the Vikings in 812 and 823. But in spite of the attacks and the plundering, the monastic community on Skellig survived. In 860 some rebuilding was done and detailed studies of the now-ruined hermitage on the southern peak suggest that this too may have been a ninth-century construction.

How these ascetic monks ever contrived to live on this 18-hectare crag is a mystery by today's standards. In summer, no doubt, they enjoyed seabirds, eggs and fish, but winter must have brought months of lean isolation. Very little evidence survives to give any insight into the occupations of the Skellig monastic community.

The Welsh priest and historian, Giraldus Cambrensis, reported at the end of the twelfth century that the Skellig community moved base to Ballinskelligs 'on the continent', but the island monastery did remain occupied and in repair, and it is a fact that one particular church building in the monastic enclosure was extended in the Middle Ages. The ecclesiastical taxation of 1300 refers to 'the Church of St Michael's Rock' having a valuation of 20s.

PILGRIMAGE

Occupied or otherwise, Skellig Michael featured as a place of pilgrimage and penance for many years. Early in the sixteenth century the Register of Primate Dowdall of Armagh lists Skellig Michael as one of the principal penitential stations for the performance of public penance. Writers refer to pilgrims coming from all over Ireland and Europe at Easter – not so much to visit the monastery, but to perform the nerve-racking, difficult climb to follow the Stations of the Cross and finally kiss a standing stone slab overhanging the sea near the isolated hermitage of the Needle's Eye, on the 217m southern pinnacle of the island. Sadly the stone slab disappeared in 1977, and so this hazardous and dangerous part of the ancient pilgrimage is discouraged today.

To reach the monastery today, one normally follows the lighthouse road from the landing point at Blind Man's Cove to a junction just beyond Cross Cove where the real ascent to the monastery begins *via* the old southern stairway of some 600 steps. Access to the monastery terrace is by a tunnel in the retaining wall, and upon emerging within the shelter of this enclosure – some 100m x 30m – one finds the old stone dwellings and oratories huddled close together at various levels, almost as perfect as when first built.

There are six corbelled, beehive-shaped huts and two boat-shaped oratories as well as many stone crosses and slabs, some graves, two wells and the ruin of the medieval church. Tradition tells that there is also a deep subterranean tunnel leading away from the monastic site but although there are two features in the enclosure which could be associated with this idea, there is no clear evidence of any tunnel as such today.

The monastery huts are more or less rectangular in plan at floor level and take on a circular shape as the corbelling progresses upwards:

CELL A

Cell A has a floor area of 4.5m × 3.8m and a height of 5m. The internal walls are almost straight to a height of 1.5m before the dome begins to narrow, and all around the interior of the walls at about 2.5m are protruding stone pegs which may have supported a wooden upstairs floor. The windows high up in the east

and west walls would have given light at this level. On the exterior of the hut other stone pegs protrude and these may have been anchorages for protective sods or thatch. The door is 1.2m × 0.8m and the walls are 1.8m thick.

CELL B

Cell B is 2.7m × 2.7m × 3m high. There are two cupboard recesses in the internal walls, but no windows or portruding pegs inside or out. The door is 1.3m × 0.6m and the walls are 1.06m thick at the door.

CELL C

Cell C is 2.7m × 2.6m × 3.4m. It is quite like Cell B, being without windows or protruding stones. The door is also the same size.

CELL D

Cell D is only a ruin which may have been circular in plan. Its collapse is not of recent times.

CELL E

Cell E is very similar to Cell A. It also has the internal stone pegs on the walls. The floor, which is very well laid, is 3.6m × 3.5m, and the height is 3.9m. The door is 1.4m × 0.9m and the walls are 1.2m thick.

CELL F

It is thought that the roof of this cell collapsed between 1871 and 1891, and that the dome was reconstructed inaccurately, some 0.9m less than originally. This cell is now 2.5m × 2.7m × 3m.

There are three cupboard recesses in the internal walls and again the internal stone pegs. The door is 1.2m × 0.6m and the walls are 1.1m thick at the door.

LARGE ORATORY

The building is boat-shaped with a door in the western wall. Its measurements are 3.6m × 2.4m × 3m. The stone altar which occupied the eastern wall was removed during the renovations of 1990. There is also a small window in the eastern wall.

SMALL ORATORY

The building is on a substantial artificial terrace some distance away from the group. It is 2.4m × 1.8m × 2.4m and there is a window, 0.6m × 0.3m, in the north-eastern wall. The door is only 0.9m × 0.5m and the walls are 1m thick.

MEDIEVAL CHURCH

This is quite a ruin but its eastern window still stands. As distinct from the other buildings of the monastery, the construction of this medieval church contains imported stone – a feat of transport and labour which is almost incredible. In the centre of the church is a comparatively modern gravestone which refers to the lighthouse families of 1868, and was erected in this position some time after 1871.

PRACTICAL INFORMATION

- *The Skellig Experience:* The Skellig Experience Visitor Centre on Valentia Island is a major, weatherproof attraction which opened in 1992. As well as being the launching point for a 90-minute cruise around the Skellig Islands, the Skellig Experience also 'transports' the Skellig Islands across 8 miles of ocean. In a purpose-built interpretation centre on the waterfront of Valentia Island, the sights, sounds and stories of Skellig are readily available.

   Access: 6km off Ring of Kerry route; signposted Portmagee

Suggested Devotion

Revelation 12.7–12: St Michael Attacks the Dragon
From an eighth-century simple rule for a solitary in Kenneth Jackson, *Studies in Early Celtic Nature Poetry* (Cambridge, 1935), pp. 105–6:

> *All alone in my little hut without any human being in my*
>   *company . . .*
> *Dear has been the pilgrimage . . .*
> *All alone in my little hut, all alone I came into the world . . .*
> *Alone I shall go from it.*

Opening times: Heritage Centre daily, April – Oct 10am – 6.15pm

- The Cruise: 3 cruises daily between mid May and end of August (weather permitting). Open boats carrying 12 persons 12 noon (3hr cruise) / 3pm (2hr cruise) / 4pm (2hr cruise)

Charges vary considerably

Contact number: 00353 66 76306

- Killarney Travel Information: 00353 64 31633
- Cork/Kerry Travel: 00353 21 273251
- Ordnance Survey Map: Ireland Discovery Series no. 70
- Video: *The Edge of Europe* (Riochta Productions, Killarney)

Croagh Patrick, County Mayo

Croagh Patrick is 6 miles from Westport in Co. Mayo, on the Louisburgh Road.

The beautiful mountain of Croagh Patrick, overlooking Clew Bay, has been a sacred mountain for almost 5,000 years. As far back as 3,000 BC the people of the Megalithic period worshipped there. In pre-Christian times, Croagh Patrick was already the centre of a joyful festival in honour of Lug, a god worshipped at the time particularly by the Druids. The Christian Church changed this into an annual pilgrimage on the same day in honour of St Patrick. Like Moses, he is said to have spent 40 days upon the summit in the year 441 communing with God and interceding with him on behalf of the Irish people. Every year, pilgrims climb 'The Reek', as it is known locally, carrying a stick, like the staff of their medieval forebears, on the traditional day, the last Sunday in July. It is the most popular of all Irish pilgrimages. The happy atmosphere of the pilgrims, young and old, continues the festival atmosphere of the early Christian gathering with which it started its life.

During his retreat on this mountain in 441, Patrick was tormented by black birds which surrounded him and which in later stories became demons and serpents. Ancient chroniclers say that Patrick threw his bell at them and banished them into the hollow known as *Lag na nDeamhan* which is located on the north side of the mountain below the first station. It is a common belief that this is the reason why no poisonous snake or reptile can be found in Ireland to this day.

TOCHAR PHADRAIG (PATRICK'S CAUSEWAY)

For hundreds of years pilgrims following in St Patrick's footsteps began their climb at Aughagower which is on the ancient pilgrims' route known as *Tochar Phadraig*. Tochar Phadraig or Patrick's Causeway pre-dates St Patrick. It was probably built around 350 AD and was the main route from Cruachan, near Downpatrick Head, the seat of the Kings of Connaught, to Cruachan Aigle or Croagh Patrick. Since St Patrick's time the route has become a Christian Pilgrim Route and today the pilgrim can still walk in part on the original flagstones with which the walk was paved. The full route runs from Ballintubber to Croagh Patrick, and is 22 miles long. Anyone wishing to walk the full route should consult the book *Tochar Phadraig* (published in 1989 by Ballintubber Abbey Productions) and walk back into history. It is difficult to say if there was a church on the summit at the time of St Patrick, but there are references to a chapel on the summit from 824. The present church was built in 1905.

THE PILGRIMAGE TODAY

Every year on the last Sunday of July many thousands of people flock to Croagh Patrick, climb its rugged sides and perform exercises of penance and prayer. These thousands of pilgrims are carrying on an unbroken tradition, following in the footsteps of their race for whom all down the centuries Croagh Patrick has been a holy mountain. Some pilgrims endure the utmost hardship and penance by climbing the mountain in their bare feet. Mass is celebrated continuously in the open air on Reek Sunday, confessions are heard in the small St Patrick's chapel and pilgrims perform the three traditional stations. Until the 1970s the pilgrimage was made during the hours of darkness, but in the interest of safety it now takes place in daylight.

The ascent is usually made from Murrisk and this is the recommended route though some begin the climb from the Drummin or Lecanvey side of the mountain. A short distance from the road at Murrisk there is a statue of St Patrick which is meant to signify St Patrick's welcome. Pilgrims are advised to do the first part of the climb slowly as it is comparatively easy, consisting of a long gradual ascent. At the end of the first portion, there is a level stretch of ground which leads to the first station, *Leacht Benain*, that is, the monument of Benen or Benignus, a disciple of St Patrick. Leacht Benain consists of a heap of stones readily identifiable from the path worn down to it by the feet of thousands of pilgrims.

At the station the pilgrim recites 7 Our Fathers, 7 Hail Marys and the Creed, and walks around the Leacht 7 times, after which he or she walks up the precipitous path called

Casan Phadraig to the summit.

Having reached the summit the pilgrim performs the second station (St Patrick's Bed) – a pile of rocks enclosed by a rectangle of low metal poles like a grave.

The third station, *Roilig Muire*, is situated some distance from the summit down the Lecanvey side of the mountain. Full details of the prayers to be recited for the proper performance of the stations are provided at the base of the mountain at Murrisk.

PRACTICAL INFORMATION

- The mountain is well signposted and takes approximately two hours to climb.
- Service times: Garland Friday (before the last Sunday in July/Reek Sunday): 10am For pilgrimages (from last Sunday in July): 8am – 3pm, half hourly
- Contact number: 00353 98 28871 or 00353 98 26900
- For the guided walks and pilgrimages: 00353 94 30934
- Croagh Patrick Tourist Information: 00353 98 25711
- Ordnance Survey Map: Ireland Discovery Series no. 31
- St Patrick's Church on the summit is kept locked; key available on request from the administrator of Westport Church.
- There is a good car park at Murrisk.
- There is an excellent Croagh Patrick Information Centre with many facilities: guided tours / secure lockers / craft shop / coffee shop / exhibitions: 00353 98 64114.

Suggested Devotion

Matthew 10.16–23: Jesus Sends Forth the Disciples

A section from St Patrick's 'Confessio', in Thomas O'Loughlin, *Saint Patrick* (Triangle, 1999):

I am the sinner Patrick.
I am the most unsophisticated of people, the least of Christians,
And for many people I am the most contemptible.

The Burren and Kilfenora

THE BURREN

The word *Burren* derives from the Irish word *Boirreann*, which means a rocky place. The story of the Burren began over 300 million years ago when layers of shells and sediment were deposited under a tropical sea only to be thrust above this many millions of years later and left open to the erosive power of rain and weather to produce the limestone landscape that appears today.

As early as 7,000 years ago, people began to leave their mark on this landscape in the form of Stone Age burial monuments such as Poulnabrone Dolmen and Gleninsheen Wedge Tomb, or in the Iron Age ring-forts such as Cahercommaun or Ballykinvarga, some of which remained in use until the early Christian period. In the Burren, the blend of Celtic and Christian tradition produced a distinctive art form in stone, an excellent example of which is Kilfenora Cathedral with its famous High Crosses, grave slabs and east window.

The Burren is one of the most enigmatic regions in Ireland and the Burren Centre is a good place to begin exploring the area. The Centre's landscape models, displays and audio-visuals reveal the mysteries and complexities of this unique place. Not only is it a place of Christian pilgrimage from early days, but the geology and geography, the rich diversity of flora and fauna, as well as the history of humanity are all fascinating to explore at the Burren.

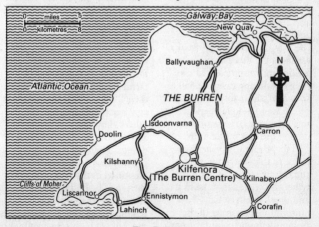

The Burren

Kilfenora, home to the Burren Centre, boasts one of the greatest concentrations of High Crosses in Ireland, including the famed Doorty Cross (twelfth-century). Not only has this picturesque village its own medieval cathedral, but can also claim the Pope as bishop.

THE CHRISTIAN PERIOD

The legacy of about 1,500 years of Christian worship remains very tangible as a story in stone in the Burren. There are up to 82 ecclesiastical sites in the Burren, covering a millennium of worship. As well as church ruins, cemeteries, hermitages and monastic enclosures we have holy wells, saints' seats or 'beds', and penitential stations, all rooted in the Christian past.

When Christianity came to the Burren is uncertain, but by the eighth century, the territory of the Corcu Modruad tribe had shrunk to the region of the modern Burren and Corcomroe and some parts of Inchiquin, and in the twelfth century this was defined in ecclesiastical terms as the diocese of Kilfenora, comprising 13 civil parishes. In any case, the 450 or so *cahars*, those fortified houses of the well-to-do farmers, point to a relatively large population during the first millennium.

The people who gave their name to this district were the Corcu Modruad, a Celtic tribe who settled in western and north-western Co. Clare around the beginning of the first millennium. Not far from

Kilshanny is a very large monument, 8m high and nearly 100m in base diameter, known as Carn Connachtach. According to some experts this is 'Carn Mac Tail' – the inauguration place of the chieftains of Corcu Modruad. A battle was fought here in 1573 between rival factions of the O'Briens.

The Celts were a remarkable people – imaginative, cultured, obsessed with honour and glory, war-like and boastful. Their societies were tribal, rural, hierarchical and familiar. The basic territorial unit was the *tuath*, roughly translated as the 'tribe', and it has been estimated that there were, in all, about 150 of these small kingdoms in Celtic Ireland. Celtic society was almost exclusively rural, although there were certainly coastal settlements where the extensive trade carried on with Britain and other countries had its base.

The most common structural reminder of the Celts is the distinctive dwellings they built. Known generally as ring-forts, they were roughly circular, fortified enclosures where a farmer and his family – and their livestock – lived. Some are constructed from stone, while others show the earthen banks and ditches that formed their design. The remains of over 170 of these forts have been identified in the area of the Burren. The best examples are in Caherballiny, east of Killonaghan Church, where one can still see high stone walls.

One of the most interesting areas of the Burren lies to the north of Oughtdarra Church. It is a valley, surrounded by cliffs on the east and north, and opening, with a spectacular view of the Aran Islands, to the west. Here are found hut sites, forts, and early cultivation sites. Rising up from the valley floor is Croghateeaun – a tower-like hill, pointing like a stumpy finger at the sky; an earthen fort rests on top. Not far from Ballinalackan Castle are three Iron Age (500 BC–500 AD) burial sites, associated with the Celts, called ring or bell barrows.

From what we know of them through their myths and ritual practices, the Celts were a profoundly religious people. They appear to have taken to Christianity with the enthusiasm and creative energy they brought to everything they encountered. Dates, once again, are difficult to establish. So, again, are directions. St Patrick, whose missionary work was in the north, never got as far as Clare, although his disciples may have.

It is possible that the new faith came from the south, from the Continent or, more interestingly, from the eastern Mediterranean and North African centres of early Christianity. The tradition of desert monasticism comes from this part of the world, a practice that seems to translate quite effortlessly into the stern monasticism of Aran and the far-flung Skelligs off the coast of Kerry. And it was the Aran saints – Enda, Columba, Mac Dara – who either founded or had dedicated to them some of the oldest churches along this part of West Clare.

None of the ruined churches of the present Burren go back much before the ninth or tenth centuries. But it is probable that many of them occupy sites of much earlier churches. Evidence suggests that primitive Irish churches were built of wood and obviously none of these have survived.

Altogether, nine church ruins are found in the district. Another four or five sites, with names containing the Irish prefix *kil* (church), are possible church sites, though nothing now remains of them.

In no particular order, four churches with some claim to occupy much older sites are Oughtdarra, dedicated to St Sionach Mac Dara (sixth-century); Killeany Church, founded by St Enda (fifth-century); Killonaghan, dedicated to St Colm Cille (sixth-century); and Crumlin Church, dedicated to St Columba (sixth-century). With the exception of Killeany, these churches are all close to the coast and, in most cases, within sight of Aran. Killeany, though further inland, actually takes its name from the founder of Aran monasticism. Whatever the exact nature of the connection, that it was a close one can hardly be questioned. The other remaining five churches all belong to the fifteenth and sixteenth centuries.

THE HIGH CROSSES

Kilfenora Cathedral is not a remarkable piece of unique and splendid architecture. On the whole it is plain and relatively unadorned. However, the High Crosses in the churchyard are very impressive. From the beginnings of Celtic Christianity, crosses were erected for various purposes, mostly for sepulchral monuments and to define the limits of sanctuary of the church. The crosses at Kilfenora were erected for these two purposes, but as to the number that stood here we will never know, although a deeply rooted tradition to which the older generations very much adhered is that there were seven crosses, and we know that Kilfenora was often referred to as 'the city of the seven crosses'.

Two of the crosses deserve special mention:

- The first is the best preserved of all and stands in the open field about 200 yards west of the cathedral. It faces the village and the cathedral. The cross is elaborately carved out of one solid slab of limestone. It stands about 14ft high and at least another two or three feet must be sunk into the ground. It has a raised figure of the crucified Christ, vested in a long tunic reaching to below the knees; the head is tonsured in the Roman style, and there is a square panel in the centre of the figure. The arms are fully extended and the head erect. It has been suggested that this is a figure of the triumphant Christ against the background of the cross. As well as this, the cross also contains the intricate Celtic knot and a depiction of the lamb.

- The second is the Doorty Cross which stands near the west front of the cathedral. The west face is very faint and worn, making it difficult to see the detail. Near the base of the cross one can see the small figure of a man sitting sideways on a horse, but it is hard to distinguish his head. On the upper part is seen a figure of Christ, head erect, surrounded by four birds, probably doves: one is standing on each shoulder, their bills resting on the side of the head above the ears, where the crown of thorns was, while of the other two, one is under each arm. The east face of the cross depicts three figures, one at the top wearing an unusual mitre, and two immediately below carrying different style croziers. Below these three bishops is a winged, presumably mythical, beast devouring what looks like human skulls. The croziers are interesting; the left-hand figure is holding a crook-headed crozier of Irish type and the other a tua–crozier (one without a crooked top). Tua–croziers are still in use in some Eastern churches, and they were in use in the Western Church by abbots and bishops up to the twelfth century. There are very few tua–type crozier examples in Ireland.

PRACTICAL INFORMATION

- Ennis Tourist Information Centre: 00353 65 28366
- Ordnance Survey Map: Ireland Discovery Series no. 51
- The Burren Centre: 00353 65 88030 or e-mail: burrencenter@tinet.ie
- Facilities at the Burren Centre: tearooms, gardens, crafts and bookshops, Tourist Information Point, Bureau de Change, ample parking, toilets and good wheelchair access
- The Burren Exposure: the story of the stones of the Burren in Whitehorn, Ballyvaughan: 00353 65 77277
- The Centre is open daily: March – Oct: 10am – 5pm June – Sept: 9.30am – 6pm
- Burren Tours: 00353 65 81168
- Doolin Ferry to Aran Islands: 00353 65 74455 / 74189
- Sunday services: St Fachnan's Catholic Church: 9.30am / 11am The Cathedral (Anglican): 10am

---

Suggested Devotion

Matthew 3.7–9: What God Can Make of Stones

Some words from the writings of the Monks of Kilcrea, from John Flanagan, *History of Kilfenora* (Ennistymon Printers, 2000):

> *Upon the left was Corcomroe, and next not far away*
> *Was Kilfenora's holy shrine, and towers of Llemanagh*
> *While full in front spread bleak and wild*
> *Grey Burren's rocks all shattered piled*
> *Rugged and rough and dear and lone*
> *A weary waste of barren stone.*

Lough Derg, County Donegal

St Patrick's Purgatory, Lough Derg, is a unique pilgrimage site in a small lake in Co. Donegal – once considered to be at the end of the earth and therefore on the threshold of the other world. Tradition has it that the first abbot of the monastery of Lough Derg was St Davog, a disciple of St Patrick. The tradition of pilgrimage in this place certainly dates back to the early days of Christianity – and possibly even further. Some aspects of this pilgrimage – fasting, vigil, bare feet – make the fact that it is still popular in the twenty-first century all the more surprising. A constant feature of Lough Derg has always been the widely representative group of people who come there on pilgrimage.

The small lake of Lough Derg in south-east Donegal was the only Irish place of pilgrimage known throughout Europe during the Middle Ages. Its fame stemmed from a vision of purgatory which St Patrick is said to have seen in a cave on one of the lake's islands. The pilgrimage involves a three-day or one-day programme of penance and prayer. The austerity practised by the pilgrims is more reminiscent than most pilgrimages today of the harsh conditions experienced by their medieval counterparts.

THE ORIGINS OF THE PILGRIMAGE TO LOUGH DERG

The origin of the name *Lough Derg* is the word *Derc* (or in some cases *Gerc*) which means a pit or a cave. This interpretation fits in well with what we know of the origins of the Lough Derg Pilgrimage.

The pilgrimage today is centred on the tiny island called Station Island. The earliest Christian settlement was, however, founded on Saints' Island, a much larger island lying about two miles north-west of Station Island. Here in the fifth century a monastic community was established. There is very little by way of archaeological or documentary evidence about the precise origins of the monastery of Lough Derg, although St Patrick was traditionally believed to have been its founder. This tradition only became firmly established in the twelfth century and hard evidence to associate the saint directly with the lake is practically non-existent. There is some evidence to suggest that St Patrick travelled in the vicinity of Lough Derg. It is quite possible that he may have been attracted by the remoteness of the place to escape the cares of his mission and spend some time in prayer in the bleak countryside which surrounds the lake.

The harsh beauty of lake and landscape may very well have been an important factor in the decision of the early Celtic monks to create a community on what came to be known as Saints' Island. It is worth noting also that Celtic pagan cults seem to have been very strong in the area between Lough Derg and Lough Erne. We know that many of the most significant pagan sites of worship in Ireland were taken over and Christianized by the early missionaries.

The first abbot of the monastery of Lough Derg is reckoned to have been St Davog, supposedly a disciple of St Patrick. Davog is also the name of another saintly abbot of Lough Derg who lived in the seventh century. The name is preserved locally to this day both in St Davog's Chair and the neighbouring Seadavog mountain. Old Irish writings such as the *Annals of Ulster* and the *Annals of the Four Masters* make passing reference to the monastery. We are told that in 721 Cillene of 'Locha Gercc' died, possibly a reference to one of the early abbots of Lough Derg. The famous Round Tower on the monastic island of Devenish on Lough Erne reminds us of the vulnerability of the Irish monasteries to plundering raids. It is unlikely that the monastery of Lough Derg escaped the attentions of the Vikings who, according to the *Annals of the Four Masters*,

destroyed all the churches of Lough Erne in 836. The *Annals* also refer to the plundering of Lough Derg by Irish chieftains in 1070 and again in 1111.

The twelfth century was a century of transformation. We do not know for certain when Lough Derg first became a centre of pilgrimage. What we do know is that by the end of the twelfth century the island was well on its way to becoming one of the most renowned places of pilgrimage in the Christian world. The rapid rise of St Patrick's Purgatory to a position of fame rivalling any of the great medieval shrines seems to have depended on several factors. Chief among these was the great change that began in the Irish Church in the middle of the twelfth century.

It was with the coming of the Augustinians to Lough Derg in the 1140s that we first find hard evidence of a pilgrimage dedicated to St Patrick and reputedly founded by him. This is at least in part because the Irish Church was now more integrated into the fabric of Roman Christendom. The international nature of religious orders such as the Augustinians supported easier communications, as well as a natural tendency to promote as widely as possible those shrines and pilgrimages in their care. It is at this time too that the earliest written accounts of the pilgrimage appear.

THE PILGRIMAGE TODAY

What is it about this remarkable pilgrimage which has allowed it not just to survive but to grow, in spite of the many difficulties it has faced? Why does Lough Derg continue to exercise such a strong fascination, even attraction, in the twenty-first century? The answer to both these questions lies in the nature of the pilgrimage itself.

In many ways Lough Derg is a place of contradiction. It contradicts the accepted values of the contemporary world, by offering people the opposite of what human beings are supposed to want. Comfort, nourishment and sleep are discarded in favour of hardship, hunger and exhaustion. But the fact remains, thousands are attracted annually.

The attraction cannot be ascribed to the island itself – it is a bleak and inhospitable place. Nor are pilgrims drawn to Lough Derg to see ancient relics or monuments. The simple fact is that, for the pilgrims, Lough Derg is as much an experience as a place.

If Lough Derg has the power to speak in this way to the modern age, it is because, as in every age, it addresses a real spiritual need in human beings. Perhaps the most contradictory aspect of the Lough Derg Pilgrimage is the fact that for many pilgrims, the need which it fulfils is to find some measure of peace.

The Pilgrimage Centre is open to the public from 1 May until 30 September. The traditional three-day pilgrimage season runs from 1 June until 15 August. This involves three days of fasting, praying and keeping vigils. Boats are available from 11am until 3pm. One-day retreats are held during May and September. These are structured days of prayer particularly suited to those who, for various reasons, are unable to make the three-day pilgrimage. Boats during this time are available from 9.15am to 10.30am and advance booking is essential. For the three-day pilgrimage, intending pilgrims must be at least 15 years of age, in normal good health and able to walk and kneel unaided. Participating pilgrims must be fasting from the midnight prior to arrival.

The Lough Derg Heritage Centre is excellent and it encourages the pilgrim to explore the Celtic origins of St Patrick's so-called 'Purgatory'. This archaic sanctuary which so fascinated the medieval world, drawing its penitents and pilgrims from every corner of the world, is recreated in the exhibits and the presentations on display. Lough Derg has also inspired poets throughout the ages and extracts of many poems are used as an alternative to the traditional story boards. A visit to the centre can be combined with a boat trip to the island which will enable the pilgrim to experience the tranquility of the site which attracts over 30,000 pilgrims annually.

PRACTICAL INFORMATION

- Access: *via* Pettigo village then by boat – the *St Davog* and the *St Columba* are licensed to carry 75 persons each
- Frequent sailings 11am – 12 noon and 12.45pm – 3pm (sailing time 5 mins)
- Opening times: 1 June – 15 August
- Duration: two and a half days (pilgrims may arrive on any day of the week)
- Service times: individually chosen as this is a place of private pilgrimage
- Admission charges: £18 / £16 concessions / £11 day retreat
- Contact numbers: 00353 72 61518 / 72 61546
- Daily bus from Dublin and Sligo

Suggested Devotion

Mark 1.12–13: The Temptation in the Desert

A poem written by Alice Taylor at Lough Derg and published in Mary McDaid and Pat McHugh, *Pilgrim's Tales . . . and More* (Columba Press, 2000):

Needs

Give me space
To roll out my mind,
So that I can open
The locked corners
Where lost thoughts
Are hidden.
I need time
In a quiet place
To walk around
The outer edges
Of my being,
To pick up
Fragmented pieces,
To put myself
Back together again.

The Irish Pilgrimage Roads

Just like the religious sites associated with the beginnings of Christianity in Ireland, there are many pilgrim paths. There are seven which are currently well known and restored:

1 *TOCHAR PADRAIG*, CO. MAYO

Tochar Padraig is the longest of all the surviving Irish pilgrimage roads. This is a pilgrim road from Ballintubber Abbey, *via* Aghagower, to Croagh Patrick. There are many stiles and stone flags along the way as markers for the pilgrims. It is all on one level through boggy countryside. Aghagower has a Round Tower and a medieval church. In the centre of the village is *Dabhach Phadraig*, a circular 'bath' surrounded by a stone wall. Beside it is an ancient tree, the clay at the base of which is said to have curative powers. Also along the Tochar is a raised altar stone in Lankill and a holy well dedicated to St Brendan.

2 THE SAINT'S ROAD, DINGLE PENINSULA, CO. KERRY

St Brendan's Way probably started initially from Ventry. Today the starting point is Baile Breac car park and it leads through fields and roads *via* Kilmalkeder, a twelfth-century church, to Mount Brandon. Close to the road is Gallarus Oratory, built between 800 and 1200 in fine masonry, without any obvious use of mortar. The modern pilgrim must only attempt the walk with good guidance and when the mountain is clear. Pilgrims walk this road throughout the summer but in particular on 16 May, the feast of St Brendan.

3 THE PILGRIM'S WAY, CLONMACNOIS, CO. OFFALY

The shortest of the pilgrim roads is the Pilgrim's Way. The way probably started at the Nuns' Church leading towards the monastery and ending at the tomb of St Ciaran. Ten miles east-south-east of Clonmacnois is Lemanaghan, where there appears to be another short pilgrim road.

4 ST PATRICK'S WAY, CO. DONEGAL

A pilgrimage road led from the village of Pettigo to Lough Derg and beside it, at Drumawark, was a round enclosure like a ring-fort, with a cross within. Pilgrims still visit Lough Derg in great numbers from May to August each year.

5 ST DECLAN'S WAY, CO. WATERFORD

An extensive road is reported from Ardmore to Lismore. This is almost the same as the present modern road. Ardmore stands sentinel over a fine sandy bay on the south-east coast of Ireland. It boasts a Round Tower and St Declan's Cathedral, house and holy well.

6 *SLI CHAOIMHIN* (ST KEVIN'S WAY), CO. WICKLOW

This road brought pilgrims eastwards from Hollywood over the Wicklow Gap to Glendalough. There are several markers along the way, the most notable being a large granite Labyrinth stone, now in the National Museum in Dublin. The labyrinth is known from the floors of the medieval French cathedrals, such as Chartres and Amiens. It was walked by penitents on their knees as an equivalent of a pilgrimage to the holy places; it was also called the 'Jerusalem Mile'.

7 *TURAS CHOLMCILLE* (ST COLUMCILLE'S WAY), CO. DONEGAL

Other than Derry (*Doire Cholmcille*) one place which still bears the name of Colmcille is this beautiful secluded glen in west Donegal. Here the saint is still venerated annually by a *turas* (pattern) or pilgrimage, on his feast day, 9 June, and on Sundays between 9 June and 15 August. *Turas Cholmcille* is one of the few traditional *turasanna* still faithfully observed in Ireland and seems to hold resolutely to the traditions which surround it. There are remnants of what may once have been a more extensive pilgrimage road through boggy terrain traversed after the eighth century. The *turas* has 15 stations, some marked by early Christian standing stones at which certain prayers are said. The prayerfulness of the stations in this charming valley evoke more than anything the essence and the spirit of medieval pilgrimage in Ireland. The *turas* covers about three miles and takes about three to four hours.

Scotland

Introduction to Scotland

In late Roman times, Scotland was a patchwork of Celtic kingdoms, whose people were led by chieftains or kings. Those in the north and east were Picts, while south of the Antonine Wall were the Britons of Strathclyde. This was a kingdom that stretched from Dumbarton at the mouth of the River Clyde eastwards to the Scottish Borders, and into northern England and the Lake District. In 360 the political scene shifted: Gaels from Ireland raided the west coast of Scotland, while Picts attacked Strathclyde from the north. Seven years later, Angles attacked from the east. In 369 the Emperor Theodosius repelled the invaders, and Strathclyde enjoyed 20 years of peace, but in 410 the Romans withdrew officially, leaving the Britons to defend themselves.

Rome laid down Britain's northern frontier twice, each time spanning an east–west constriction. Hadrian's Wall ran from the Solway to the Tyne, and the Antonine Wall from the Clyde to the Forth. It is a measure of the non-Romanization of North Britain that the more southerly, Hadrianic, frontier was the one eventually maintained and that the intervening Lowlands up to the Antonine Wall, as a buffer zone, alone held those tribes with whom any kind of stable agreement was possible.

The conversion of Scotland to Christianity was piecemeal. The differing chronological horizons in the component regions are of some importance, because the advent of Christianity meant the introduction both of external influences and of Christian literacy with its accompanying art and specialized archaeology.

To the Britons between the Walls, the presence of fourth-century Christianity in Carlisle and sporadically among the Hadrianic garrisons with their civil settlements must have been apparent. It is on the western flank, along the coastal plain of Dumfries and Galloway, that tradition and archaeology combine to suggest the first implantation.

At Whithorn, St Ninian became the first bishop north of Hadrian's Wall. From here, Christianity spread amongst the fierce peoples of Northern Britain and Ireland. It was through Christianity, not the legions, that Roman culture made an enormous impact on the native people of Scotland.

In Ninian's day (362–432), Britain was fragmenting into many kingdoms of Britons, Scots, Picts and Saxons. In Cumbria and Dumfries and Galloway, the kingdom of Rheged emerged. Descended from the native Celtic tribes that lived around the Solway, Ninian's people, the Christian

Britons of Rheged, saw themselves as the inheritors of Roman culture.

From the beginning, stone memorials were erected and inscribed by local Christians at Whithorn. The Latinus Stone, praising God, commemorates Latinus and his daughter. The Latinus Stone and the Kirkmadrine Stones are the earliest Christian memorials in Scotland. They show that these communities were literate. Although the Britons of Rheged spoke a form of ancient Welsh, they wrote in Latin using Latinate names. Roman culture was still valued, despite the collapse of the Roman Empire. Perhaps Christianity was attractive to the Britons because of the Roman status it gave them.

Although more and more local people were gradually converted to Christianity, they did not entirely give up their pagan beliefs. The Celtic tribes had venerated watery places such as lochs, rivers, bogs and springs. Some of these sites may have been adopted into local Christian customs. In this way, Christianity blended into the lives of ordinary people. During the seventh and eighth centuries when Cumbria and Dumfries and Galloway became part of the Anglian kingdom of Northumbria, even greater vigour and energy was brought to Christianity in this region. The newly converted Northumbrians built a new church at Whithorn in the eighth century, establishing it probably for the first time as an important pilgrimage site.

An important question emerges at this stage: how did this early focus of Christianity affect the rest of Scotland? By the late sixth century, all the successor native kingdoms are presented as Christian; Rheged had Christian rulers and of course Whithorn, under whatever Cumbrian place name, would have been one of the several noted Christian centres within it. The Gododdin rulers, in Edinburgh and any other Lothian or Forth-region citadels, were Christians. The Strathclyde Britons had their own founder-bishop and saint, Kentigern, and a focus equivalent to Whithorn lay below the present Glasgow Cathedral.

Early chronicles refer to the peoples south of the Antonine Wall as Britons and to those north of the Wall as Picts. The Picts also inhabited the Scottish islands, where many of their circular stone-walled forts, or *brochs*, are found. These are tower-shaped houses with double walls which taper inwards, built prior to the second century AD.

The Picts used an Ogham alphabet, but none of their written records survive, apart from a few names on tombstones and a Gaelic list of their kings, which demonstrates a matrilineal succession. The Romans called them *Picti*, meaning 'Painted Ones', which may describe how their warriors painted or tattooed their bodies.

The Picts were perhaps at their most powerful in the seventh century. By this time their leaders had established a stronghold on the mainland beside the northern shore of Loch Ness, at Castle Urquhart, a native Pictish word which means 'woodland'.

Although the Picts left few inscriptions, they carved symbols on their monuments; their regular combinations approach a form of writing. On earlier stones, which are generally unshaped boulders or natural slabs, groups of three or four symbols are depicted: human figures, animals, fantastic beasts and bands of decoration. On later stones, figures are often centred around an elaborate knotwork cross, showing the influence of Christian sculptors from Northumbria; these stones are carefully shaped and dressed.

Bede records that he knew people who had visited the Picts. He also once met a delegation from the Pictish king Nechton which visited the Northumbrian monasteries of Wearmouth and Jarrow (Bede's home) in 710. These Picts, clerics among them, wished to be instructed in certain more regular observances and they also wanted skilled masons to help build them 'a stone church after the Roman fashion'.

It was the northern Picts, who had received the Christian faith from the Irish settlers, the Dalriadic Scots, that brought Christianity to Pictland. This does not mean that all Picts were Christian. In 563 the Pictish king, Bruide son of Maelchon (ruler of all lands north of the Forth and Clyde), gave the small island of Iona to Columba. The Picts considered that Columba had crossed to Iona in order to convert those Picts who dwelled in the north, and that his mission was primarily Pictish in purpose.

Adomnan, the ninth abbot of Iona, wrote Columba's life around 690. He mentions journeys from Iona into Pictland. Elsewhere in the *Life*, a few Pictish families, among a nation depicted as overwhelmingly pagan, were converted and baptized. Clearly, the status of Iona emerges as that of a principal monastic centre for the Irish colonies, contact with the Picts being a secondary element.

Iona
St Columba

ST COLUMBA

Born in Co. Donegal in 521, St Columba, probably one of the most influential Celtic saints, founded monasteries at Derry, Durrow and Kells. He was a prince of the royal Ui Neill family and could have been High King of Ireland if he had not decided to become a monk. He is often called Columcille to distinguish him from other saints called after the 'dove of God', Columba. *Kille* means a monastic church, and he bears the epithet as the founder of the monastic rule that spread to northern England.

Columba studied the Bible under St Finian of Moville and learned the art of poetry alongside Gemman. He later went to Clonard to study under another Finian and was ordained priest by St Mobhi at Glasnevin in Dublin.

When he was 41, he left Ireland and sailed to Iona, an island off the west coast of Scotland, a place from which Ireland cannot be seen. He had copied St Finian's prayer book without permission and, when he was forced to give the copy to its proper owner, St Finian was so enraged that a battle ensued, leading to Columba's exile.

When he arrived on the old Druidic island St Columba expelled the resident women of Iona, so that he could set up an exclusively male monastery. The work of this monastery spread until there were several new foundations on the island and in mainland Scotland.

There are seven main sources for the life of St Columba:

- *Amra Choluimb Chille* (the Elegy of Colum Cille) – probably written around 600 by Dallan Forgaill, an Irish poet.
- *Fo Rreir Choluimb* and *Tiugraind Beccain* – two poems probably written around 650 by Beccan mac Luigdech, a hermit associated with the Iona community and possibly living on Rum.
- *The Irish Annals* (especially those of Ulster and Tigernach) – chronicles recording events in Ireland which were started around the middle of the seventh century, possibly earlier. Some argue that a chronicle written on Iona and possibly started during Columba's life may underlie the earliest stratum of *Irish Annals* up to about 740.
- *The Book of the Miracles of Columba* – written probably in the 630s or 640s by Cummine, seventh abbot of

Iona, who died in 679. Only a tiny fragment of this survives.

- *Vita Columbae* (the Life of Columba) – the classic life written by Adomnan, eighth abbot of Iona, between 688 and 692.
- *The Ecclesiastical History of the English People* – written by the Venerable Bede in Jarrow and completed in 731.
- *The Irish Life of Columba* – an Irish homily based on Genesis 12.1 and probably written in Derry around 1150.

THE IONA COMMUNITY

The key strands of Columba's faith and Christian practice were pilgrimage, penitence and politics. Similarly, these are the central concerns of the present Iona Community.

The Iona Community is an ecumenical community of men and women seeking new ways of living the gospel in the world. It was founded in 1938 by George MacLeod, at that time a parish minister in Glasgow, who was concerned at the church's lack of impact in local communities at a time of high unemployment. The rebuilding of the ruined abbey buildings on Iona was a sign of hope in dark times, expressing also the necessary integration of work and service, prayer and politics.

The Community continues to see its first task as being the building of community in a world marked by division, injustice and isolation. Although the historic island of Iona is the Iona Community's place of inspiration and renewal, and the symbol by which it has become best known, it seeks to be faithful to its task in every place of human need.

The Community has at present about 250 members, 900 associates and 2,000 friends, drawn from a range of denominations and working backgrounds, with the biggest single group in ordained ministry. It is a dispersed community; members live all over Britain and beyond. The Community shares a common discipline in the keeping of which all are mutually accountable – a five-fold Rule of daily prayer and Bible study, economic sharing, planning the use of time, meeting together, and working for peace and justice.

There is a resident group on Iona which welcomes more than 400,000 visitors who come to the island each year. The Community maintains three residential centres on Iona and Mull which offer week-long programmes for guests from March to October – Iona Abbey and the MacLeod Centre on Iona, and Camas Adventure Camp on the Ross of Mull. Its administrative headquarters are in Community House, Govan, in Glasgow, where it also supports work with young people; the Wild Goose Resource and Worship Groups; a publishing house, Wild Goose Publications; and its bi-monthly magazine, *Coracle*.

But why Iona?

Why should a modern community seeking to discover new and relevant ways of relating the gospel to living in the world decide to be associated with a small and seemingly remote Scottish island? There are three main reasons:

- Iona has a most important place in the history of Scotland and of Western Christianity. It was to Iona that St Columba came in 563 to establish a monastic settlement which became one of the leading centres of Christian mission in Europe. Monks from Iona went out to evangelize the Scots of Dalriada (Argyll), the Picts of northern Scotland, and the Britons of north-east England – and on into Europe, penetrating as far as north Germany and Russia. As part of the Celtic Church, and maintaining close links with Ireland, the monks of Iona had a dynamic, robust spirituality, which combined a profound mysticism and sense of the goodness and beauty of creation with an earthy realism. Perhaps these two strands are demonstrated best in the two things which, along with their missionary activity, characterized their life on Iona: the agriculture and fishing by which they lived, and in which they displayed considerable expertise; and their work of illuminating and copying sacred manuscripts, for which they were renowned.

- The second reason for coming to Iona was that there was a clear task to be accomplished. It was a task that had meaning for craftsmen, for the ministers, and for the volunteer workers who shared in the rebuilding of the ancient abbey. They believed that the restoration would act as a hopeful sign for the Church and for the world.

- Finally, there is the spirit of Iona itself.

PILGRIMS TO IONA

Iona has been a place of pilgrimage for centuries, a meeting-point for countless people and possibilities. It still is. It is a place of refreshment, of encouragement and engagement, of taking stock and finding new ways, of reaching inwards and moving outwards, of personal growth and building community, of song and searching, of justice and joy. On Iona there is something that touches the soul, and the soul of the world as well, for it is a place of many dimensions – of welcome and challenge, of healing and community, of prayer and acceptance, of risk-taking and vision.

From Oban the ferry takes the modern pilgrim to Mull, which is crossed by coach, and then there is a further small ferry from Fionnphort on Mull to Iona. As one draws near to the island the image of

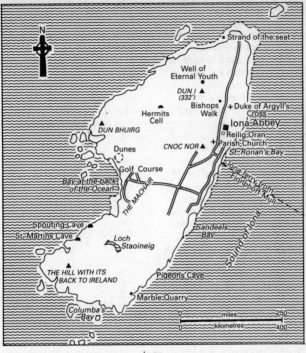

Iona

the present rebuilt abbey will become clearer. The disembarkation point is near Martyr's Bay where tradition has it the Vikings slaughtered a large number of the Celtic monks. Here the pilgrim may reflect on the cost of early coastal monasticism and consider our debt to these people of faith.

As one then walks up towards the abbey past the ruins of the thirteenth-century nunnery, one is reminded of the contribution of female saints. Nearby is Maclean's Cross, only

about 400 years old, but a very fine example of carving. St Oran's Chapel near the abbey takes its name from a cousin of Columba who was buried alive (willingly) in order to consecrate the ground, but was dug up again and found to be still alive!

The King's Walk leads across the churchyard, reflecting on the tradition of how many Scottish and Scandinavian kings are buried here. St Martin's Cross (17ft high) and St John's Cross will impress by their sheer scale, knotwork patterns and biblical scenes. The Torr, a large mound just east of the abbey, is reputed to be the site of Columba's cell.

The abbey itself, rebuilt by George Macleod and helpers during the late twentieth century, was founded about 1200 and has an atmosphere all its own with good information, guides, an excellent bookshop and fine examples of inscribed and patterned stonework in the museum. The small shrine to the north of the main entrance is identified as the place Columba was laid to rest, and this is quite possible. During the worship times in the abbey, each day of the week different themes and issues are explored, led by various members of the community.

Those who stay on the island can join a planned pilgrimage each Wednesday with a member of the Community which will take in the site of a hermit's cell, a disused marble quarry, St Columba's Bay (traditionally the place Columba landed on arrival from Ireland), and other places. The pilgrimage will take most of the day and at each stop there will be prayer, information and singing.

To stay on the island is most certainly to be preferred to a hurried day trip, where little of the atmosphere can be taken in, and to stay with the Community taking part in a rhythm of work, worship and rest is an experience few will forget.

PRACTICAL INFORMATION

- The Iona Community: 01681 700404
- Wild Goose Publications: 0141 4400985
- Glasgow Main Office: 0141 4454561
- Argyll and the Isles Tourist Board: 01369 701000
- Oban Tourist Information: 01631 563122
- Mull Tourist Information: 01688 500123
- Craignure Tourist Centre (Mull Pier): 01680 812377
- Caledonian MacBrayne Ferries: 01631 566688
- Ordnance Survey Map: Landranger Series no. 48

Suggested Devotion

Genesis 12.1–2: The Call of Abraham

A closing prayer from Iona's Evening Liturgy D, in *A Wee Worship Book* (Wild Goose Publications, 1999), p. 73:

> Bless to us, O God,
> The Moon that is above us,
> The Earth that is beneath us,
> The friends who are around us,
> Your image deep within us,
> The rest which is before us. Amen.

Dunadd, the Valley of Kilmartin, Argyll

Dunadd, about 80 miles north-west of Glasgow, is a lumpy rock rising above the River Add. It takes its name from the Scottish *dun Add*, meaning the hillfort situated above the River Add. The river's multiple serpentine bends loop inward from Loch Crinan to form an enormous flat peat bog, the *Moine Mhor* (Great Moss). Also flowing through the Moine Mhor is the Kilmartin Burn, and the relatively isolated hump Dunadd is thus in a position to control the entire Y-shaped valley. Excavations have shown the valley to have been occupied as early as 3000 BC and Dunadd itself from about 600 BC.

In fact in the landscape that surrounds Kilmartin people have lived, loved, danced, mourned, farmed, hunted, played and prayed for about 10,000 years. Before the Egyptian pyramids were built (over 5,000 years ago) the inhabitants of this wide area had constructed the first of the burial cairns that make up the Linear Cemetery on Nether Largie South. These Neolithic and Bronze Age monuments, together with the stone circle at Temple Wood, and the standing stones at Ballymeanoch and other sites, are all part of the ritual landscape of the Valley of Kilmartin. Although found in many areas in Western Europe the enigmatic cup-and-ring-marked rock art is most prolific in this small area of mid Argyll.

Dunadd can claim a clear connection with St Columba. Stretching northward up the valley from Dunadd toward Kilmartin village lies the Linear Cemetery, consisting of seven burial cairns in a roughly straight line about three miles long. The oldest of these is the Nether Largie South cairn, which is dated as far back as the fourth millennium BC. Excavations have demonstrated that it served several generations of inhabitants who used different burial practices over the years. The cairn was built with four internal compartments totalling about 20 feet in length, with stone slabs on the sides as uprights and flat stone slabs above as a kind of ceiling. The whole area was then covered over with loose stones and dirt to form the typical rounded mound, or cairn, probably with an open area or 'court' at the entrance. One description says Nether Largie South is built 'like a house of cards', but the huffing and puffing of winds and storms for 3,000 years have not been able to blow it down. Since this cairn today is open at both

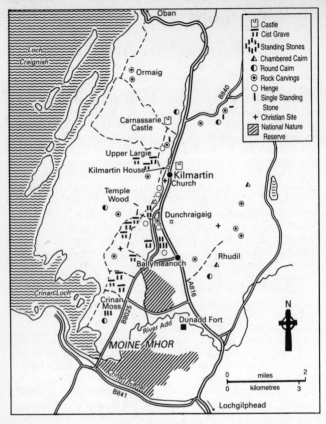

Kilmartin

ends, pilgrims can see one end through to the other, but in order to wriggle through the compartments, a person would have to be very tiny indeed.

Dunadd is mentioned in the *Annals of Ulster*, whose Scottish material up to about 740 is based largely on a set of annals

kept at Iona. The entry for 683 mentions the 'siege of Dun At and the siege of Dun Duirn'; a longer entry in 736 records that 'Aengus son of Fergus, king of the Picts, laid waste the territory of Dal Riata and seized Dun At and burned Creic and bound in chains two sons of

Selbach, that is Donngal and Feradach'. Such military action between the Picts and the Scots in the seventh and eighth centuries provides the context for fortifications such as Dunadd.

At the northern end of the valley is Kilmartin Church, the third or possibly fourth building to be constructed on this site. There is little doubt as to its originally having been a Celtic foundation, most likely a Celtic monastery, possibly founded by Columba. A reasonable conclusion is that this may have been the church serving the people of Dunadd and the rest of the Kilmartin Valley in the early Christian centuries. Its dedication to St Martin (*kil Martin*,'Church of Martin') is significant, since it is known that dedications to Martin were common in this area. The present Kilmartin church building, however, dates only from 1835. In the churchyard are about 25 West Highland grave slabs, some with intriguing early medieval carvings. Inside the church, and in the care of Historic Scotland, are some very fine Celtic Crosses from the same school of carving as those found on Iona.

It is easy to understand why the entire valley is one of the most prolific archaeological sites in all Scotland. Fascination with the area continues because even the most expert of the experts, after years of excavations and research, still do not know exactly why the multiple standing stones are aligned the way they are, why the stone circles are positioned where they are, what the mysterious cup-and-ring marks mean, or when the burial cairns were first built. Perhaps most significant of all, no one knows why this particular valley, appropriately referred to as a 'ritual landscape', was selected as an obviously sacred space.

Why bring a Christian pilgrim party here?

Other than the connection of Columba with Dunadd and the carved stones in Kilmartin Church, what is here that would justify a Christian Celtic pilgrimage? Nearly all the sites are long pre-Christian, and most are even pre-Celtic. Yet, if a pilgrimage is a journey undertaken in search of that which is holy, then surely that is justification enough to visit this exceptional valley. That it has been an area of religious observance, a place sacred to our forebears, can hardly be questioned. When we limit our own understanding of God to Christian doctrine and the worship of God to Christian practice, we limit our appreciation of such holy sites. It may be another century before all the mysteries of Kilmartin are understood – if then – but mystery and numen are certainly abundantly present for those who are sensitive to such things and consciously seeking the holy for their own lives.

PRACTICAL INFORMATION

- To find the Valley of Kilmartin: from Glasgow take the A82 to Tarbet on Loch Lomond. Then follow the Argyll Tourist Route (A83) via Inveraray to Lochgilphead. Just a few miles north on the Oban road (A816) one enters the Valley of Kilmartin.

- Kilmartin House: Centre for Archaeology and Landscape Interpretation:
    artefacts from the nearby sites, reconstructions and interactive displays; audio-visual: awe-inspiring time travel experience with imagery and music.
The Kilmartin sessions introduce music that would have been familiar to our Celtic forebears – the eighth-century iron bell of St Adomnan, the ninth-century Pictish triple pipes and a traditional Gaelic quern song used as a melody for St Columba's visionary poem, the 'Altus Prosator'.
Kilmartin House is two hours from Glasgow on the A816 between Lochgilphead and Oban – information centre, bookshop, café, education centre.
Open all year: 10am – 5.30pm. Admission prices vary (good concessions). Allow 1–3 hours per visit. Disabled access, toilets and car park.
Further details and bookings: 01546 510278 and www.kilmartin.org

- Lochgilphead Tourist Information Office: 01546 602344

- Oban Tourist Information Office: 01631 563059

- Cycle hire: 01546 603511

- Taxis: 0370 812795

Suggested Devotion

John 1.1–5: Prologue to St John's Gospel

Angels and archangels and all the company of heaven surround us. An extract from Robin Flower, *The Irish Tradition* (Oxford, 1947), p. 48:

Angels

> *The maker of all things,*
> *The Lord God worship we:*
> *Heaven white with angels' wings,*
> *Earth and the white-waved sea.*

Whithorn

St Ninian

Whithorn is a small and delightful fishing harbour out of everyone's way in Galloway, south-west Scotland. It is hard to imagine now that here in 397 St Ninian built his *Candida Casa* (White House) which was to be the first Celtic monastic community from which all others would trace their roots.

As the Whithorn Dig continued into the 1990s, it gradually became possible to trace the outline of a circular Celtic monastery. There were any number of Christian graves. Many other artefacts, such as fragments of glass, pieces of pottery and shards of amphorae, implied a lively trade with the Mediterranean world and a wealthy and sophisticated society. Most exciting was the discovery of a pile of builders' rubble consisting of stones of grey lime coated with a thick skin of calcium carbonate. Any building made from such stones would indeed have been a shining white hut, especially when wet. And, not long after that discovery, the foundation wall of a small building constructed of those same stones was found beneath the western end of the medieval

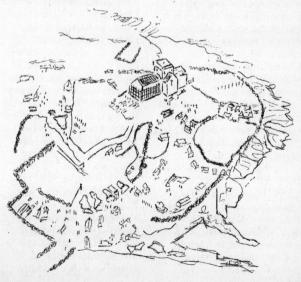

cathedral. Most scholars today, therefore, are satisfied that there was indeed a *Candida Casa* and that the remains of it can still be seen at Whithorn.

Today, as the pilgrim passes through a sixteenth-century archway in the main village street, there is a superb heritage centre. This offers both a 'slide and sound' presentation, which is excellent, and informative guided tours of the site. Here visitors are shown where early wooden huts were sited and remnants of a thick whitewashed wall found, and there is a superb display of early Celtic carved crosses. By far the most important of the Whithorn stones is the Latinus Stone. In 1922 an important archaeologist, after exhaustive research and years of comparative studies, suggested that the Latinus Stone was not a memorial stone on a tomb, but instead was a place marker denoting the presence of a church. Most of the Priory Church ruins date from the sixteenth century and are associated with the powerful medieval monastery which sold its questionable theology in the form of dubious relics and papal bulls, simply trading on the heritage of Ninian.

Further along the coast is the thirteenth-century St Ninian's Chapel, marking the place where pilgrims first landed on their way to this site. There is also St Ninian's Cave which can only be reached by footpath, and time must be allowed for this. In this cave lots of

crosses carved on stones were found, and these have now been transferred to the heritage centre.

It seems that Ninian set about his work of sharing the light of Christ from this monastery in the heart of the Druidic culture. There is little evidence of violence between the two and Ninian appears to have been peacefully successful in his mission in Scotland, his successors even engaging as far as the Orkney and Shetland Islands in the sixth century.

ST NINIAN

The Venerable Bede, writing in the eighth century, remains the earliest literary source for Ninian. Bede asserts that Ninian, a 'most holy man', had studied in Rome, thereby implying Ninian's total theological orthodoxy. Bede also tells us that this Ninian built a *Candida Casa*, or White House, of stone, something most unusual for the Britons. Bede does not tell us how he got this information, but most scholars tend to think he may have learned it from his friend Bishop Pechthelm of Whithorn, who was passing on to Bede a strong local tradition that Ninian was the founder of Whithorn.

Only two other early literary sources of information about Ninian exist. One is a poem, also from the eighth-century monastery at Whithorn, the 'Miracula Nynie Episcopoi' (the Miracles of Bishop Ninian), which, even while drawing on the same local tradition as did Pechthelm, tells us more about life in the monastery of that time than it does about the historical Ninian. The other source, from the twelfth century, is Ailred of Rievaux's prose *Life of Ninian*. This latter work, more hagiographical than historical, is the source for most of the Ninian stories set forth today as authentic.

PRACTICAL INFORMATION

- The Whithorn Interpretation Centre: 01988 500508
  A visitor centre, shop, audio-visual show, exhibitions, original dig site, picnic area, toilets, priory museum and crypts. Admission charges vary / discounts for pre-booked groups.
  Open 10.30am – 5pm daily, Easter – 31 Oct (last tour 4pm).
- Dumfries and Galloway Tourist Board: 01387 245550
- Ordnance Survey Map: Landranger Series no. 48

Suggested Devotion

Luke 24.44–49: Jesus' Last Instructions to the Apostles

From Esther De Waal, *The Celtic Vision: Prayers and Blessings from the Outer Hebrides* (Darton, Longman and Todd, 1988), p. 155:

Journey Blessings

May God shield you on every step,
May Christ keep you in every path,
May Spirit bathe you in every pass.

The Ruthwell Cross

This unique 18ft-high cross stands in an apse in Ruthwell Church which is just north of the Dumfries–Annan B724 road, 10 miles from Dumfries and 7 miles from Annan. It is probably a seventh-century preaching cross and has carved on it many biblical scenes and quotations in Anglo-Saxon runes and Latin.

Antiquarians believe it to be the oldest and most interesting monument of its kind in the British Isles. Its story is briefly told in its sculpture. From the day on which it was first completed by a great unknown artist, who designed and executed its beautiful vine tracery and its noble sculptured panels, it has never ceased to declare its message. Alike as a literary document and as a work of art, it is of great and enduring value. It is the only document of the kind, dating back for twelve centuries, the message of which can be clearly read today.

The cross was designed to tell the story of the Life and Passion of Christ. Both on the narrower and broader faces of the cross-shaft the subject matter of the sculpture, and of the inscriptions – whether in rune-stave or in Roman character – is the same.

It is not a churchyard memorial but a preaching cross; a sermon in stone. Miracle and teaching, the preaching of John the Baptist, the washing of Jesus' feet, and the healing of the man born blind, as well as the crucifixion itself and the writing of the gospel story – these were all depicted upon the sculptured stone in a manner so vivid and picturesque, and so true to life and fact.

So truly classical in style is the sculpture, and so skilfully has the work been executed, that one of the greatest puzzles connected with the cross, as a relic of early Christian art, is to explain and account for the production of a work of such high artistic merit in a land which had been, only half a century earlier, inhabited by people who were rude and unlettered barbarians.

As a preaching cross it was designed simply to mark the spot which had been consecrated for divine service and worship, and where the sacraments of the Church were to be celebrated. There can be little doubt that, in course of time, a primitive building of wood and mud would be constructed to shelter the pilgrims who came to worship at the shrine. But such a temporary structure might be levelled by a storm from the Solway shore at any time and might not be rebuilt for years. The massive cross remained secure. It continued to declare, from one generation to another, the great message of salvation and of eternal life.

The period when the cross was completed and first set up is, in the opinion of the best informed scholars, in the last quarter of the seventh century, about 680.

The siting of the cross is also of some interest. It belongs to the time when the northern Angles held the region north of Hadrian's Wall. To the early church in the Celtic period, the Irish Sea was a Mediterranean lake, and the Solway Firth was but an arm of her home waters. Round the Solway Firth the old Romano–British tradition had been transmitted to the

Celts: at the head of the Firth was Carlisle, with its impressive Roman ruins, and while Hadrian's Wall led away to the east, through Camboglanna and Corbridge, the coastline to the west, the southern bank of the Firth, was studded with Roman forts; Clannaventa, from which port Patrick was abducted by Irish pirates, lay just to the south. On the northern bank of the Solway lay Whithorn and Kirkmadrine. The Ruthwell Cross, not a mile from the sea, and near the famous church and minster of Hoddom on the Arranwater, was a preaching and votive cross for those travelling around this important early Christian area.

THE PICTURES ON THE CROSS

THE SOUTH SIDE
- St John the Evangelist and the Eagle
- The Archer
- The Visitation
- Washing of Jesus' Feet
- The Healing of the Man Born Blind
- The Annunciation
- The Crucifixion

THE NORTH SIDE
- The Bird on Topmost Twig of Vine
- Two Evangelists
- John the Baptist with the 'Lamb of God'
- Christ Standing on the Heads of Swine
- The Meeting of Paul and Antony in the Desert
- The Flight into Egypt

THE NARROWER SIDES OF THE CROSS: THE RUNIC TEXT AND VINE TRACERY

In the depiction of the crucifixion on the south side of the cross, it has been suggested that there is a special significance in the fact that the sun finds beautiful alliterative lines, all of which may have been originally inscribed upon the cross but are now no longer to be read there.

Prior to the time when the correct translation of the runic characters was first made, it was generally supposed that the Latin inscriptions, upon the broad faces of the cross-shaft, provided an interpretation of the mysterious rune-staves inscribed upon the margins of the narrow edges.

The complete text is given in 'The Dream of the Rood' a poem possibly written by Caedmon, a north England poet of the seventh century. The extract below is taken from Professor Stephens' *The Runic Roods of Ruthwell and Bewcastle* (quoted in J. L. Dinwiddie, *The Ruthwell Cross*, Solway, Dumfries, 1999); it is part of a much longer poem and the words as translated here are a rendering of the runic text now to be seen upon the narrower edges of the cross. The letters are the earliest existing example of Anglo-Saxon script.

Also on the narrow edges is the vine scroll, a form of decorative sculpture which from the earliest Christian times was characteristic of Christian art. It is found upon the walls of the catacombs at Rome, as well as in many other places on the Continent.

PRACTICAL INFORMATION

- The key to the church in which the cross is displayed is available at the farmhouse on the corner just as you turn for the church – guide book and history also available at the farmhouse
- Tourist Information: 01387 253862

Suggested Devotion

Matthew 4.23–25: Jesus Begins His Teaching Ministry

From the seventh-century poem 'The Dream of the Rood' (part of which can to be seen on the narrow edges of the Ruthwell Cross):

> *Girded Him then*
> *God Almighty*
> *When he would*
> *Step on the Gallows,*
> *Fore all mankind*
> *Mindfast, Fearless,*
> *Bow me durst I not.*

The Isle of Man

Introduction to the Isle of Man

The Isle of Man was clearly an important place during the early Celtic period. No fewer than 12 of the 17 ancient parish churches of the island are dedicated to Celtic saints and many of the numerous *keeils* (early oratories or small chapels) and holy wells are dedicated to the Celtic saints. The ruins of over 200 *keeils* have been recorded and there is a wealth of early crosses and inscriptions. Indeed, the island shows a greater concentration of early Christian remains than can be found in any other area of comparable size in the British Isles.

Celtic saints associated with Manx churches and *keeils* include Maughold, Lonan and Brigid, who gave her name to the parish of Kirk Bride as well as to several *keeils*. Other parishes whose names are derived from Celtic saints are Arbory (St Cairbre), Santan (St Sanctan), Braddan (St Brendan), Onchan (St Conchenn), and German (St Germanus).

The cultural influences on the island originate from the indigenous Celtic peoples who were converted to Christianity by the early missionaries of the Celtic Church around 500. However, the Vikings arrived on the island around 800 and a significant fusion of cultures took place, one which is still evident in the archaeology, language, place names and parliamentary traditions of the island today.

Possibly the very earliest churches in Man were built of sods, or of wattle and mud, and there is now no trace of them. Graves have been found together with crosses, some of which have been dated to the fifth century, and it is possible that they mark the sites of buildings which have disappeared. Later, stone buildings were erected, the stones at first being held together with earth. Afterwards clay was used as a cement, and finally lime or shell-mortar.

The earliest *keeils*, being so small, could not have been intended for congregational worship but rather as places in which the first Christian missionaries could offer up their simple service of prayer and praise. Preaching would have been conducted out of doors, and so too would baptism, for a holy well is usually found near these old chapels. Many of the *keeils* that have been examined are known to have been built on sites that had been sacred for a long time previously, thus illustrating that respect for tradition which was a marked characteristic of Celtic Britain.

St Maughold is probably the most honoured of the Manx saints. Tradition has it that he and Patrick did not get on.

Patrick banished him to the sea in a coracle without rudder, oars or sail, and through his trust in God's guidance he landed on the Isle of Man. There he apparently repented of whatever it was that he had done in Ireland and founded a monastery on the site that still bears his name, in due time becoming a bishop.

The island was occupied by hunter-fishermen of the Mesolithic Age (5000–3000 BC) and archaeology gives evidence of human occupation through the succeeding periods. From the Neolithic period there are standing stones, cairns and burial chambers scattered all over the island. Much later, during the pre-Christian Celtic period, perhaps in the second/first centuries BC, an Iron Age promontory fort was built on the headland at what is now Maughold.

When St Maughold founded his monastery in the fifth century, he was building on land that had been sacred space for many hundreds of years. The Maughold site is clearly a holy place. In the churchyard are the visible remains of three *keeills*, a fourth is marked by a granite pillar and there was a fifth beneath the foundations of the porch of the church. These date from the eighth to the twelfth centuries. Typically a *keeill* has a rectangular shape, about 10ft wide by 15ft long, and sometimes the remains of an altar can be seen at the east end. But it is not only the *keeills* that remind us of the Isle of Man's early Christian past. Superb collections of carved Christian cross-slabs are found at a number of places on the island.

THE VIKINGS: when the Vikings raided the monastic settlements of Britain and Ireland there was great confusion; a great many communities were scattered and destroyed. The Vikings were not overtly anti-Christian but were attracted by the riches of the monasteries. They were not the first Germanic raiders to threaten the Celts. In a series of migrations in the fifth century, Angles from Schleswig-Holstein, Jutes from Jutland and Saxons from Lower Saxony in north-west Germany had overrun Britain. The Vikings of Norway and Denmark were their kinsmen. The word 'Viking' probably comes from the Old Norse word *vik*, meaning a bay or creek: Vikings were associated with the sea. Part of their success was attributed to their ability to develop long, flexible and lightweight boats that could handle rough seas, yet travel up rivers in water only a metre deep.

The Manx Celtic Crosses

The Isle of Man has its unique crosses. As in other Celtic countries, the earliest Manx crosses are inscribed standing stones, some of which bear inscriptions in Ogham or Roman script.

Since the fifth century crosses have served in the Isle of Man as grave markers and memorial stones. To date, 204 decorated stones have been found, representing the largest concentration of such stones for this period. The great majority remain in the churches and churchyard 'cross shelters' of their parish of origin. Cast copies of all the stones are kept at the Manx Museum, forming an invaluable reference collection. Wherever the stones are housed, they are treated as Ancient Monuments and as such are under the protection and guardianship of Manx National Heritage.

The earliest slabs show Celtic styles, from simple cross designs to the later complicated interlace. Inscriptions in Ogham, Celtic lettering, or very occasionally Latin, commemorate the dead. A large number of these Celtic Crosses can be seen in the cross shelter at Kirk Maughold, with others at Old Kirk Lonan, Old Kirk Braddan and Onchan Parish Church. The bilingual nature of many of the Manx crosses is interesting. For example, the one at Knoc-y-Dooneee,

Andreas, which dates from the sixth century, has on one face the Latin *Ammecat filius Rocat hic jacet* (Ambecatos son of Rocatos lies here), and on the left side the fragmental Ogham Celtic inscription, *(Am)b(e)catos magi Rocatos*.

After the Vikings settled on Man, and later converted to Christianity, Norse sculptors decorated their stones with images from their pagan mythology and with interlace. A standing stone from Maughold is interesting in being a transitional form from the standing memorial stone to the classical Celtic Cross. Inside a circle surrounded by an inscription in the manner of a seal is a six-leafed pattern that was the symbol of the goddess Juno in Roman religion. Beneath the pagan goddess symbol are two *Chi-Rho* crosses with accompanying inscriptions.

Also in this period the practice of erecting carved cross-slabs on the graves of the dead was readopted in the tenth and continued into the early eleventh century. Outstanding examples of the new designs were produced by Gaut, the earliest and best known of the Scandinavian sculptors, who was responsible for the ring-chain pattern. Memorial runes link Norse and Celtic names with families, providing evidence of intermarriage. Fine examples of Norse Crosses can be seen at the parish churches of Andreas, Maughold, Jurby, Michael and Old Kirk Braddan. However, the most outstanding collection of the earlier Celtic Crosses is that at Maughold.

Throughout the period of the erection of the crosses, the Isle of Man formed an important part of the early church in Celtic Britain. The simplest incised crosses cannot be closely dated, and the earliest dateable carvings are small slabs with simple compass-arc decoration which may be ascribed to between 650 and 800, perhaps representing the continuation of the Christian tradition of the former Roman provinces of Britain and Gaul. In the ninth century larger slabs of more monumental proportions were erected, bearing in low relief representations of the Celtic ring-headed cross, usually on a rectangular slab, showing Scottish rather than Irish affinities. Closely knit interlacing patterns became characteristic of the decoration.

The remarkable and outstanding Calf of Man Crucifixion carving (probably from an altar or shrine rather than a grave memorial) may be regarded as the supreme creation of the Celtic art tradition in stone carving in the Isle of Man.

The following is a list of some of the important crosses. The numbering of the crosses refers to the Manx Museum's official registration:

- Early Celtic Cross-Slab, Maughold (46)
- Irneit's Cross-Slab, Maughold (47)
- Altar Front, Ballavarkish, Bride
- Branhui's Cross-Slab, Maughold (169)
- Crux Guriat, Maughold (69)
- Cross-Slab with Monks, Maughold (96)
- Cross-Slab with Dog-Headed Figures, Onchan (92)
- Wheel-Headed Cross-Slab, Braddan (72)
- Wheel-Headed Cross-Slab, Lonan (73)
- Calf of Man Crucifixion (61)
- Gaut's Cross-Slab, Michael (101)
- Olaf Liotulfson's Cross, Ballaugh (106)
- Sandulf's Cross-Slab, Andreas (131)
- Crucifixion Cross-Slab, Michael (129)
- Boar Fragment, Maughold (133)
- Gerth Fragment, Michael (123)

- Heimdall Cross-Slab, Jurby (127)
- Thorwald's Cross-Slab, Andreas (128)
- Joalf's Cross-Slab, Michael (132)
- Dragon Cross-Slab, Michael (117)
- Dragon Fragment, Michael (116)
- Thorleif Hnakki's Cross, Braddan (135)
- Odd's Cross, Braddan (136)

PRACTICAL INFORMATION

- For good background reading: A. M. Cubbon, *The Art of the Manx Crosses*, (Manx National Heritage, 1996)
- Isle of Man Dept of Tourism: 01624 686766 / 01624 686801
- Airport: 01624 821600
- Maughold Parish Church: 01624 812070
- Ordnance Survey Map: Landranger Series no. 95
- Manx National Heritage, Douglas: 01624 648000 / www.gov.im/mnh

---

Suggested Devotion

Romans 16.25–27: Preaching the Good News

Part of 'The Cross of Christ', in Alexander Carmichael, *Carmina Gadelica* (Floris Books, Edinburgh, 1992), p. 278:

> *Be the cross of Christ between me and the fays*
> *That move occultly out or in,*
> *Be the cross of Christ between me and all ill,*
> *All ill-will, and all mishap.*

Glossary of Terms

Abbey: The building(s) occupied by a community of monks or nuns.

Abbot: A man who is the head of an abbey of monks.

Arianism: The heresy which denied the true divinity of Jesus Christ, so called after its author Arius who was a Libyan and lived between 250 and 336.

Asceticism: A technical term which denotes a system of practices designed to combat vice and develop virtues. It comes from the Greek word for 'exercise' or 'training'.

Athanasius: Bishop of Alexandria in Egypt. He attended the Council of Nicaea and wrote the life story of St Antony the Great of Egypt. He was the main obstacle for the success of Arianism. He lived between 296 and 373.

Augustinian Canons: Religious followers of St Augustine of Hippo popular in the eleventh century.

Benedictine: The historical and present-day monastic followers of Benedict of Nursia (480–550), the main influence on Western monasticism and author of the monastic rule.

Brythonic: The major language of the Celts of Britain and Brittany in the early part of the first millennium until it broke up into different Celtic languages such as Welsh and Irish.

Cairn: A mound of rough stones as a monument, landmark or burial place, particularly common in the Bronze Age (*c.*2300–800 BC).

Canonry: The office, benefice or dwelling of a canon (a clerical office).

Chancel: Normally the entire area within the main body of the church east of the nave and transepts. Traditionally a screen separated nave and chancel.

Chantry Priest: A priest who said mass for the souls of various people.

Chapter House: A building used for meetings of a cathedral or monastic group of priests responsible for that particular ecclesiastical institution.

Cistercians: The order of 'white monks' founded originally at Citeaux in 1098 by Robert of Molesme who intended to found a strict Benedictinism. St Bernard of Clairvaux was one of its most celebrated monks.

Clas: A distinctive feature of the Welsh Church: an important and responsible body similar in many ways to a monastic establishment, but without any particular rule; an association of clergy serving the church, working in co-operation, and leading a common life under an

acknowledged head.

Cloister: An enclosed area forming a means of communication between different parts of cathedrals, monasteries or other religious buildings.

Corbel: A projection of stone, timber etc. jutting out from a wall to support a weight.

Council of Nicaea: The first major council of the Church following the official acceptance of Christianity in the Roman Empire, summoned by the Emperor Constantine in the year 325 primarily to deal with the Arian heresy.

Cromlech: An ancient stone marking a place of burial.

Crusade: A title that originated to describe the military expeditions undertaken by Christians of the eleventh, twelfth and thirteenth centuries for the recovery of the Holy Land from Islam. The name comes from the cross which the Crusaders bore upon their clothing.

Culdees: Certain Irish monks of the eighth century and beyond who aimed to purify and consolidate the Celtic monastic tradition.

Diocletian: Roman Emperor from 284 to 305. At the end of his period Christians seemed to have been severely persecuted.

Dissolution of the Monasteries: In the later Middle Ages the wealth of many monasteries had made them an object of criticism. Henry VIII took action to abolish the monastic system. In 1536 an Act of Dissolution was passed, the king's principal adviser being Thomas Cromwell (1485–1540). This was a different Cromwell to the later Oliver Cromwell (1599–1658), the great Puritan of the English Civil War of 1642.

Edict of Milan: An agreement made by the emperors Constantine and Licinius at Milan early in 313 to recognize Christianity and end the persecution of the Christians.

Frank: A member of the Germanic nation that conquered Gaul in the sixth century.

Gildas: A monk and the first British historian (500–70). He spent most of his adult life in Wales and Ireland and became a student of St Illtud. His most famous work is the *De Excidio et Conquesto Brittaniae* (On the Fall of Britain) written between 516 and 547 and the only real history of the Celts.

Giraldus Cambrensis: Archdeacon of Brecon and a historian (1147–1223), the author of some very important books telling the story of Britain during the twelfth century.

Heresy: The formal denial or doubt of any defined doctrine or teaching of the Catholic Church.

Isthmus: A narrow piece of land connecting two larger bodies of land.

John Chrysostom: Bishop of

Constantinople, ascetic, author and theologian and one of the Fathers of the Church (347–407).

Justin Martyr: An early Christian apologist, teacher and theologian (100–65).

Martin of Tours: Bishop of Tours and a patron saint of France who died at about 397. Once a Roman soldier but later a Christian and monk under Hilary of Poitiers (315–67) who had himself spent some years in the Egyptian desert and probably knew Athanasius. He probably founded the first monastery in Gaul (Liguge). He encouraged and promoted the spread of monasticism.

Missal: The book containing all that is necessary to be sung or said at the celebration of the mass throughout the year.

Nave: That part of the church, between the main front and the chancel and choir, which is generally assigned to the laity. The term comes from the Latin word for 'ship', *navis*, this being the symbol of the church.

Normans: The inhabitants of Normandy who, in 1066 under the leadership of William the Conqueror, defeated the English.

Norwich Taxatio: A taxation on churches to aid the Crusades. This is a valuable document showing the existence of twelfth- and thirteenth-century churches and the amount they gave.

Origen: An Alexandrian biblical exegete and theologian who lived between 185 and 254. He mainly adopted an allegorical interpretation of Scripture.

Pelagianism: The theological system which held that a person took the initial and fundamental steps towards salvation by his own efforts apart from divine grace. It was on this point that Pelagius and Augustine of Hippo disputed.

Penitential Books: A set of books containing directions to confessors. Of Celtic origin, they spread with the Celtic and Anglo-Saxon missions all over Europe. The earliest are the two series of canons ascribed to St Patrick and dating from the fifth century.

Portionary Church: A natural development of the Welsh *clas* system, but differing in that these had no definite leader, and were little more than benefices held by a number of independent clerics. The revenues of these churches were divided as portions between these clerics who effectively acted as the clergy in charge of the district. They were later called collegiate churches.

Presbytery: The eastern part of the chancel of a church beyond the choir.

Priory: A religious house presided over by a prior or prioress. In the Benedictine tradition the prior ranked next to the abbot.

Provost: In early Christian usage the official next in dignity to the abbot, but later the head of an ecclesiastical chapter.

Reformation: A loose term to describe a series of changes in the Western Church between the fourteenth and seventeenth centuries. In general, the break-up of the Catholic Church which led to the formation of other churches such as Anglicanism and Protestantism.

Roman Patriarchate: The see (ecclesiastical area) based in Rome. Before the crucial eleventh-century divide of the world Church into East and West, it was generally believed that there were five ancient patriarchates: Constantinople, Alexandria, Antioch, Jerusalem and Rome.

Romanesque: A style of architecture prevalent in Europe between about 900 and 1200, often with massive vaulting and round arches.

Rood Screen: Usually a wooden carved screen separating nave and chancel.

'Rood' is an ancient English word for a cross or crucifix, often raised on a screen at the entrance to the chancel.

Runic/Rune: The letters of the earliest Germanic alphabet used by Scandinavians and Anglo-Saxons from about the third century and formed by modifying Roman letters to suit carving.

St Antony: One of the earliest hermits of the Egyptian desert (251–356) whose life was written by Athanasius in about 357.

Scriptorium: The room, especially in a monastery, which was set apart for the scribes to copy manuscripts.

Tertullian: An African church father and a native of Carthage who wrote many apologetic, theological and ascetic writings in Latin. He lived between 160 and 220.

Transept: Either arm of the part of a cross-shaped church at right angles to the nave.

Uncial/Half Uncial Script: A form of large-lettered script used for books in Greek and Latin from about the fourth to the eighth centuries.

Bibliography

Several books have been invaluable resources and have greatly enriched the writing of this book; I have made extensive use of the following:

Almost all the sites and churches mentioned produce excellent notes and guides for pilgrims. I have made use of these. The *Pitkin Guides* are especially useful. Please see also the books mentioned in the Introduction to this book.

John Adair, *The Pilgrims' Way*, Book Club Associates, 1978
Oliver Davies, *Celtic Spirituality*, Paulist Press, 1999
Basil Hume, *Footprints of the Northern Saints*, Darton, Longman and Todd, 1996
Martin Palmer and Nigel Palmer, *Sacred Britain*, ICOREC/Piatkus Press, 1997
Cintra Pemberton, *Soulfaring: Celtic Pilgrimage Then and Now*, SPCK, 1999
Nigel Pennick, *The Celtic Saints*, Thorson/HarperCollins, 1997
Nigel Pennick, *The Celtic Cross*, Blandford, 1998
Elizabeth Rees, *Celtic Saints Passionate Wanderers*, Thames and Hudson, 2000

At the end of each section quotations are offered as suggested devotions. Books from which the non-biblical readings come are cited at the end of the particular sections, and so are not repeated here.

Index